Fifth Edition

Harmonic Materials in Tonal Music

A PROGRAMED COURSE

Part I

Paul O. Harder CALIFORNIA STATE COLLEGE, STANISLAUS

Allyn and Bacon, Inc. Boston   London   Sydney   Toronto

Production Coordinator: Jane Schulman
Production Services: Helyn Pultz

Library of Congress Cataloging in Publication Data

Harder, Paul O.
   Harmonic materials in tonal music.

   Includes indexes.
   1. Harmony—Programmed instruction. I. Title
MT50.H26 1985   781.3'07'7   84-14594
ISBN 0-205-08290-4 (v. 1)
ISBN 0-205-08292-0 (v. 2)

Printed in the United States of America

10 9 8 7 6 5   89 88 87

Contents

Preface

The refinements incorporated into the fifth edition are designed to make this book an even more useful aid for learning the materials and practices of tonal harmony. One change concerns the summaries that follow the expository section of each chapter: many have been expanded for a more complete overview of the main points covered. The summaries, plus all new mastery frames, help the learner assess or comprehend the material in each chapter before proceeding to the next. Another change involves the supplementary assignments, which are also all new. In addition, they are now organized so that each may be removed from the book as a separate entity, facilitating their submission to the instructor for evaluation.

The chief emphasis in this two-part study of tonal harmony is on the basic elements of harmony that have retained their validity throughout the period from about 1600 to 1900. Music from this period is still very much a part of our musical life. Not only does a large part of the current repertoire consist of eighteenth- and nineteenth-century music, but tonal harmony is the basis of practically all commercial music. All composers, no matter what style they generally may employ, turn to tonal harmony when such material is appropriate to their expressive purpose. This book is not devoted to the study of any one composer's works, nor is it limited to four-part writing; various applications of harmonic principles are shown in musical examples drawn from a variety of periods and compositional types.

Since most of the music we hear and perform is based on tonal harmony, it is essential that serious students become familiar with this system. For the composer, competence in writing requires thorough understanding of techniques practiced by composers of previous generations. For the performer, the ability to convey delicate nuances and subtleties of phrasing often stems from a cultivated sensitivity to harmonic processes.

Experience has shown that the type of programed instruction used in this book can lead to rapid, yet thorough mastery of musical concepts and techniques. Also, it has proved to be versatile in that it can be used not only by a single student working independently, but also by students in large classes. Still more important is the flexibility that programed material brings to the instructor. The core of knowledge contained in this book may be expanded by emphasis upon creative writing, analysis, or the study of music literature. Because students evaluate their own exercises, the instructor is free to prepare more vital and creative supplementary learning experiences.

The development of this course was supported by the Educational Development Program at Michigan State University. The author is grateful to Dr. John Dietrich, Assistant Provost, and Dr. Robert Davis, Director of the Educational Development Program, for their assistance; also to Drs. Jere Hutcheson, Clifford Pfeil, and Gary White, who helped develop practical classroom methods. Particular tribute, though, must be paid to the many students who, over a period of several years, assisted in proving out the approaches incorporated in this book. Thanks also go to Rita Fuszek, Professor of Music at California State University, Fullerton, the diligent pianist who recorded the examples contained in the cassettes that accompany this book. And finally, special thanks go to my wife, Mildred, who has not only typed countless pages over the years, but provided helpful comment and moral support.

How to Use This Book

This book features the use of programed instruction to convey conceptual information and provide drills to develop techniques for handling harmonic materials. In programed instruction, information is presented in small, carefully sequenced parcels which combine in cumulative fashion to give students mastery of the subject. The parcels into which the material is divided are called *frames*. Most frames require a written response, which may be a word or two, or consist of the solution of a musical problem. Since correct answers are provided by the book itself, this type of material is self-correcting; thus students may work entirely alone and proceed at their own pace. When used in class, supplementary examples and lessons may be supplied by the instructor as he or she sees fit.

The principal part of each frame is located on the right-hand side of the page. The answers, which appear on the left-hand side, should be covered with a slip of paper or a ruler (merely the hand will do). After the response is written, the appropriate answer is uncovered so the response may be checked immediately. Since each step in this process is small, few mistakes are made. Because of this, learning is reinforced and misconceptions have little chance to become part of the student's thinking.

To the Student

Do not begin this study of tonal harmony without thorough knowledge of the fundamentals of music including scales, key signatures, intervals, and triads. You may wish to review the author's *Basic Materials in Music Theory*, also published by Allyn and Bacon, Inc.

This book features the use of programed instruction to convey conceptual information and provide drills to develop techniques for handling harmonic materials. In programed instruction, information is presented in small, carefully sequenced parcels that combine in cumulative fashion to help you master the subject. The parcels into which the material is divided are called *frames*. Most frames require a written response, which may be a word or two, or perhaps the solution to a musical problem.

The principal part of each frame is located on the right-hand side of the page. The answers, which appear on the left-hand side, should be covered with a slip of paper or a ruler (or merely the hand will do). After you write your response, uncover the answer and check your work immediately. There are many cases in which your answer need not be exactly the same as that supplied by the text. You should consider your response correct if it conveys the same meaning as the one given. Use common sense to decide whether or not you comprehend a particular item. Because each step is small, you should make few mistakes.

Each chapter ends with a series of "mastery" frames. These frames allow you to evaluate your mastery of key points—concepts and skills essential to coping with matters that lie ahead. *Do not proceed unless your handling of the mastery frames assures you that you are ready to continue.*

Mastery frames are identified with double numbers to prevent confusion with the frames that constitute the body of the text. References to the frames that cover the subject of each question are provided along with the correct answers. Avail yourself of these references in order to focus remedial study precisely upon the points missed.

Many musical examples are given in the text to acquaint you with the way various composers use harmonic devices. You should play these at the piano so that they are actually *heard*. It is not sufficient to approach this study on an intellectual level alone; you must have command of the harmonic vocabulary as an aural phenomenon as well. The purpose of conceptualizing musical processes is to render more understandable the responses elicited by the auditory stimuli of music. Remember, music is an *aural* art; it is comprehended better by the ear than by the eye.

A bullet before a frame indicates that the music in that frame is reproduced on the cassettes.

A Perspective for the Study of Harmony

One would suppose that, by now, the study of tonal harmony would be passé. After all, traditional harmonic tonality, with its attendant vocabulary of chords, was pretty thoroughly done in by the assault of both the impressionists of the late nineteenth century and the atonalists of the early twentieth century. The impressionists—Debussy in particular—caused a progressive decay of tonality through the use of nontertian chords and nonfunctional streams of chords, as well as by the expansion of tonal frontiers. By the end of the first decade of the twentieth century, Arnold Schönberg had shown in works such as *Pierrot Lunaire* that expressive music could indeed be created without resorting to either tonality or tertian harmony. The dodecaphonic, or twelve-tone, system was designed to effectively negate any lingering influences of traditional harmonic practices. This system, as employed by members of the second Viennese School (Webern and Berg, in addition to Schönberg), as well as by countless others during the succeeding three decades, led to a large body of music, including many highly expressive works.

Harmonic music, however, is still with us. Far from being dead, it is alive and well. Most of the music heard through mass media, and practically all commercial music, is based on traditional harmonic practices. This is true, also, of music performed in churches and studied in schools. Even concert and recital programs reveal a stubborn adherence to the standard repertoire, with the inclusion of only an occasional nontonal work. There is, of course, the all-too-rare program devoted exclusively to advanced music. Unfortunately, such programs have little impact, considering the overwhelming amount of more traditional music heard.

What accounts for the persistence of traditional music? Reasons can only be stated as speculation. A few follow:

1. There are those who would point to the "natural" basis of harmonic music. Because the natural harmonic series is a phenomenon of nature, the generation of chords by thirds and the relation of roots to the tonic according to precepts derived from the series can be seen not only as being ordained by nature, but also as possessing special moral sanction.
2. Perhaps because most people in our society, from birth, have heard little other than harmonic music, preference is given to the familiar; choice is made on the basis of conditioning, which produces an inertia of values.
3. Music in which tones bear relatively simple acoustical relations to one another is easier both to sing and to apprehend. Much folk music, for example, displays preference for limited range and relatively small intervals, as well as emphasis on the perfect fourth and fifth—intervals which have special tonal significance.
4. It is apparent that the expressive resources of tonal music have not been exhausted. The rapidly changing styles of commercial music demonstrate that fresh draughts of musical expression still remain to be drawn from the well of harmonic resources.

Rationale aside, harmonic music clearly constitutes the bulk of what is heard by our society at large. It also dominates the music studied and performed by students in our schools of music. These realities justify the continued study of tonal harmony. And the time is not yet in sight when this study will be without meaning and thus disappear from the standard music curriculum.

The two basic parameters of music are *temporal* and *sonic* (time and sound). With respect to the sonic parameter, two principal methods of organization have evolved in Western music: counterpoint (linear) and harmony (chordal). The technique of counterpoint developed much earlier than the concept of harmony as an independent musical principle. From about the beginning of the tenth century to nearly 1600, the chief organizing principles were related to counterpoint. But from the beginning, the effect of voices sounding together was recognized as an important factor. This is evidenced by the changing preferences for intervals during the course of musical evolution.

Early in the development of counterpoint, the chief consonances were perfect unisons, octaves, fourths, and fifths. Open sonorities such as 1-5-8 were the main consonant sonorities, with complete triads (1-3-5) appearing as passing occurrences. The frequency of triads gradually increased after 1300, occurring even at cadence points, except for the final cadence where perfect consonances (1-5-8) were still preferred. From about the middle of the fifteenth century, complete triads in both root position and first inversion predominated, but music from this period displays no systematic approach to harmonic progression, except at the cadences, where plagal, authentic, and Phrygian cadences are used.

After 1600, the preeminence of the first, fourth, and fifth scale degrees began to be established, and greater consistency of root movement developed. This led to the establishment of major/minor tonality, which supplanted the modal system of the medieval and Renaissance periods. During the baroque period, the vocabulary of chords was enlarged to include various altered chords such as the Neapolitan sixth and secondary dominants. Chromaticism and systematic modulation also developed at this time. In response to the classical ideals of clarity, lightness, and balance, harmonic action tended to be simpler and more formula driven. The form-defining function of contrasting tonalities, however, became even more important. Also, there was more frequent modulation to distant keys.

Harmony received its fullest development during the romantic period (1825–1900), during which time the tonal horizon was pushed back to the very limits of equal temperament, and the repertoire of chords was expanded by the use of the complete chromatic scale. Frequent use of altered chords, coupled with modulations to distant keys, led to the eventual disintegration of tonality, and the fall of tonality brought down the whole structure of tonal relations and chord structures associated with tertian harmony. But, as we have seen, harmonic music refuses to die; its emotive power is still strong. And, although it appears that the evolution of harmony was complete by 1900, harmonic materials may still be exploited for new ends.

The evolution of harmony may also be traced through the writings of various theorists. For this purpose we shall review briefly some of the major contributions to the field of harmonic theory. It is surprising that recognition of harmony as an independent musical parameter occurred so late. After all, several contrapuntal lines produce simultaneous sounds, and for several centuries prior to 1600, many of these sounds resulted in chords. But pre-baroque technique exploited the interval as the basic constructive unit—the concept of chord did not exist. What we recognize as chords were viewed then as conglomerations of intervals. The first recognition of the chord as an entity occurred in Gioseffo Zarlino's *Istituzioni armoniche* of 1558. In this work Zarlino refers to the *harmonia perfetta*, which results from the first six tones of the natural harmonic series. It is, in effect, the major triad. Being the first to recognize the triad as a harmonic entity, Zarlino is the father of modern harmonic theory.

A still greater contribution to harmonic theory was made by Jean-Philippe Rameau, whose treatise *Traité de l'Harmonie* was published in 1722. Many of the principles set forth by Rameau are still employed today to explain harmonic processes. Rameau's writings are extensive and involved. His chief contributions however, are threefold:

1. He postulated that the lowest note of the triad in 1-3-5 position is the root and is the generator of the 3rd and 5th. Also, this note (1) remains the root when the chord is inverted to either 3-5-8 (first inversion) or 5-8-10 (second inversion).
2. The roots of chords, as opposed to the actual bass line, constitute the "fundamental bass," and the fundamental bass is the true motivator of the harmony. The result of this principle is to reduce the number of harmonic entities and provide a simple method for relating chords to one another and to the tonal center.
3. The symmetrical structure of harmonic tonality was identified by Rameau, who, recognizing the fundamental accoustical nature of the perfect fifth, also saw the subdominant and dominant as straddling the tonic (IV-I-V), the dominant a fifth higher, the subdominant a fifth lower. It was Rameau who first used the term *sous-dominante* to designate the "lower" dominant.

Rameau, like Zarlino, based his theories on the natural harmonic series and mathematics. Most later harmonic theorists did likewise. Some, however, chose other bases for their speculations. For example, in 1754 Giuseppe Tartini published his treatise *Trattato di musica*, in which reference is made not only to the natural harmonic series and mathematics, but also to geometry. In 1853, Moritz Hauptmann published his *Die Natur der Harmonik und Metrik*, in which a philosophical approach based on Hegel's dialectical metaphysics is employed.

The theorists reviewed here, plus many others, felt that they were dealing with harmony as a science, that basic principles which would explain music phenomena, and more, lay hidden, waiting only to be discovered and proved. But this has proved to be a chimera; for no harmonic theory, including Rameau's, is free of inner contradictions. There have been many near misses; but nature has not cooperated by providing a closed system to tone relations, at least in terms of the kinds of music with which people have to date been concerned.

chapter one

Some Definitions

The elements of music include rhythm, melody, timbre, texture, and harmony. Some of these are virtually universal; they are exploited in music of all ages and cultures. Music without rhythm, for example, can hardly be imagined. Harmony, on the other hand, is missing from much primitive and oriental music. Even in Western music harmony was established as an independent element in the relatively recent past. From only about 1600 did consistent usage gradually establish patterns of harmonic and tonal relations, which eventually were codified by theorists to form a "science of harmony." But harmony quickly became a central concern, and ultimately superceded even counterpoint, which had provided the technical basis for musical composition since about the ninth century.

During the eighteenth and nineteenth centuries composers were so preoccupied with the expanding harmonic system, that other musical elements—particularly rhythm—were neglected. But harmony served these composers well. It provided the fountainhead of style and expression—from harmony stemmed not only melody, but form. Most of the music heard today (this includes nearly all commercial music) is either from the eighteenth or nineteenth centuries, or is based on similar harmonic principles. For this reason the study of harmony is essential for those who wish to be knowledgeable listeners or competent performers.

Harmony has two dimensions. One is "vertical"—several tones sounding simultaneously (chords); the other is "horizontal"—successions of chords within a tonal system. Thus the study of harmony involves two things: types of chords; and how chords relate to one another. We shall begin by explaining what is meant by tonal music. Next, some terms which relate to tonality and chords will be defined. Some basic analytical symbols will also be introduced.

tonal	1. Most of the music composed between 1600 and 1900 is based upon major and minor scales. Music of this type is called TONAL music. In tonal music one tone (the keynote) predominates over the other tones of the scale. The keynote is the same as the first note of the scale. Music in which one tone predominates over the other tones of the scale is called _____ music.
B-flat.	2. What is the keynote of the B-flat major scale? _____
E.	3. What is the keynote of the E minor scale? _____
	4. Music which is based upon the C major scale is said to be in the key of C major. The KEY of a composition corresponds to the keynote of the scale which is used.

F-sharp

A composition in the key of F-sharp minor is based primarily upon the _____ minor scale.

■ 5. But being "in a key" involves more than merely using the notes of a particular scale. The melody below, for example, uses some of the notes of the G major scale, and the prominence of the keynote (G) is heightened because the melody begins and ends on G.

Carey, *America*

Only five notes of the G major scale are used. Count the number of times each note occurs and list them below:

		F♯	_____
F♯	2	G	_____
G	6	A	_____
A	4	B	_____
B	3	C	_____
C	1		

---

keynote

6. Iteration is an important means of causing one tone to predominate over other tones. In simple tonal music the tone which receives the greatest stress through iteration is often the _____ _____.

---

tonality

7. It is common to speak of music as being in a particular key. This is a way of identifying the scale which serves as the basis for the music. The term TONALITY means practically the same thing as *key*. This term is often used in a broader sense, however, to refer to any music which centers on a single tone regardless of the tonal system employed. Within the context of this study the terms *key* and *tonality* will be used synonymously.

A composition in the key of C major may also be said to be in the _____ of C major.

A major.

8. What is the tonality of a composition which is based primarily upon the A major scale? _____

key	9. Music in which a single tone predominates over the others is said to be TONAL. In tonal music one tone takes precedence over all the others; this tone is called the TONAL CENTER. What is another name for the tonal center? The _____ center.
first	10. The keynote is which note of the scale? The _____.
Yes.	11. Do the terms tonal center, key center, and keynote have approximately the same meaning? _____
(No response.)	12. The points made thus far are these: The *key* of a composition may be established by using the notes of a particular scale; by beginning and ending on the keynote; and by iteration of the keynote. The *tonal center* is that tone which predominates over all the others. This tone is also called the *keynote*. Any music which is orientated to a tonal center is said to be *tonal*. The *tonality* of a composition corresponds to the tonal center.
tonal	13. Harmony which is associated with tonal music is called TONAL HARMONY. Within the limits of this study tonal harmony will mean harmony based upon major and minor scales. Harmony based upon the major-minor scale system is called _____ harmony.
tones	14. Before continuing with the study of tonal harmony we must make some important distinctions. In the next few frames we shall note the difference between *intervals*, *chords*, and *triads*. The basic component of harmony is the chord. These, in turn, are the result of several tones sounding simultaneously. Chords are vertical structures consisting of several _____.
	15. The simultaneous sounding of two tones produces a *harmonic interval*, but do not confuse an interval with a chord. Although a single interval may occasionally imply a chord, <u>*at least three tones are required to*</u> produce a complete chord.* *In impressionist music as well as some later twentieth century styles, two tones do occasionally function as a chord. In such cases the term *dyad* may be used.

chords	Vertical structures form either intervals or _____.
three	16. Two tones sounding together produce an interval. A chord, however, consists of at least _____ tones.
Yes.	17. Are all of the structures below chords? _____ 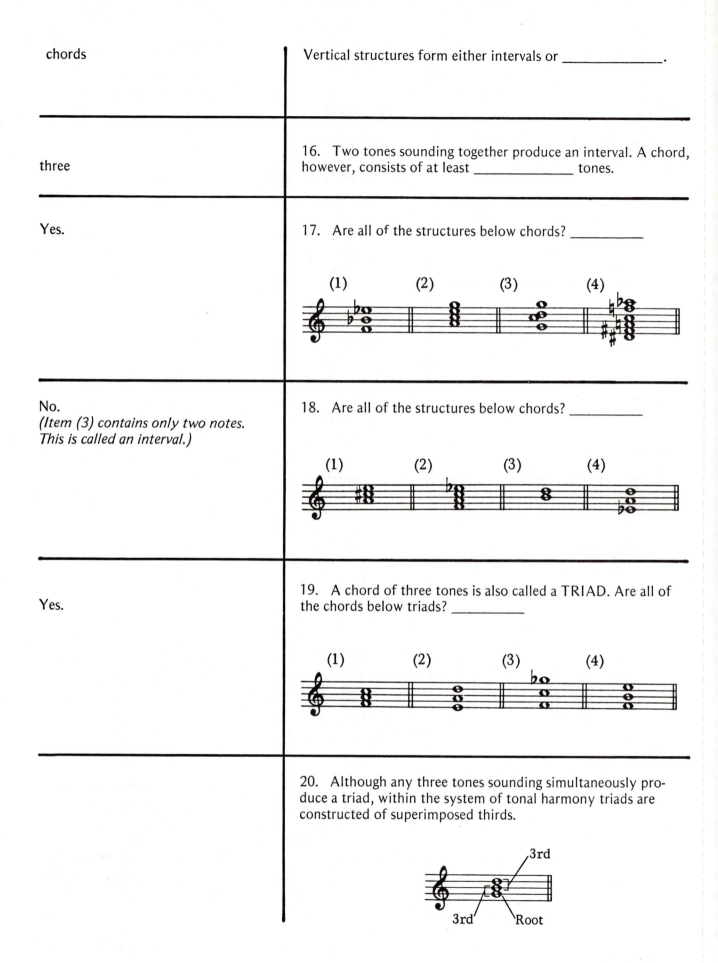
No. *(Item (3) contains only two notes. This is called an interval.)*	18. Are all of the structures below chords? _____
Yes.	19. A chord of three tones is also called a TRIAD. Are all of the chords below triads? _____
	20. Although any three tones sounding simultaneously produce a triad, within the system of tonal harmony triads are constructed of superimposed thirds.

tonal	The note on which a triad is built is called the ROOT. Triads consisting of superimposed thirds are part of the system of _____ harmony.
	21. Consider each note of the C major scale below to be the root of a triad. Write a triad on each note. *(Use no accidentals.)* KEY OF C MAJOR
diatonic	22. The triads you have just written use only the notes of the C major scale. These are called DIATONIC triads. Diatonic triads are constructed only of notes contained in the scale being used. Triads which utilize only the notes of the scale are called _____ triads.
(3). *(E-flat is not a diatonic tone in the key of G major.)*	23. Which of the triads below is NOT a diatonic triad? _____ (1) (2) (3) (4) (Key of G major)
(1). *(B-natural is not a diatonic tone in the key of B-flat major.)*	24. Which of the triads below is NOT a diatonic triad? _____ (1) (2) (3) (4) (Key of B♭ major)
No.	25. If a triad contains a tone which is foreign to the key, can it be called diatonic? _____

26. A triad may be constructed on each of the seven degrees of the major scale.

KEY OF D MAJOR

Yes.

Is each of these triads a diatonic triad? _____

27. How many diatonic triads are contained in a major key? _____

Seven.

28. Construct a diatonic triad on each degree of the E-flat major scale.

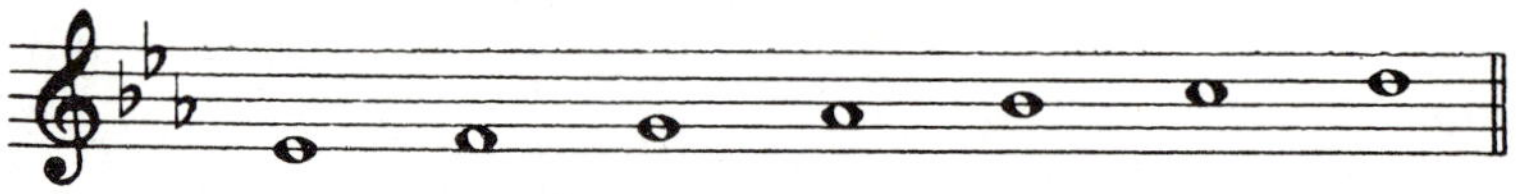

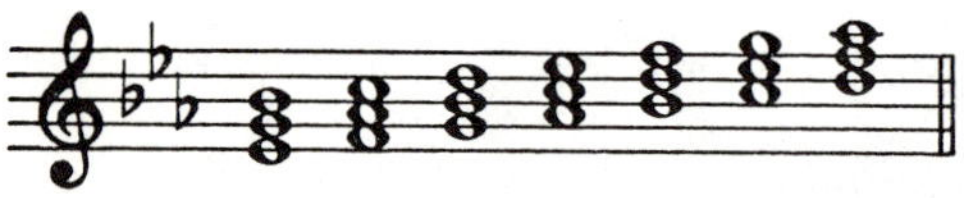

29. Construct a diatonic triad on each degree of the B major scale.

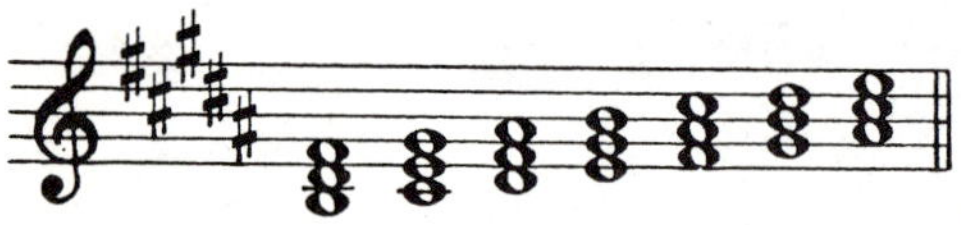

30. Diatonic triads utilize only the notes which are included in the scale being used. In the *harmonic* minor scale the raised seventh degree is considered diatonic since it is part of the scale. The seven diatonic triads in the key of D harmonic minor are shown below.

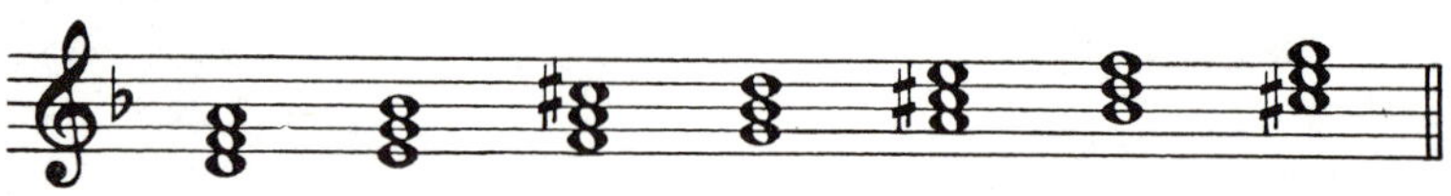

Yes.
(C-sharp is a diatonic note in the D harmonic minor scale.)

Some of the triads above contain an accidental (C-sharp). Are these diatonic triads? _____

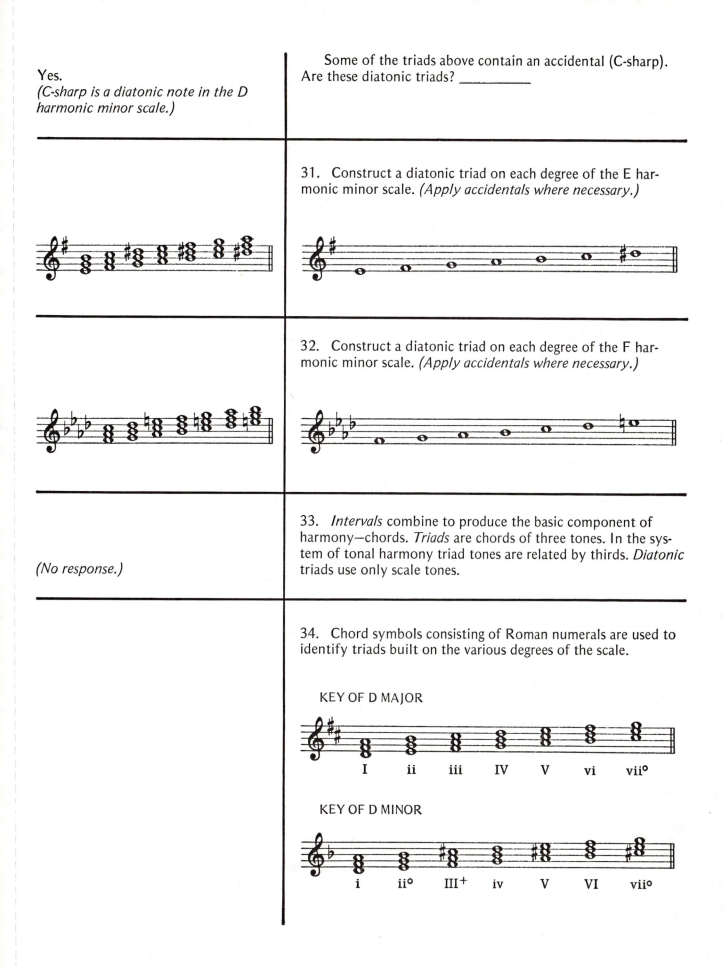

31. Construct a diatonic triad on each degree of the E harmonic minor scale. *(Apply accidentals where necessary.)*

32. Construct a diatonic triad on each degree of the F harmonic minor scale. *(Apply accidentals where necessary.)*

(No response.)

33. *Intervals* combine to produce the basic component of harmony—chords. *Triads* are chords of three tones. In the system of tonal harmony triad tones are related by thirds. *Diatonic* triads use only scale tones.

34. Chord symbols consisting of Roman numerals are used to identify triads built on the various degrees of the scale.

KEY OF D MAJOR

I   ii   iii   IV   V   vi   vii°

KEY OF D MINOR

i   ii°   III⁺   iv   V   VI   vii°

scale	The Roman numerals used to identify the various triads of a key correspond to the degrees of the _____.
	35. Notice in the preceding frame that the Roman numerals have different forms depending upon the quality of the triads. *Study the chart below:* | TYPE OF TRIAD		SYMBOL
---	---	---
Major	=	I, IV, V
Minor	=	ii, iii, vi
Diminished	=	ii°, vii°
Augmented	=	III⁺	 A Roman numeral consisting of capital letters denotes a _____ triad.
major	
plus *(or cross)*	**36.** An augmented triad is indicated by a large Roman numeral followed by a _____ sign.
circle	**37.** A diminished triad is indicated by a *small* Roman numeral followed by a _____.
True.	**38.** A minor triad is indicated by a *small* Roman numeral. (True/False) _____

Major
Diminished
Augmented
Minor
	39. Name the triad *quality* (major, minor, diminished, or augmented) indicated by each chord symbol.
	    (1) IV _____
	    (2) ii° _____
	    (3) III⁺ _____
	    (4) vi _____

No. *(Item (3) represents a diminished triad.)*	**40.** Do all of the Roman numerals below represent triads of identical quality? _____ (1) vi (2) iii (3) ii° (4) iv
Yes.	**41.** Do all of the Roman numerals below represent triads of identical quality? _____ (1) I (2) VI (3) IV (4) V

Major.

42. What type of triad is indicated by the Roman numerals in the preceding frame? _____

---

(3).

43 Which Roman numeral represents a *minor* triad? _____
   (1) V   (2) III⁺   (3) ii   (4) vii°

---

(4).

44. Which Roman numeral represents an *augmented* triad? _____
   (1) ii°   (2) III   (3) vi   (4) III⁺

---

(2).

45. Which Roman numeral represents a *diminished* triad? _____
   (1) ii   (2) vii°   (3) III⁺   (4) V

---

(3).

46. Which Roman numeral represents a major triad? _____
   (1) III⁺   (2) ii   (3) IV   (4) iv

---

47. Write the remaining Roman numerals to represent the triads built on the seven degrees of the E-flat major scale. *(Be sure the quality of each triad is reflected by the form of the Roman numeral.)*

I   ii   iii   IV   V   vi   vii°

I   __ __ __ __ __ __

---

48. Write the Roman numerals to represent the triads built on the seven degrees of the E-flat harmonic minor scale. *(Be sure the quality of each triad is reflected by the form of the Roman numeral.)*

i   ii°   III⁺   iv

V   VI   vii°

__ __ __ __ __ __ __

49. Complete the list below:

THE QUALITY OF TRIADS IN MAJOR

1st: major   The triad on the 1st degree is _____.
2nd: minor   The triad on the 2nd degree is _____.
3rd: minor   The triad on the 3rd degree is _____.
4th: major   The triad on the 4th degree is _____.
5th: major   The triad on the 5th degree is _____.
6th: minor   The triad on the 6th degree is _____.
7th: diminished   The triad on the 7th degree is _____.

---

50. Complete the list below:

THE QUALITY OF TRIADS IN HARMONIC MINOR

1st: minor   The triad on the 1st degree is _____.
2nd: diminished   The triad on the 2nd degree is _____.
3rd: augmented   The triad on the 3rd degree is _____.
4th: minor   The triad on the 4th degree is _____.
5th: major   The triad on the 5th degree is _____.
6th: major   The triad on the 6th degree is _____.
7th: diminished   The triad on the 7th degree is _____.

---

minor

51. The quality of the triad on the fourth degree of the harmonic minor scale is _____.

---

major

52. The quality of the triad on the sixth degree of the harmonic minor scale is _____.

---

minor

53. The quality of the triad on the first degree of the harmonic minor scale is _____.

---

major

54. The quality of the triad on the fifth degree of the harmonic minor scale is_____.

False.
(This triad is minor.)

55. The triad on the sixth degree of the major scale is major. (True/False) _____

True.

56. The triad on the second degree of the harmonic minor scale is diminished. (True/False) _____

False.
(This triad is augmented.)

57. The triad on the third degree of the harmonic minor scale is major. (True/False) _____

I   ii   iii   IV   V   vi   vii°

58. Analyze with Roman numerals the triads built on the seven degrees of the G major scale.

___   ___   ___   ___   ___   ___   ___

---

i   ii°   III⁺   iv   V   VI   vii°

59. Analyze with Roman numerals the triads built on the seven degrees of the G harmonic minor scale.

___   ___   ___   ___   ___   ___   ___

(No response.)

60. The benefit gained from using various forms of Roman numerals is that you are thereby made aware of the *specific quality* of each chord. This, in turn, increases your sensitivity to the actual sounds represented by the notes.

---

major

61. When analyzing with Roman numerals the key is identified by an abbreviation of its name followed by a colon (:).
Compare the designations below:

E-flat major = E♭:
E-flat minor = e♭:

Notice that a *capital* letter is used to indicate a major key, whereas a *lower case* letter is used for a minor key.
The symbol (B:) represents the key of B _____.

---

(1) F:
(2) a♭:
(3) E:

62. Write the proper designation for each key.

(1) F major   _____
(2) A-flat minor   _____
(3) E major   _____

(1) g♯:
(2) D:
(3) b♭:

63. Write the proper designation for each key.
   (1) G-sharp minor _____
   (2) D major _____
   (3) B-flat minor _____

---

(1) A major.
(2) C-sharp minor.
(3) D minor.

64. What key is indicated by each symbol?
   (1) A: The key of _____
   (2) c♯: The key of _____
   (3) d: The key of _____

---

(1) B minor.
(2) G-flat major.
(3) C-sharp major.

65. What key is indicated by each symbol?
   (1) b: The key of _____
   (2) G♭: The key of _____
   (3) C♯: The key of _____

---

66. Write the proper chord symbol in each case. *(Be sure to check the quality of each triad.)*

(1)   (2)   (3)

(1) (2)   (3)
I   III⁺ ii

Bb: ___   e: ___   D: ___

---

67. Continue as in the preceding frame.

(1)   (2)   (3)

(1) (2) (3)
iv iii V

d: ___   Eb: ___   f#: ___

---

68. Continue as in the preceding frame. *(Note use of bass clef.)*

(1)   (2)   (3)

(1) (2) (3)
IV   VI   V

Ab: ___   c#: ___   Bb: ___

69. Continue as in the preceding frame.

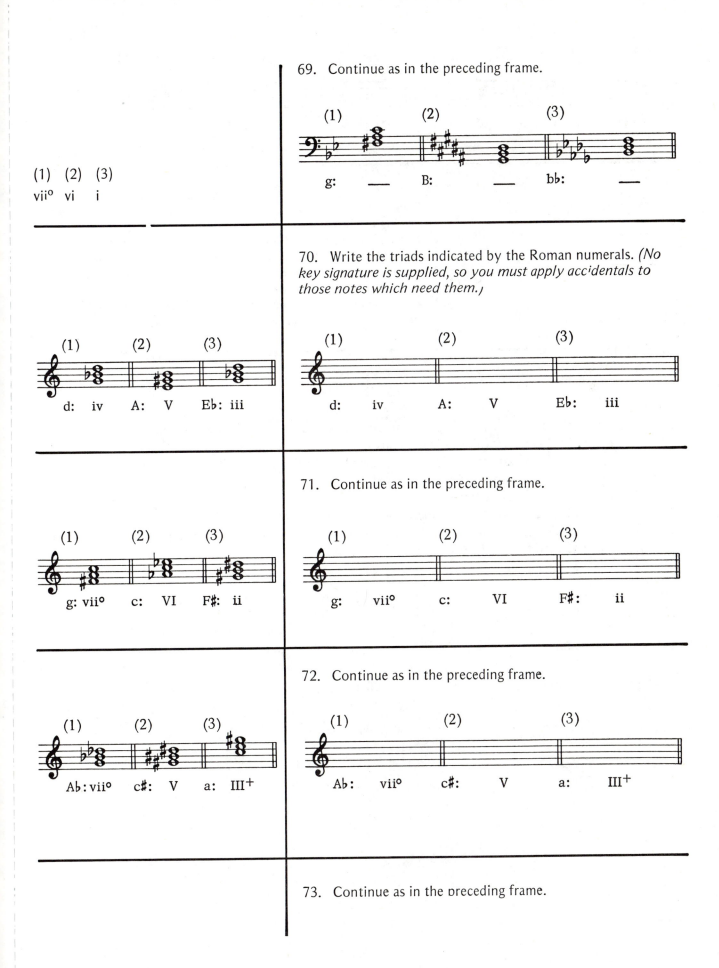

(1)   (2)   (3)

(1)   (2)   (3)
viiº vi   i

g: ___   B: ___   b♭: ___

70. Write the triads indicated by the Roman numerals. *(No key signature is supplied, so you must apply accidentals to those notes which need them.)*

(1)   (2)   (3)

d: iv   A: V   E♭: iii

(1)   (2)   (3)

d: iv   A: V   E♭: iii

71. Continue as in the preceding frame.

(1)   (2)   (3)

g: viiº   c: VI   F#: ii

(1)   (2)   (3)

g: viiº c: VI   F#: ii

72. Continue as in the preceding frame.

(1)   (2)   (3)

A♭: viiº c#: V   a: III+

(1)   (2)   (3)

A♭: viiº c#: V   a: III+

73. Continue as in the preceding frame.

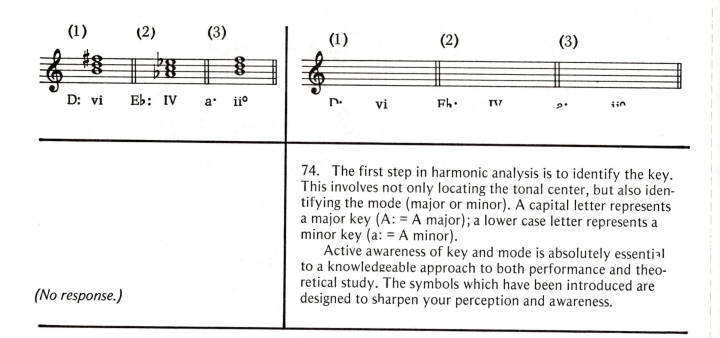

(1)   (2)   (3)

D: vi   Eb: IV   a: ii°

(1)   (2)   (3)

D: vi   Eb: IV   a: ii°

(No response.)

74. The first step in harmonic analysis is to identify the key. This involves not only locating the tonal center, but also identifying the mode (major or minor). A capital letter represents a major key (A: = A major); a lower case letter represents a minor key (a: = A minor).

Active awareness of key and mode is absolutely essential to a knowledgeable approach to both performance and theoretical study. The symbols which have been introduced are designed to sharpen your perception and awareness.

SUMMARY

In tonal music a single tone is caused to predominate over the others. This tone is called the *tonal center* and is the same as the *keynote* of the scale being used.

Two superimposed intervals of a third produce a chord of three tones called a *triad*. There are four types of triads in the major-minor scale system (major, minor, diminished, and augmented). These four types of triads provide the basic harmonic material of tonal music.

For the purpose of analysis triads are identified by chord symbols consisting of Roman numerals. These correspond to the scale degrees on which the triads are built. Various forms of chord symbols are used to show the quality of each triad as below:

TRIAD QUALITY	SYMBOLS	
Major	I, IV, V	(capital letters)
Minor	ii, iii, vi	(lower case letters)
Diminished	ii°, vii°	(circle added to lower case letters)
Augmented	III⁺	(plus sign added to capital letters)

The terms that are explained in this chapter are listed in chronological order below:

tonal	tonal center	harmonic interval
keynote	tonal harmony	root
key	intervals	diatonic (triads)
iteration	chords	chord symbols
tonality	triads	Roman numerals

Mastery Frames

3. Tonal center. (1–12)	1-1. Indicate the term on the right that conveys practically the same meaning as the one on the left.
	
	Keynote____ 1. Tonality
	                     2. Root
	                     3. Tonal center

2. Key. (4–13)	1-2. Indicate the term on the right that conveys practically the same meaning as the one on the left.
	
	Tonality____ 1. Chord
	                     2. Key
	                     3. Tonal harmony

(1) Interval (2) Chord (3) Chord (4) Interval (14–19)	1-3. Identify each example as either an interval or a chord. (1)_____ (2)_____ (3)_____ (4)_____
3. (19)	1-4. How many tones are required to produce a triad?____
thirds (20)	1-5. Triads within the system of tonal harmony are based on a note called the *root*, and they are constructed of superimposed _____.

diatonic (22-33)	1-6. Triads that employ only the notes of the prevailing key are called _____ triads.
(2), (3) (22-33)	1-7. Which are diatonic triads in the key of B-flat major? _____ 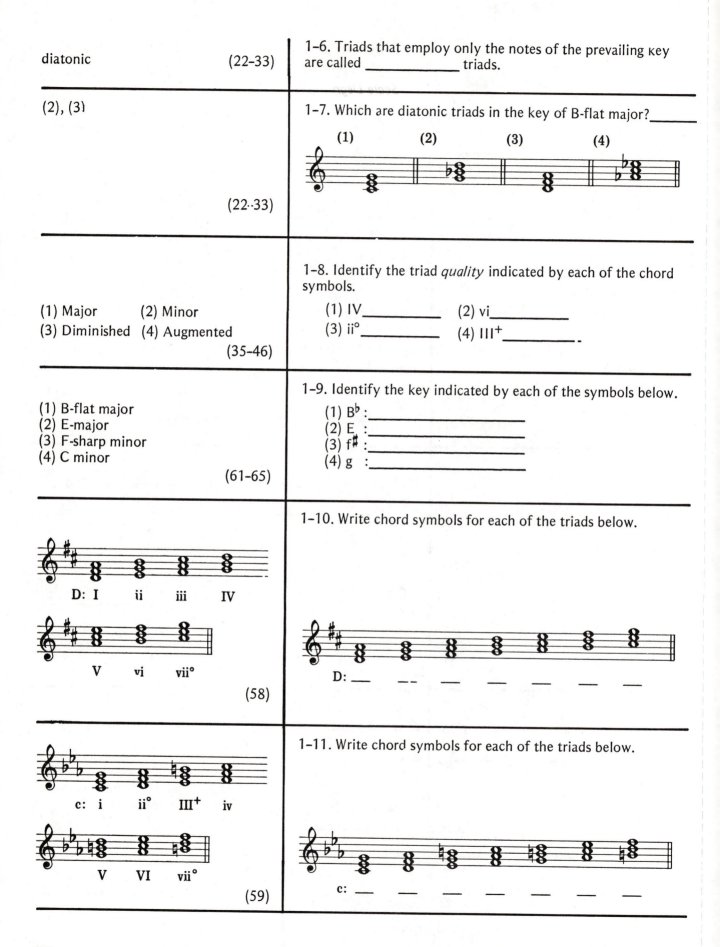
(1) Major (2) Minor (3) Diminished (4) Augmented (35-46)	1-8. Identify the triad *quality* indicated by each of the chord symbols. (1) IV _____ (2) vi _____ (3) ii° _____ (4) III⁺ _____ .
(1) B-flat major (2) E-major (3) F-sharp minor (4) C minor (61-65)	1-9. Identify the key indicated by each of the symbols below. (1) B♭ : _____ (2) E : _____ (3) f♯ : _____ (4) g : _____
(58)	1-10. Write chord symbols for each of the triads below.
(59)	1-11. Write chord symbols for each of the triads below.

(1) Major
(2) Minor
(3) Minor
(4) Major
(5) Major
(6) Minor
(7) Diminished

(49)

1–12. Indicate the type of triad that occurs on each degree of the *major* scale.

Scale Degrees	Triad Types
(1)	_____
(2)	_____
(3)	_____
(4)	_____
(5)	_____
(6)	_____
(7)	_____

(1) Minor
(2) Diminished
(3) Augmented
(4) Minor
(5) Major
(6) Major
(7) Diminished

(50)

1–13. Indicate the type of triad that occurs on each degree of the *harmonic minor* scale.

Scale Degrees	Triad Types
(1)	_____
(2)	_____
(3)	_____
(4)	_____
(5)	_____
(6)	_____
(7)	_____

Supplementary Assignments

ASSIGNMENT 1–1   Name_____

1. What note is the tonal center of the melody below?_____

2. Write a brief justification for your answer to question 1.

_____

_____

3. Write a single line melody that clearly establishes the key of B-flat major.

4. Identify the specific features of your melody that contribute to the establishment of the tonality.

_____

_____

5. Identify each example as either an interval or a chord.
   (1)_____   (2)_____
   (3)_____   (4)_____
   (5)_____   (6)_____

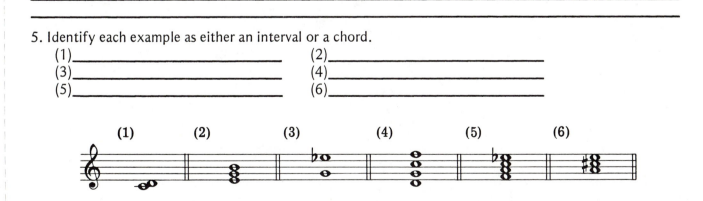

6. List the examples in the preceding question that are triads._____

7. What interval is the basic building block of triads in the tonal harmonic system?_____

8. Write all of the diatonic triads in the key of E major.

9. Write all of the diatonic triads in the key of G minor (harmonic form).

1. List the *quality* of the diatonic triad on each degree of a major scale

Scale degree
(1)_____
(2)_____
(3)_____
(4)_____
(5)_____
(6)_____
(7)_____

2. List the *quality* of the diatonic triad on each degree of a minor scale (harmonic form).

(1)_____
(2)_____
(3)_____
(4)_____
(5)_____
(6)_____
(7)_____

3. Write the chord indicated by each chord symbol. *(Provide the necessary accidentals.)*

Ab: vi   ii   vii°   IV   iii   V   I

4. Write the chord symbol for each chord.

b: __   __   __   __   __   __   __

5. Which chord matches the chord symbol?_____

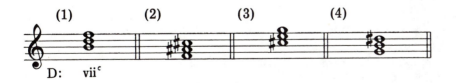

(1)   (2)   (3)   (4)

D: vii°

6. Which chord matches the chord symbol?_____

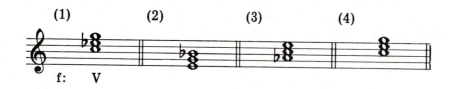

7. Provide the correct chord symbol for each chord.

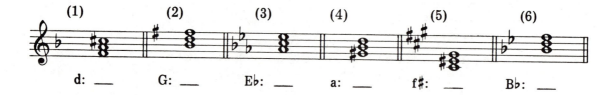

8. How many *major* triads occur in a major key?_____

9. How many *minor* triads occur in a major key?_____

10. On which scale degrees do major triads occur in the harmonic minor scale?_____

11. Does the augmented triad occur in the major scale?_____

12. Does the diminished triad occur in both the major and harmonic minor scales?_____

chapter two

The Structure of Tonality

Chords built on the various scale degrees differ not only in quality, but also possess different functions resulting from their position in the scale. Function means two things: the tendency for each chord to relate to the others in a consistent way; and the particular position each chord has in the edifice known as the "structure of tonality." Through chord function, harmony plays a role in the establishment of tonality. We may, in fact, speak of "harmonic tonality"—the result of consistent patterns of harmonic action, which cause a particular tone (or chord) to gain preeminence over the others. By noting the position of the chords in the tonal structure and examining their functions, we shall begin to understand the subtleties of the "language of harmony."

75. Roman numerals are used chiefly for harmonic analysis. In addition to Roman numeral terminology, each triad has a proper name. The name in each case is either derived from the harmonic function of the triad or determined by its position in the scale. You will understand the full significance of these names later in this study, but the diagram below will shed some light upon their meaning and also the structure of tonality.

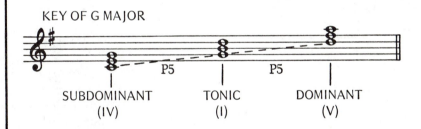

KEY OF G MAJOR

SUBDOMINANT (IV)   P5   TONIC (I)   P5   DOMINANT (V)

The triad which is built on the first degree of the scale (the keynote) is called the _____.

tonic

76. The word TONIC means "tone." This is the proper name given the triad built on the keynote of the scale. Since the keynote predominates over the remaining tones, *the tonic triad is the principal triad of the key.*

The tonic triad is built on the _____ degree of the scale.

first

dominant	77. Notice in Frame 75 that the root of the DOMINANT triad is a perfect fifth *above* the keynote (G). Triads whose roots are related by the interval of a perfect fifth have a close relation to one another. This is due to the "fundamental" nature of the perfect fifth.* The triad whose root is a perfect fifth above the keynote is called the _____. --- *In acoustics (the scientific study of sound), intervals are expressed by the ratio of frequencies between two tones. The ratio of the perfect fifth is 3:2. This represents the simplest relationship of all intervals except the unison (1:1), and the octave (2:1).
perfect fifth	78. The *dominant* triad is so called because of its "dominant" position in the tonality. The root of the dominant triad is the interval of a _____ _____ above the keynote.
above	79. Notice in Frame 75 that the root of the SUBDOMINANT triad is a perfect fifth *below* the keynote. The subdominant triad is so called because it occupies the same position *below* the tonic that the dominant has _____ the tonic.
subdominant	80. The triad whose root is a perfect fifth *below* the keynote is called the _____.

False.
(The tonic triad is relatively inactive.)
	81. The *tonic, dominant,* and *subdominant* triads are the PRIMARY triads in any key. The importance of this statement will become clear as we progress.
	      Since the tonic triad is built on the keynote (the center of the tonality), it has less harmonic activity than triads built on other degrees of the scale. It is the final chord of most compositions. Because of its position at the center of the tonality the tonic triad may be regarded as a "chord of repose."
	      The three primary triads possess harmonic activity of approximately the same degree. (True/False) _____

Perfect fifth.	82. The *dominant* and *subdominant* triads are both active and tend to progress to the *tonic.* The structure of tonality rests upon the three primary triads. This is due to the fundamental interval by which the roots of the dominant and subdominant chords are related to the tonic. What is this interval? _____

83. The structure of tonality rests upon the foundation of three chords. Name these chords.

   (1) _____

   (2) _____

   (3) _____

(1) Tonic
(2) Dominant
(3) Subdominant
(Any order.)

---

84. Write on the staff the *tonic* triad in the key of E minor Supply, also, the appropriate Roman numeral.

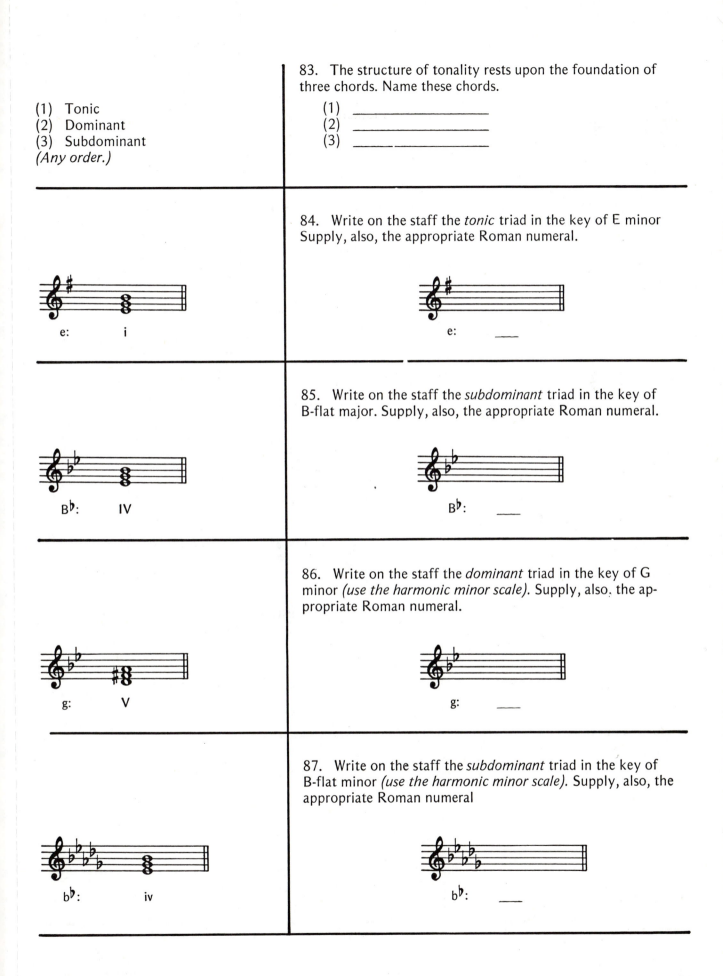

e: i

e: ___

---

85. Write on the staff the *subdominant* triad in the key of B-flat major. Supply, also, the appropriate Roman numeral.

B♭:   IV

B♭:   ___

---

86. Write on the staff the *dominant* triad in the key of G minor *(use the harmonic minor scale)*. Supply, also, the appropriate Roman numeral.

g: V

g: ___

---

87. Write on the staff the *subdominant* triad in the key of B-flat minor *(use the harmonic minor scale)*. Supply, also, the appropriate Roman numeral

b♭:   iv

b♭:   ___

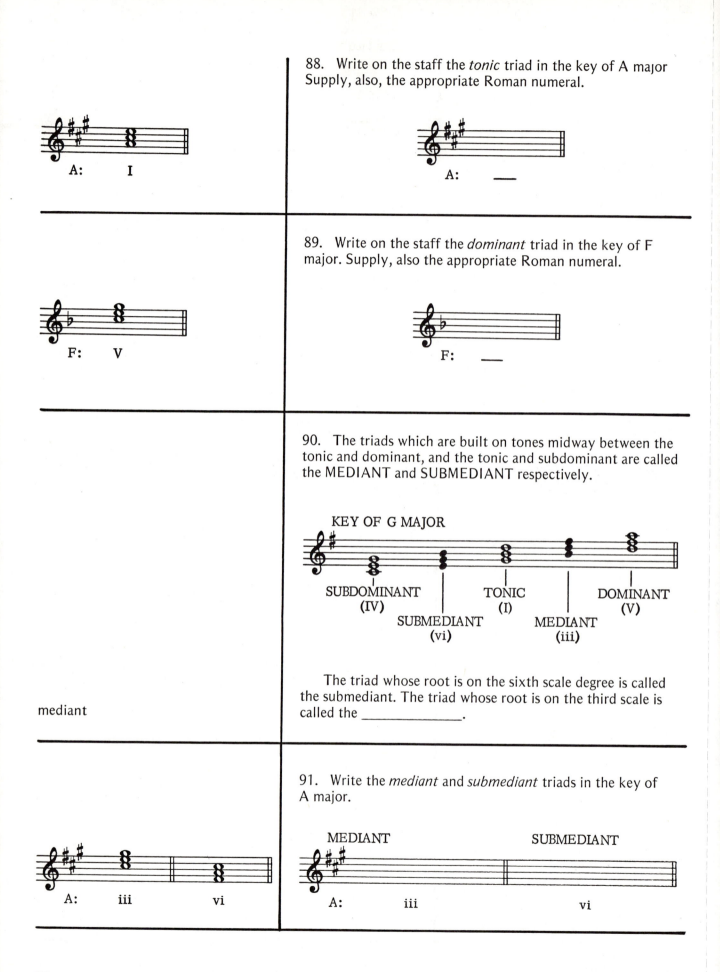

88. Write on the staff the *tonic* triad in the key of A major Supply, also, the appropriate Roman numeral.

A: I

A: ___

89. Write on the staff the *dominant* triad in the key of F major. Supply, also the appropriate Roman numeral.

F: V

F: ___

90. The triads which are built on tones midway between the tonic and dominant, and the tonic and subdominant are called the MEDIANT and SUBMEDIANT respectively.

KEY OF G MAJOR

SUBDOMINANT (IV)   SUBMEDIANT (vi)   TONIC (I)   MEDIANT (iii)   DOMINANT (V)

The triad whose root is on the sixth scale degree is called the submediant. The triad whose root is on the third scale is called the _____.

mediant

91. Write the *mediant* and *submediant* triads in the key of A major.

A: iii   vi

MEDIANT   SUBMEDIANT

A: iii   vi

92. Write the *mediant* and *submediant* triads in the key of B minor *(use the harmonic minor scale)*.

MEDIANT   SUBMEDIANT

b: III⁺   VI

b: III⁺   VI

93. Write the *mediant* and *submediant* triads in the key of G minor *(use the harmonic minor scale)*.

MEDIANT   SUBMEDIANT

g: III⁺   VI

g: III⁺   VI

94. Write the *mediant* and *submediant* triads in the key of E-flat major.

MEDIANT   SUBMEDIANT

E♭:   iii   vi

E♭:   iii   vi

95. Five of the seven triads have been named. The relation of these triads to one another, and particularly to the key center is reflected in the special order of the list below.

Write the name for each triad.

5th: Dominant
3rd: Mediant
1st: TONIC
6th: Submediant
4th: Subdominant

The triad on the 5th degree: _____
The triad on the 3rd degree: _____
THE TRIAD ON THE 1st DEGREE: _____
The triad on the 6th degree: _____
The triad on the 4th degree: _____

96. The two triads yet to be named are shown below:

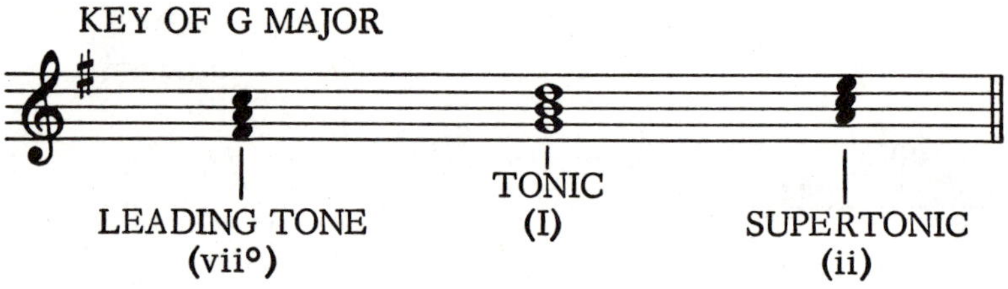

KEY OF G MAJOR

LEADING TONE   TONIC   SUPERTONIC
(vii°)   (I)   (ii)

The triad whose root is a half-step *below* the tonic is called the LEADING TONE. The triad built on the second degree of the scale is called the _____.

---

supertonic

97. The prefix *super* means over, above, or on top of. Thus it is natural that the triad whose root is a second above the tonic should be called the SUPERTONIC.

The LEADING TONE triad derives its name from the fact that its root, being a half-step below the tonic, has a very strong tendency to "lead back" to the keynote.

Which of the triads below is the *supertonic* triad in the key of E major? _____

(1)   (2)   (3)   (4)

---

(4).

98. Which of the triads below is the *leading tone* triad in the key of F major? _____

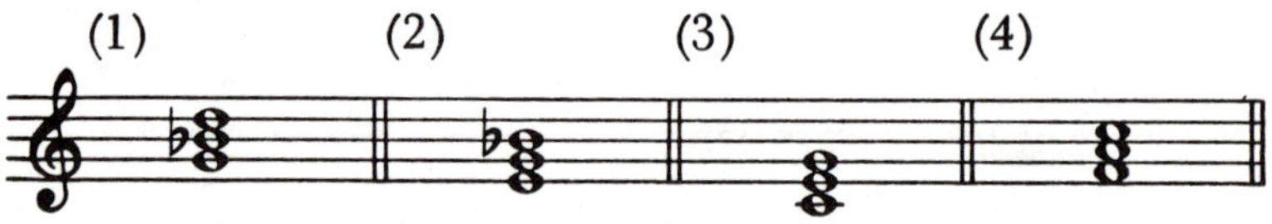

(1)   (2)   (3)   (4)

---

(2).

99. Which of the triads below is the *leading tone* triad in the key of B-flat minor? _____

(1)   (2)   (3)   (4)

---

(4).
(See next frame.)

True.

100. You may have had difficulty choosing between Items (2) and (4) in the preceding frame. The root of the leading tone triad, remember, is a *half-step* below the tonic. The triad A♭ C E♭ is a diatonic triad in B-flat natural (or melodic) minor, but it is NOT a leading tone triad. A triad built on the tone which is a *whole-step* below the tonic is called the SUBTONIC.

The *subtonic* triad does not occur as a diatonic triad in either the major or harmonic minor scales. (True/False)
_____

---

whole

101. The *leading tone* triad is built on a tone which is a half-step below the tonic. The *subtonic* triad is built on a tone which is a _____-step below the tonic.

Subtonic.

102. Which term is appropriate for the triad below? (Leading tone/Subtonic) _____

KEY OF C MINOR

Leading tone.

103. Which term is appropriate for the triad below? (Leading tone/Subtonic) _____

KEY OF F MINOR

---

(2).

104. Which of the triads below is the *leading tone* triad in the key of D minor? _____

(1)   (2)   (3)

---

(3).

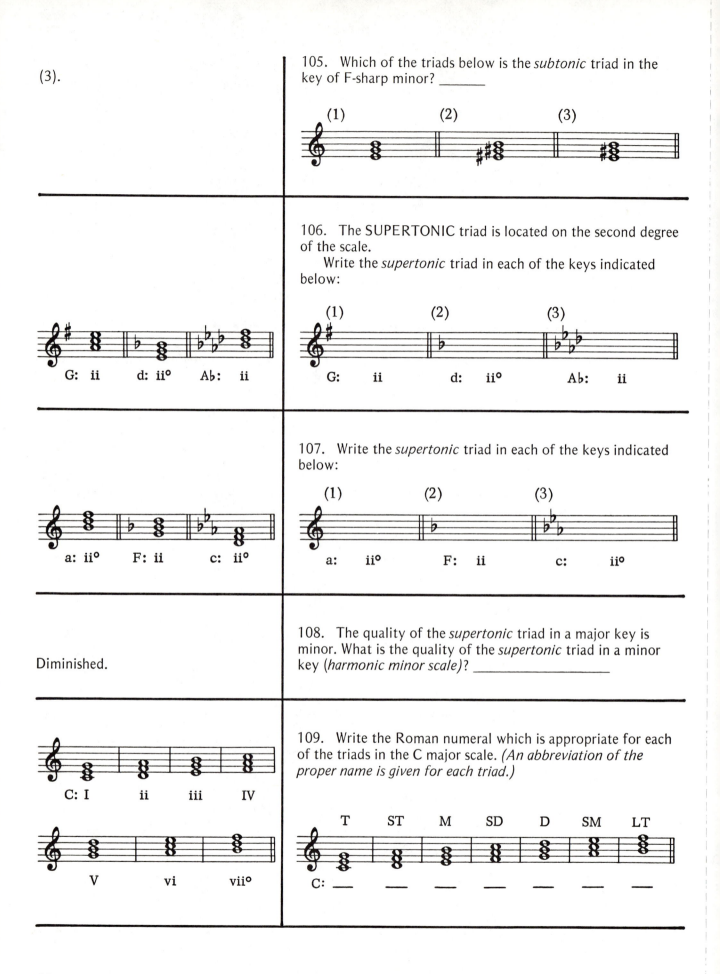

105. Which of the triads below is the *subtonic* triad in the key of F-sharp minor? _____

(1) (2) (3)

106. The SUPERTONIC triad is located on the second degree of the scale.

Write the *supertonic* triad in each of the keys indicated below:

(1) (2) (3)

G: ii   d: ii°   A♭:   ii

107. Write the *supertonic* triad in each of the keys indicated below:

(1) (2) (3)

a: ii°   F: ii   c: ii°

Diminished.

108. The quality of the *supertonic* triad in a major key is minor. What is the quality of the *supertonic* triad in a minor key (*harmonic minor scale*)? _____

109. Write the Roman numeral which is appropriate for each of the triads in the C major scale. *(An abbreviation of the proper name is given for each triad.)*

C: I   ii   iii   IV

V   vi   vii°

T   ST   M   SD   D   SM   LT

C: __   __   __   __   __   __   __

110. Write the Roman numeral which is appropriate for each of the triads in the C harmonic minor scale. *(Note the quality of each triad.)*

111. Write the Roman numeral which is appropriate for each of the triads in the C natural minor scale. *(Note the quality of each triad.)*

112. Write the proper name for each triad.

(Consider the seventh degree as being a half-step below the keynote.)

1st: Tonic
2nd: Supertonic
3rd: Mediant
4th: Subdominant
5th: Dominant
6th: Submediant
7th: Leading tone

The triad on the 1st degree: _____
The triad on the 2nd degree: _____
The triad on the 3rd degree: _____
The triad on the 4th degree: _____
The triad on the 5th degree: _____
The triad on the 6th degree: _____
The triad on the 7th degree: _____

subtonic

113. A triad whose root is a whole-step below the keynote is called the _____.

114. List the quality (major, minor, diminished, or augmented) of the triads on each degree of a *major* scale.

1st: Major
2nd: Minor
3rd: Minor
4th: Major
5th: Major
6th: Minor
7th: Diminished

The triad on the 1st degree: _____
The triad on the 2nd degree: _____
The triad on the 3rd degree: _____
The triad on the 4th degree: _____
The triad on the 5th degree: _____
The triad on the 6th degree: _____
The triad on the 7th degree: _____

---

115. List the quality (as above) of the triads on each degree of a *harmonic minor* scale.

1st: Minor
2nd: Diminished
3rd: Augmented
4th: Minor
5th: Major
6th: Major
7th: Diminished

The triad on the 1st degree: _____
The triad on the 2nd degree: _____
The triad on the 3rd degree: _____
The triad on the 4th degree: _____
The triad on the 5th degree: _____
The triad on the 6th degree: _____
The triad on the 7th degree: _____

B♭ D F.

116. Spell the *tonic* triad in the key of B-flat major. _____

A C E♭.

117. Spell the *supertonic* triad in the key of G minor. *(Use the notes of the harmonic minor scale.)* _____

D♯ F♯ A♯.

118. Spell the *mediant* triad in the key of B major. _____

C♯ E G♯.

119. Spell the *subdominant* triad in the key of G-sharp minor. *(Use the notes of the harmonic minor scale.)* _____

E♭ G B♭.

120. Spell the *dominant* triad in the key of A-flat major. _____

D♭ F A♭.

121. Spell the *submediant* triad in the key of F minor. *(Use the notes of the harmonic minor scale.)* _____

C E♭ G♭.	122. Spell the *leading tone* triad in the key of D-flat major. _____
C E G♯.	123. Spell the *mediant* triad in the key of A minor. *(Use the notes of the harmonic minor scale.)* _____
A♯ C♯ E.	124. Spell the *leading tone* triad in the key of B minor. *(Use the notes of the harmonic minor scale.)* _____
C E G	125. Spell the *subtonic* triad in the key of D minor. *(Use the notes of the natural minor scale.)* _____
(No response.)	126. Do not continue unless the proper names and chord symbols are firmly fixed in your mind. The diagram below is yet another representation which may help. 4 *Subdominant* (IV) 3 *Mediant* (iii) 2 *Supertonic* (ii) 1 *Tonic* (I) 7 *Leading tone* (vii°) 6 *Submediant* (vi) 5 *Dominant* (V)
tonic	127. The tonic triad is built on the center of a tonality—the keynote. Harmonically the tonic triad is relatively static. The other diatonic triads are attracted to it and possess various degrees of activity. The precise relation each triad bears to the tonic (and to the other diatonic triads) is unique, and the discovery of these relationships will occupy us for some time. First we shall observe some of the basic principles regarding the structure of tonality. The three primary triads of a tonality are the *tonic, dominant,* and *subdominant.* Which of these triads possesses the least harmonic activity? The _____.
■	128. Inactive in most cases, the tonic triad is a relatively "neutral" chord. Most compositions begin and end with tonic harmony, and a sense of relative repose accompanies the tonic triad whenever it appears within a harmonic phrase.

One of the most active triads is the *dominant*. This triad tends to demand resolution directly to the tonic.

Play the example below:

Beethoven, *Sonata*, Op. 2, No. 3

Allegro con brio

C: I   V

The harmonic movement is tonic-dominant—a basic progression in tonal music. Because it ends with an active chord (V), it sounds incomplete. We shall refer to such progressions as "opening" progressions.

The tonic and dominant are two of the three primary chords which provide the foundation for the structure of tonality. The root of the dominant triad is the interval of a perfect _____ above the tonic.

fifth

■   129.   The "opening" progression (I-V) illustrated in the preceding frame is completed when the dominant seventh chord* progresses back to the tonic.

Beethoven, *Sonata*, Op. 2, No. 3

Allegro con brio

C: I   V

V⁷   I

No.
(The opening progression I-V is completed by returning to the tonic.)

Tonic and dominant harmonies provide the basis for many phrases. Does a series of chords ending on the dominant sound complete? _____

*The dominant seventh chord possesses the same harmonic function as the dominant triad but has greater activity due to the dissonance provided by the seventh. This chord is treated fully in Part II of this study.

---

130.   Two of the chords which constitute the tripodal foundation of the structure of tonality are the *tonic* and *dominant*; the third is the SUBDOMINANT.

Play the example below:

Mozart, *Sonata*, K. 311

No.
(The tonic chord is required to produce a sense of finality.)

The basic harmonic movement in this example is I-IV. This is another of the common "opening" progressions. The character of the subdominant chord is quite different from that of the dominant. The need for resolution into the tonic is not as strong for the subdominant as for the dominant.
Does the phrase above end with a sense of finality? _____

---

131.   The "opening" progression I—IV is often completed by IV-I.

Play the example below:

Schumann, *Album for the Young*, Op. 68, No. 10

tonic

Both of the "opening" progressions I-V and I-IV are completed by a return to the _____ triad.

---

132. The subdominant chord often progresses to the dominant rather than returning at once to the tonic.

Play the example below:

Bach, Chorale: *In allen meinen Taten*

F: I   IV   V

This example shows another of the basic harmonic progressions (IV-V). The subdominant chord progresses as naturally to the dominant as to the tonic.

The subdominant chord may return immediately to the tonic or it may progress to the _____.

dominant (V)

---

133. Below is a list of the three *basic* progressions:

OPENING	COMPLETION
(1) I-V	V-I
(2) I-IV	IV-I
(3) (I) IV-V	V-I

Despite their seeming simplicity, these harmonic relations constitute the basic harmonic underpinning of much eighteenth- and nineteenth-century music.

Complete, in terms of the basic progressions, the statement below *(use Roman numerals)*:

The tonic (I) can progress to _____ or to _____.

IV (or to) V
(Any order.)

---

134. Complete, in terms of the basic harmonic progressions, the statement below *(use Roman numerals)*:

The subdominant (IV) can progress to _____ or to _____.

I (or to) V
(Any order.)

---

tonic (I)	135. To what triad is the dominant most likely to progress? The _____.
diminished	136. The PRIMARY triads in any key are the tonic, subdominant, and dominant triads. The remaining triads (supertonic, mediant, submediant and leading tone) are SECONDARY triads. The *primary* triads in any major key are all major triads. The *secondary* triads (in major) are either minor or _____ _____.
ii, iii (and) vi *(Any order.)*	137. List with Roman numerals the three triads (in major) which are *minor* in quality. _____, _____, and _____.
I, IV, (and) V ii, iii, vi, (and) vii° *(Any order.)*	138. Complete the chart below: *Primary triads:* _____, _____, and _____. *Secondary triads:* _____, _____, _____, and _____.
i (and) iv *(Any order.)*	139. Two of the primary triads (in harmonic minor) are minor in quality. List these triads: _____ and _____.
ii° (and) vii° *(Any order.)*	140. Two of the secondary triads (in harmonic minor) are diminished. List these triads: _____ and _____.
perfect fifth	141. The primary triads provide the foundation for the structure of tonality. This is due to the fundamental intervallic relationship of the perfect fifth between their roots. Tonic (I) — P5 — Dominant (V) Tonic (I) — P5 — Subdominant (IV) The roots of the dominant and subdominant triads are related to the tonic by the interval of a _____.

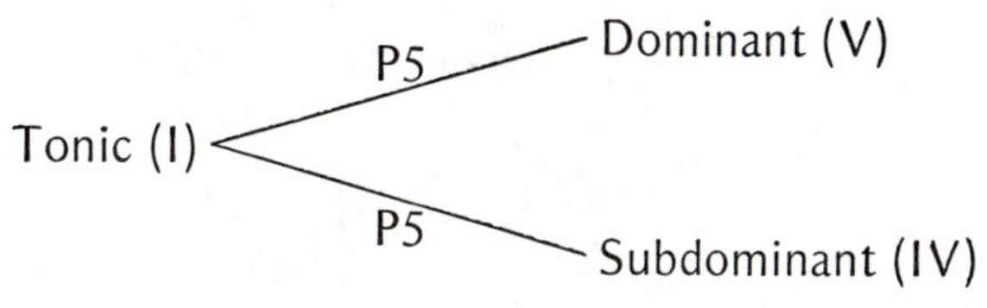

142. The relation which the various secondary triads bear to the tonic is shown here:

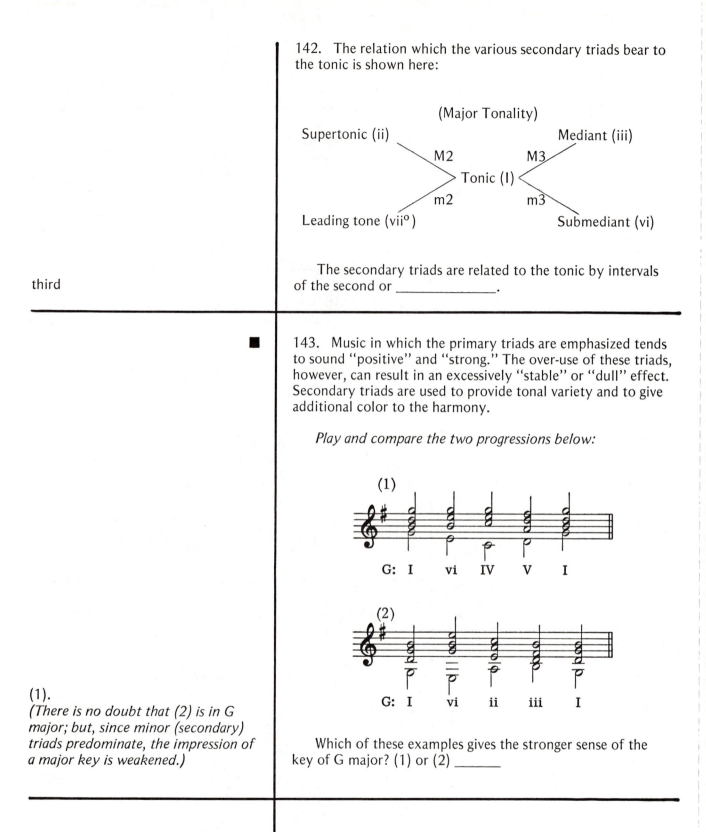

(Major Tonality)

Supertonic (ii)   M2   M3   Mediant (iii)

                        Tonic (I)

               m2   m3

Leading tone (vii°)   Submediant (vi)

third

      The secondary triads are related to the tonic by intervals of the second or _____.

---

143. Music in which the primary triads are emphasized tends to sound "positive" and "strong." The over-use of these triads, however, can result in an excessively "stable" or "dull" effect. Secondary triads are used to provide tonal variety and to give additional color to the harmony.

Play and compare the two progressions below:

(1)

G: I   vi   IV   V   I

(2)

G: I   vi   ii   iii   I

(1).
(There is no doubt that (2) is in G major; but, since minor (secondary) triads predominate, the impression of a major key is weakened.)

      Which of these examples gives the stronger sense of the key of G major? (1) or (2) _____

---

144. Observe the relation of secondary triads to the tonic in *harmonic minor* as follows:

KEY OF G MINOR
(Harmonic Minor Scale)

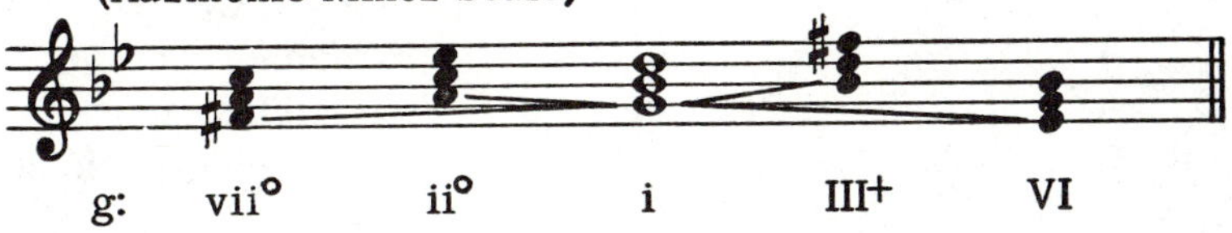

g: vii°   ii°   i   III⁺   VI

By what interval is the *mediant* triad related to the tonic in harmonic minor? *(Be specific.)* _____ _____

Minor third.

---

145. By what interval is the submediant triad related to the tonic in harmonic minor? _____ _____

Major third.

---

146. In harmonic minor the root of the *mediant* triad is a minor third above the tonic. In major the root of the *mediant* triad is a _____ third above the tonic.

major

---

147. In harmonic minor the root of the *submediant* triad is a major third below the tonic. In major the root of the *submediant* triad is a _____ third below the tonic.

minor

No.
(In major the supertonic triad is minor; but it is diminished in harmonic minor.)

148. The root of the *supertonic* triad is related to the tonic by the interval of a major second in both major and minor. Is the quality of this triad the same in major as it is in (harmonic) minor? _____

Yes.
(Both are diminished.)

149. The root of the *leading tone* triad is related to the tonic by the interval of a minor second in both major and harmonic minor. Is the quality of this triad the same in each case? _____

---

150. Each of the secondary triads associates with a specific primary triad.

Study the diagram below:

KEY OF C MAJOR

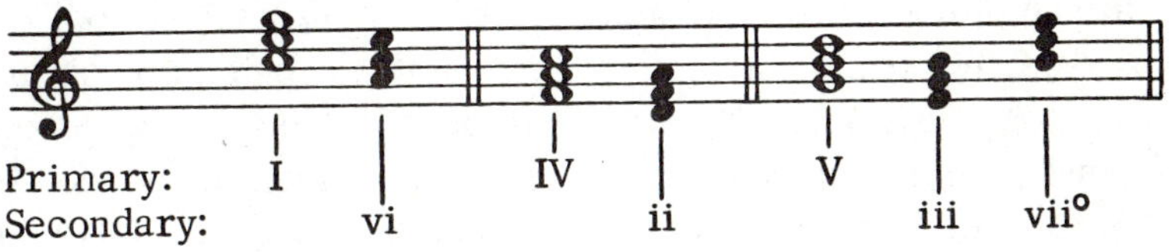

Primary: I   IV   V
Secondary: vi   ii   iii   vii°

THE STRUCTURE OF TONALITY

39

thirds	Secondary triads are used as substitutes for the primary triads with which they are associated, and have similar harmonic functions. What are the intervals between the roots of primary triads and their secondary triads? Major and minor _____.

I - vi
IV - ii
V - iii, viiº
	151. Each secondary triad is located a third *below* its primary triad with the exception of the leading tone (viiº). The harmonic functions of the leading tone and dominant triads are practically identical.* Each tends to progress directly to the tonic.
	
	Indicate with Roman numerals the secondary triad(s) associated with each primary triad.
	
	    PRIMARY TRIADS SECONDARY TRIADS
	         I - _____
	        IV - _____
	         V _____
	
	*The leading tone triad is often considered to be a dominant seventh chord with the root omitted.

subdominant (IV)	152. Which primary triad is associated with the supertonic triad? The _____ triad.
tonic (I)	153. Which primary triad is associated with the submediant triad? The _____ triad.
dominant (V)	154. Which primary triad is associated with the mediant triad? The _____ triad.
leading tone (viiº)	155. Which secondary triad has practically the same harmonic function as the dominant? The _____ triad.

SUMMARY

Roman numerals are used chiefly for harmonic analysis, while proper names (*tonic, supertonic,* etc.) are used when speaking or writing. Since both Roman numerals and proper names will be used throughout this study, it is necessary for you to become fluent in both methods of identifying chords. Whereas proper names do not reveal the quality of triads, Roman numerals do. So you must be especially careful to choose the form of Roman numeral appropriate to the quality of the triad to be represented.

Tne tnree primary triads—I, IV, and V—provide the foundation for the structure of tonality. The roots of the dominant and subdominant triads are related to the tonic by the interval of a perfect fifth. This interval is the "simplest" (see Frame 77) by which different chords can be related. This relationship accounts for the fundamental role which these triads play in the establishment of tonality. The tonic (I) is the center of the tonality; the dominant (V) is a perfect fifth *above* the tonic; and the subdominant (IV) is a perfect fifth *below* the tonic.

With respect to primary triads there are three basic harmonic progressions: I-V, I-IV, and IV-V. Each of these is an "opening" progression, which is completed by harmonic movement back to the tonic. Harmonic phrases usually begin on, and ultimately return to the tonic. Thus some typical *basic* harmonic phrases are: I-V-I, I-IV-I, and I-IV-V-I.

Secondary triads are used as substitutes for primary triads for the sake of tonal variety. With only one exception, the roots of secondary triads are the interval of a third *below* the primary triads to which they relate. The exception is the leading tone triad (vii°) whose root is located a third *above* the dominant.

The harmonic function of secondary triads is similar to that of the primary triads with which they are associated. This association is strongest in the case of the dominant and leading tone triads, for each of these triads can progress directly to the tonic. The difference between them is due not to their function, but to their quality (the dominant is major, the leading tone is diminished).

The symmetrical structure of tonality is represented in the diagram below. The tonic (I) is the center of the structure with the other two primary triads (V and IV) spaced a perfect fifth above and below. The entire structure is based on thirds.

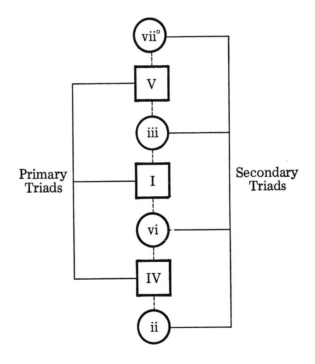

Primary Triads

Secondary Triads

Mastery Frames

(5) Dominant (4) Subdominant (1) Tonic (75–80)	2–1. Write the proper name for triads built on the indicated scale degrees. *Scale Degree* *Proper Name* (5) _____ (4) _____ (1) _____
primary (75–89)	2–2. All of the triads in the preceding frame are (primary/secondary)_____triads.
(Mediant) 3rd (Submediant) 6th (90-95)	2–3. Indicate the scale degree on which each triad is built. Mediant _____ Submediant_____
(7) Leading tone (2) Supertonic (96–108)	2–4. Write the proper name for the triads built on the indicated scale degrees. *Scale Degree* *Proper Name* (7) _____ (2) _____
Eb: I ii iii IV V vi vii° (109)	2–5. Write the appropriate Roman numeral for each triad. Eb: __ __ __ __ __ __ __

f♯:   i   ii°   III⁺   iv

V   VI   vii°

(110)

2-6. Write the appropriate Roman numeral for each triad.

f♯: ___ ___ ___ ___ ___ ___ ___

Dominant.

(128)

2-7. Which of the two triads below is more "active?"
_____

Tonic   Dominant

---

tonic (I)   (129–133)

2-8. "Opening" harmonic progressions such as I-V or I-IV are completed by eventually progressing to the_____.

P
S
S
P
P
S
S   (136–140)

2-9. Identify each triad as either primary (P), or secondary (S).

Tonic	____
Supertonic	____
Mediant	____
Subdominant	____
Dominant	____
Submediant	____
Leading tone	____

---

vi
ii
iii, vii°   (136–151)

2-10. Indicate with Roman numerals the secondary triad(s) associated with each primary triad.

Primary Triads	*Secondary Triads*
I	_____
IV	_____
V	_____

Supplementary Assignments

ASSIGNMENT 2–1   Name_____

1. Provide the proper names for the three triads represented by the Roman numerals below.

    V_____
    I_____
  IV_____

2. Name the secondary triad(s) that relate to each of the primary triads below (use proper names).

    V_____
    I_____
  IV_____

3. Write the proper Roman numeral for each triad.

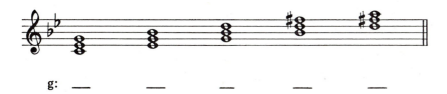

  g: ___   ___   ___   ___   ___

4. Write the proper Roman numeral for each triad.

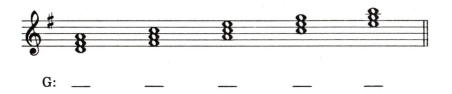

  G: ___   ___   ___   ___   ___

5. Indicate the scale degree on which each chord is built.

Subdominant	_____
Mediant	_____
Supertonic	_____
Tonic	_____

Leading Tone _____
Submediant _____
Dominant _____

6. List the scale degrees on which minor triads occur in a major tonality.

_____

7. Roots of primary and secondary triads are related by the interval of a _____.

Name_____

1. What is the name of the triad that is built on the tonal center of a key?_____

2. Write a single line melody based on the indicated harmony.

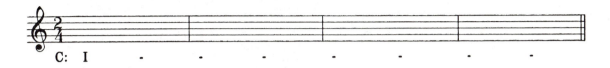

C: I   -   -   -   -   -   -   -

3. Describe the effect of the harmony underlying the melody you wrote in question 2.

_____

_____

4. Use Roman numerals to show three "opening" harmonic progressions.

_____   _____   _____

5. Write a single line melody based on the indicated chord progression.

b: i   -   -   V

6. Is the harmonic progression in question 5 an "opening" or a "closing" progression?_____

7. Write a single line melody based on the indicated harmonic progression.

F: IV   -   V (or vii°)   I

8. Is the harmonic progression in question 7 an "opening" or a "closing" progression?_____

9. Which progression is most conclusive?_____
   a. I-IV
   b. vii°-vi
   c. V-i
   d. V-iii
   e. V-vi
   f. IV-V

10. Write Roman numerals to identify the chords that underly the melody.

d: ___.　　　___　　　___　　　___

chapter three

Triads in Root Position: Doubling and Spacing

With this chapter we shall begin to master the techniques of writing chords and leading voices smoothly from one chord to another. The first step is to become acquainted with "figured bass" symbols. These symbols constitute a form of shorthand notation, and also are used for analysis. Next we shall focus on principles of doubling and spacing of triads in root position. The basis for this work will be the four-voice chorus. Although this aspect of the study of harmony is rather "mechanical," it nevertheless is vital, both to effective writing and the understanding of factors which affect linear action in harmonic music. The latter, especially, contributes to effective performance and fluent reading.

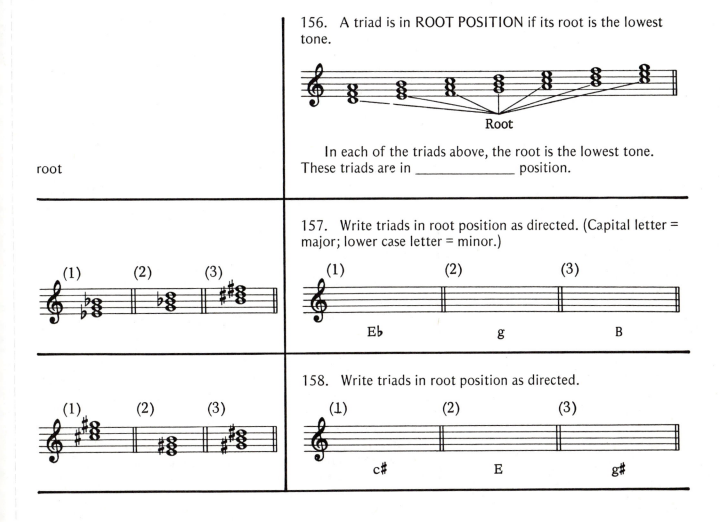

156. A triad is in **ROOT POSITION** if its root is the lowest tone.

In each of the triads above, the root is the lowest tone. These triads are in _____ position.

root

157. Write triads in root position as directed. (Capital letter = major; lower case letter = minor.)

(1)   (2)   (3)

Eb   g   B

158. Write triads in root position as directed.

(1)   (2)   (3)

c#   E   g#

(2)

159. Which of the triads below is in root position? _____

---

160. The intervals of a third and fifth occur over the lowest tone of a triad in root position. These intervals sometimes are represented by the numbers 3 and 5. These are called FIGURED BASS SYMBOLS.*

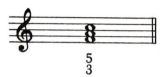

(Note that the larger number is placed above the smaller.)
Figured bass symbols are merely a listing of the intervals which occur above the lowest note. The numbers 3 and 5 beneath a note indicate a triad in _____ position.

root

---

*Figured bass symbols were widely used during the baroque era as a shorthand notation for players of keyboard instruments. They will be used here for the purpose of analysis and as an aid in teaching the principles of part writing.

---

161. Accidentals applied to the upper notes are shown in the figured bass.*

The symbol ♭5 means that the note a fifth above the lowest note is _____.

flatted
(or lowered a half-step)

---

*Accidentals applied to the lowest note, or to its duplication one or more octaves higher are not indicated.

---

162. Figured bass is a shorthand system of indicating notes above a bass (the lowest part). There are several special signs and conventions which must be learned in connection with the use of figured bass symbols.

A slash through a number means that the note represented by the number is RAISED a half-step.

Observe the use of this sign below:

Does the symbol ♯5 mean the same as the symbol ⌿5 ? _____

Yes.
(But see next frame.)

---

163. The figured bass symbols ⌿5 and ⌿3 do not always refer to the use of sharps (♯). The raising of a tone by a half-step is sometimes accomplished by a natural (♮), or a double-sharp (✖). The key signature (if any) must be taken into account. Compare the three triads below:

In (1) the fifth of the triad has been raised a half-step by the use of a natural (♮); in (2) a sharp (♯) has been used to produce the same result; in (3) a double-sharp (✖) has been used.
  The symbol ⌿3 might be used in place of *any* of the following: ✖3, ♯3, or ♮3. (True/False) _____

True.

---

164. Check (√) the correct option:

1. A slash through a number means that the note represented by the number is raised a half-step.
2. A slash through a number calls for a sharp.

True statements:
(1) _____ (2) _____ Both _____ Neither _____

(1) √

---

165. Write the triads and apply accidentals as indicated by the figured bass symbols.

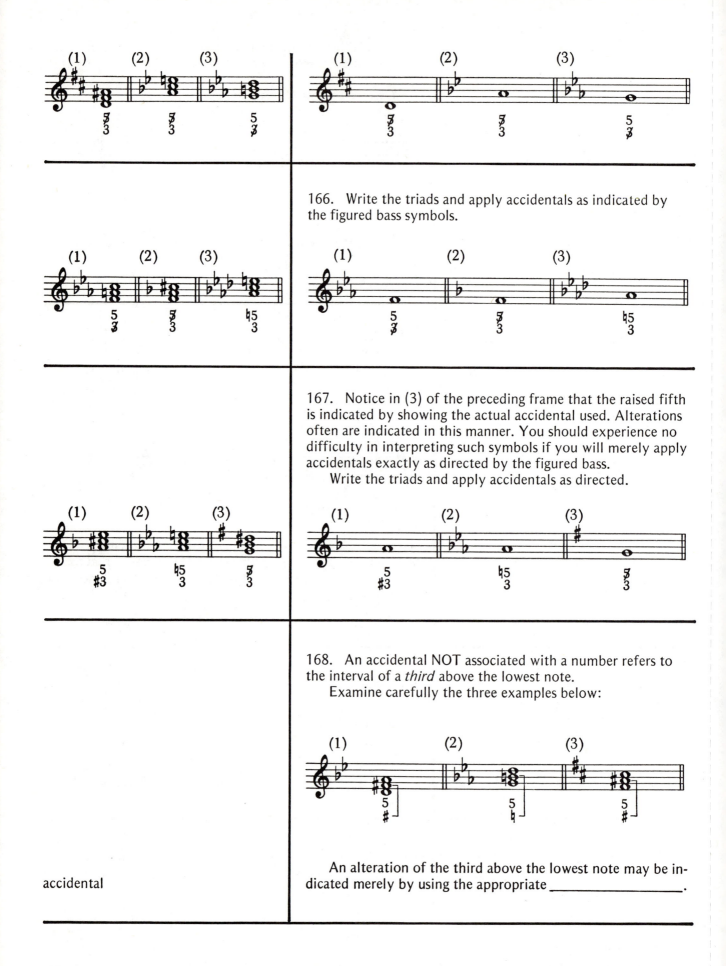

166. Write the triads and apply accidentals as indicated by the figured bass symbols.

167. Notice in (3) of the preceding frame that the raised fifth is indicated by showing the actual accidental used. Alterations often are indicated in this manner. You should experience no difficulty in interpreting such symbols if you will merely apply accidentals exactly as directed by the figured bass.

Write the triads and apply accidentals as directed.

168. An accidental NOT associated with a number refers to the interval of a *third* above the lowest note.

Examine carefully the three examples below:

An alteration of the third above the lowest note may be indicated merely by using the appropriate _____.

accidental

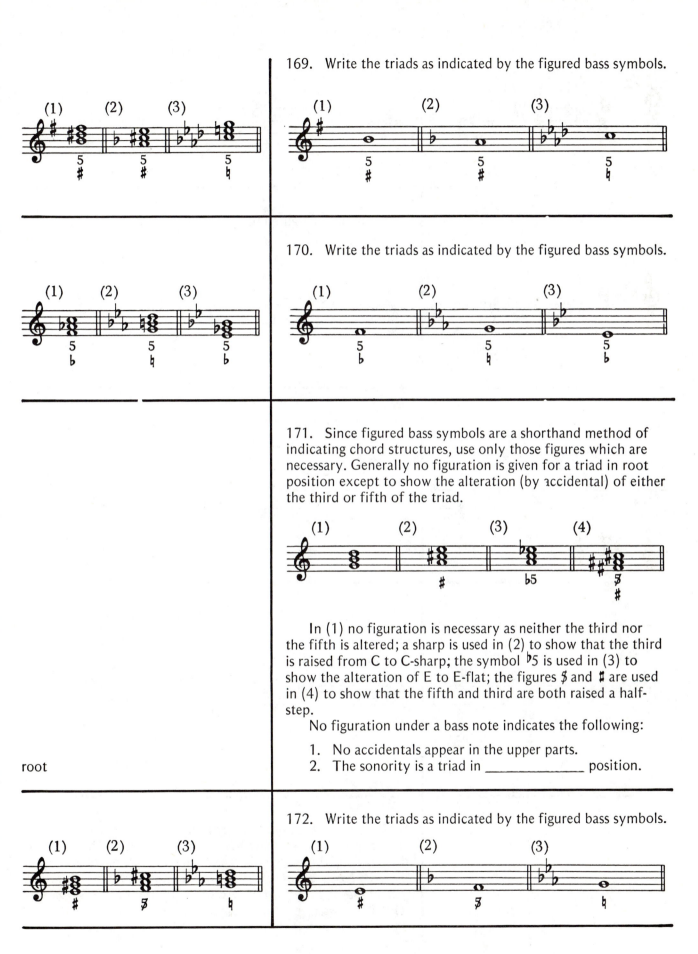

169. Write the triads as indicated by the figured bass symbols.

170. Write the triads as indicated by the figured bass symbols.

171. Since figured bass symbols are a shorthand method of indicating chord structures, use only those figures which are necessary. Generally no figuration is given for a triad in root position except to show the alteration (by accidental) of either the third or fifth of the triad.

In (1) no figuration is necessary as neither the third nor the fifth is altered; a sharp is used in (2) to show that the third is raised from C to C-sharp; the symbol ♭5 is used in (3) to show the alteration of E to E-flat; the figures ♯ and ♯ are used in (4) to show that the fifth and third are both raised a half-step.

No figuration under a bass note indicates the following:

1. No accidentals appear in the upper parts.
2. The sonority is a triad in _____ position.

root

172. Write the triads as indicated by the figured bass symbols.

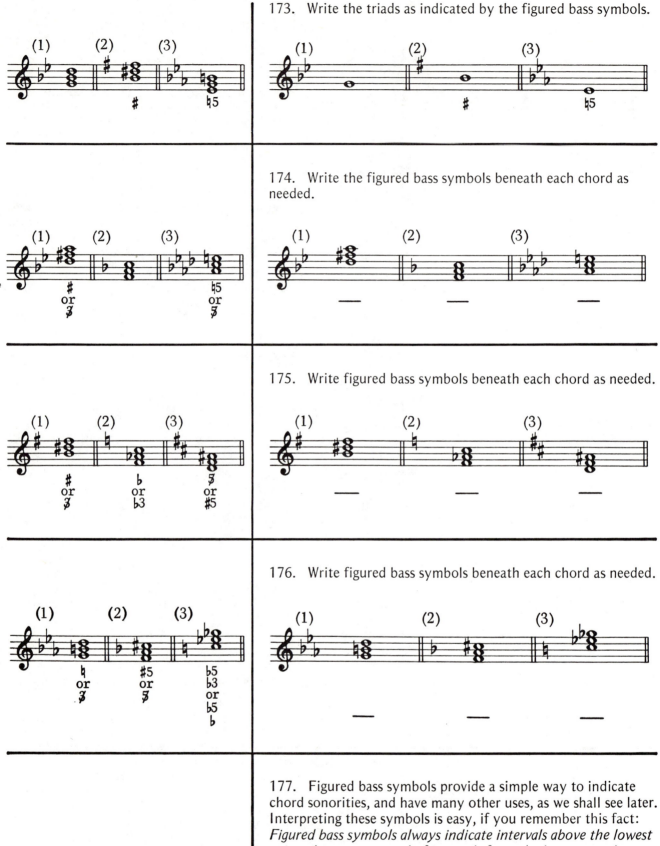

173. Write the triads as indicated by the figured bass symbols.

174. Write the figured bass symbols beneath each chord as needed.

175. Write figured bass symbols beneath each chord as needed.

176. Write figured bass symbols beneath each chord as needed.

177. Figured bass symbols provide a simple way to indicate chord sonorities, and have many other uses, as we shall see later. Interpreting these symbols is easy, if you remember this fact: *Figured bass symbols always indicate intervals above the lowest voice; they are a record of intervals from the bass upward.* Other important points to remember are these:

(No response.)

1. A triad in root position usually requires no figuration unless either the third or fifth is altered.

2. A slash through a number means that the note represented by the number is raised a half-step.

3. An accidental in the figured bass which is not associated with a number refers to the interval of a third above the bass.

---

three

178. Now let us turn to the specific techniques of *doubling* and *spacing*.

Since triads consist of three tones, no problem of doubling exists if these tones are to be given to three instruments or voices, or if a three-part texture is used in writing for a keyboard instrument. In such cases the triads are complete if the root is given to one part, the third to another, and the fifth to still another.

When working with triads, doubling is generally not a problem unless more than _____ instruments or voices are used.

---

four

179. Much of the music composed since the middle of the eighteenth century is based on a four-part texture. The utility of this texture has been proved by more than two centuries of use. It provides an agreeable sonority without imposing undue problems of doubling, or of voice leading.

The texture which has prevailed as the basis of much of the music for the last 200 years is the _____-part texture.

---

(1) Soprano   (3) Tenor
(2) Alto   (4) Bass
(Any order.)

180. Although this study is not devoted exclusively to four-part writing, this texture is so prevalent in music of the baroque, classical, and romantic eras that we must spend a considerable amount of time studying it.

The more mechanical aspects of part writing will be presented in terms of the four-part chorus, which consists of the *soprano, alto, tenor,* and *bass* voices. It is convenient to use this medium as a basis for our study since it expresses clearly the four-part texture, and the principles upon which our attention is to be focused usually are not clouded by other factors, as often is the case in music for the piano or instrumental ensembles.

Name the voices which constitute the four-part chorus.

(1) _____   (3) _____
(2) _____   (4) _____

181. You must learn the approximate range for each of the voices.

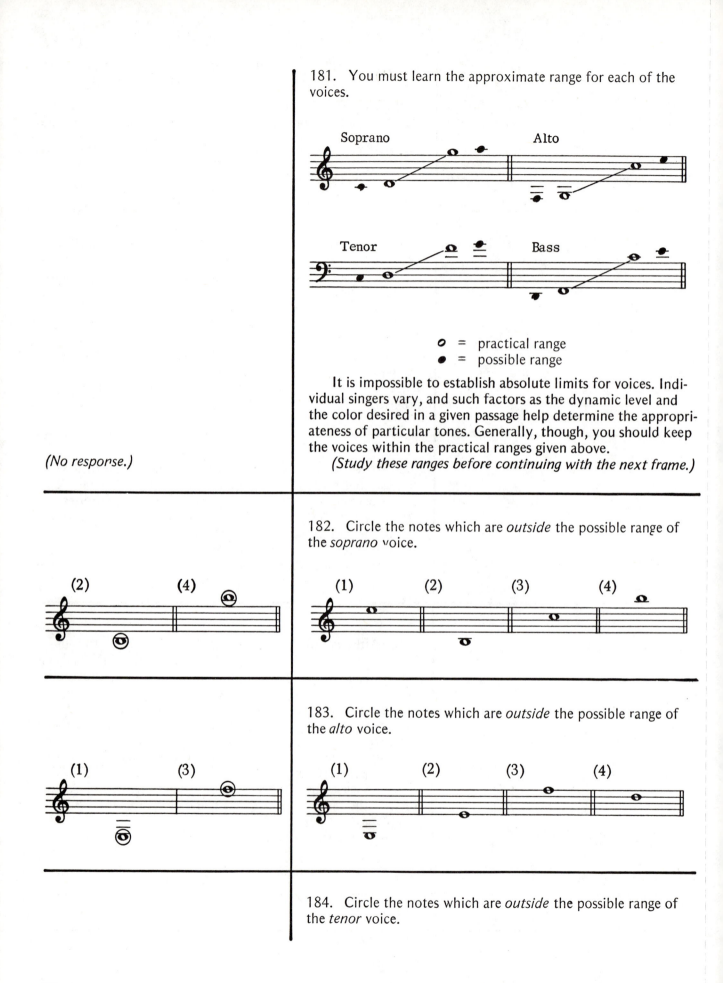

o = practical range
$\bullet$ = possible range

It is impossible to establish absolute limits for voices. Individual singers vary, and such factors as the dynamic level and the color desired in a given passage help determine the appropriateness of particular tones. Generally, though, you should keep the voices within the practical ranges given above.
(Study these ranges before continuing with the next frame.)

(No response.)

182. Circle the notes which are *outside* the possible range of the *soprano* voice.

(1)   (2)   (3)   (4)

183. Circle the notes which are *outside* the possible range of the *alto* voice.

(1)   (2)   (3)   (4)

184. Circle the notes which are *outside* the possible range of the *tenor* voice.

CHAPTER THREE

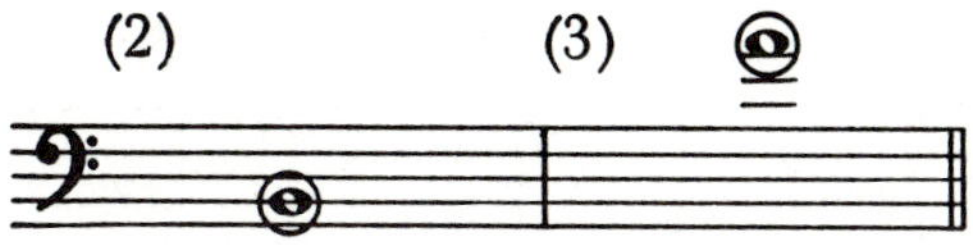

(2)   **(3)**

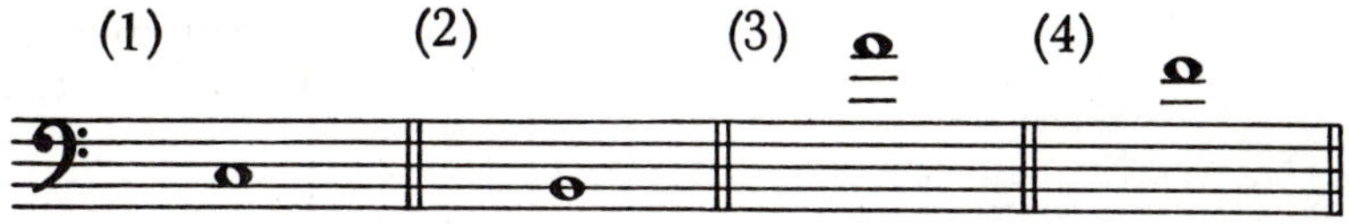

(3)

185. Circle the notes which are *outside* the possible range of the *bass* voice.

(1)   **(2)**   **(3)**   **(4)**

186. The voices of the four-part chorus are notated on the grand staff as illustrated below:

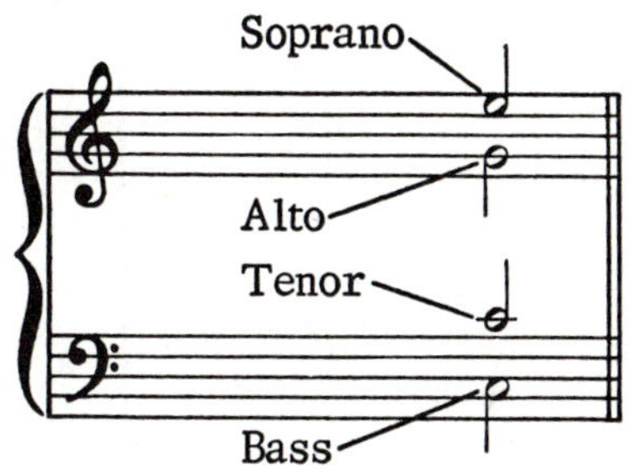

Soprano

Alto
Tenor

Bass

The *soprano* is the highest voice and is notated on the treble staff with stems going up; the *alto* is the next highest voice and is notated on the treble staff with stems going down.

The *tenor* and *bass* voices are notated on the bass staff. Upward stems are used by the tenor and downward stems are used by the bass.

Name the two voices which use upward stems.

(1) Soprano (2) Tenor
(Any order.)

(1) _____   (2) _____

187. Name the two voices which use downward stems.

(1) Alto (2) Bass
(Any order.)

(1) _____   (2) _____

188. Place stems correctly on the notes of each chord.

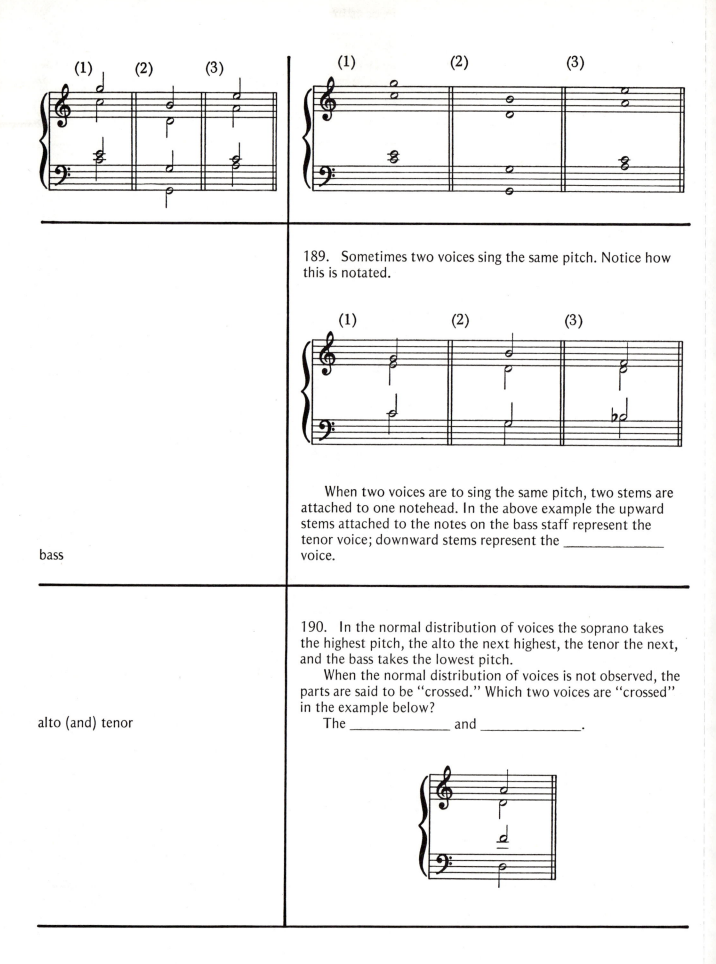

189. Sometimes two voices sing the same pitch. Notice how this is notated.

When two voices are to sing the same pitch, two stems are attached to one notehead. In the above example the upward stems attached to the notes on the bass staff represent the tenor voice; downward stems represent the _____ voice.

bass

alto (and) tenor

190. In the normal distribution of voices the soprano takes the highest pitch, the alto the next highest, the tenor the next, and the bass takes the lowest pitch.

When the normal distribution of voices is not observed, the parts are said to be "crossed." Which two voices are "crossed" in the example below?

The _____ and _____.

soprano (and) alto

191. Which two voices are "crossed" in the example below?
The _____ and _____.

192. The impetus of melodic writing will cause an occasional crossing of voices in more advanced writing. For the present, however, normal distribution should be observed.

List the voices in their normal distribution *from the highest to the lowest.*

(1) Soprano
(2) Alto
(3) Tenor
(4) Bass

(1) _____
(2) _____
(3) _____
(4) _____

193. The "spacing" of a chord concerns primarily the intervals which separate the three upper voices (soprano, alto, and tenor) from one another. Which of the four voices can *not* be called an upper voice? The _____.

bass

194. The most satisfactory spacing of a chord usually requires that the intervals which separate the soprano and alto, and the alto and tenor should not exceed an octave.

In (1) and (2) below, no two adjacent upper voices are separated by an interval greater than an octave. In (3), however, the interval between the tenor and alto voices is an eleventh. If carried on for several chords this type of spacing would cause an "empty" effect, so it should be avoided.

octave

What is the largest interval by which adjacent upper voices should be separated? The _____.

---

(2).
(There is a 10th between the soprano and alto.)

195. In which case below is there an excessive interval between adjacent upper voices? _____

Note: *Not all of the triads above are in root position.*

---

(1).
(There is a 10th between the alto and tenor.)

196. In which case below is there an excessive interval between adjacent upper voices? _____

---

197. Notice in (3) of the preceding frame that the interval between the tenor and bass is greater than an octave. *This is satisfactory.* An interval as large as a twelfth may separate the tenor from the bass without resulting in an unpleasant sonority. It is the upper voices (*soprano, alto,* and *tenor*) which must observe the octave limitation.

Are there any irregularities in the spacing of the following chords?_____

No

CHAPTER THREE

Note: *Not all of the triaas above are in root position.*

Yes.

(In (2) there is more than an octave between the alto and tenor.)

198. Are there any irregularities in the spacing of the chords below? _____

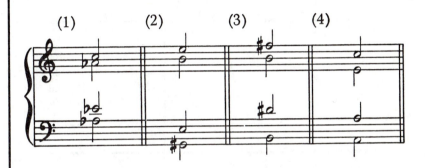

Note: *Not all of the triads above are in root position.*

---

root

199. If the three tones of a triad are to be given to four voices, it is evident that one of the tones must be doubled. Doubled tones are bracketed in the examples below. In each case the triad tone which is doubled is the (root/third/fifth) _____.

THE C MAJOR TRIAD

---

200. Draw brackets (as in the preceding frame) to indicate the doubled tones in each triad.

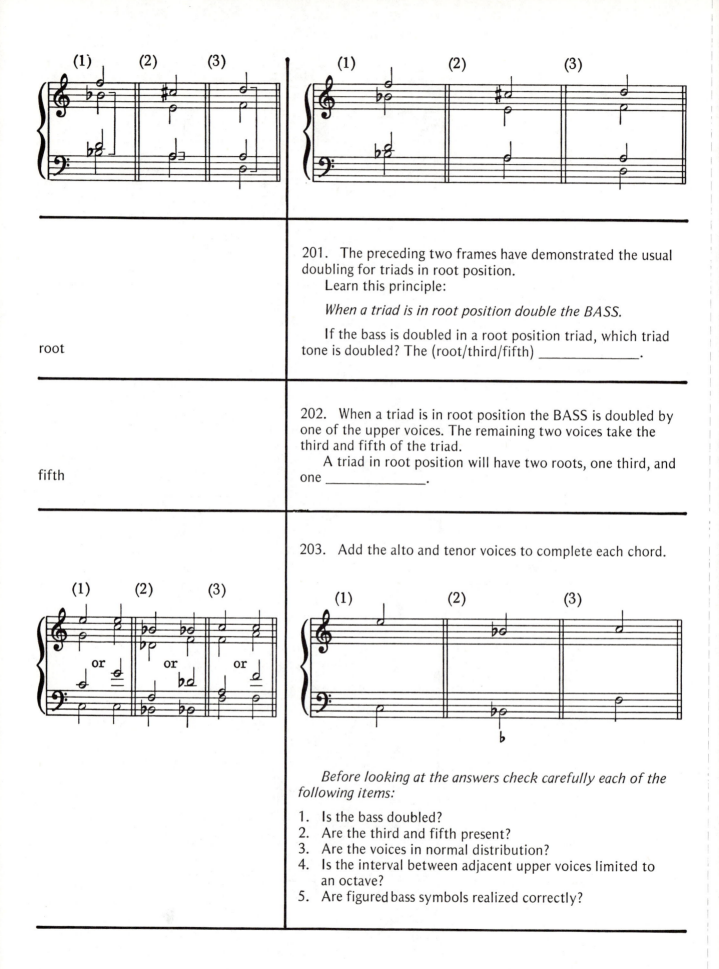

201. The preceding two frames have demonstrated the usual doubling for triads in root position.
   Learn this principle:

When a triad is in root position double the BASS.

   If the bass is doubled in a root position triad, which triad tone is doubled? The (root/third/fifth) _____.

root

202. When a triad is in root position the BASS is doubled by one of the upper voices. The remaining two voices take the third and fifth of the triad.
   A triad in root position will have two roots, one third, and one _____.

fifth

203. Add the alto and tenor voices to complete each chord.

   Before looking at the answers check carefully each of the following items:

1. Is the bass doubled?
2. Are the third and fifth present?
3. Are the voices in normal distribution?
4. Is the interval between adjacent upper voices limited to an octave?
5. Are figured bass symbols realized correctly?

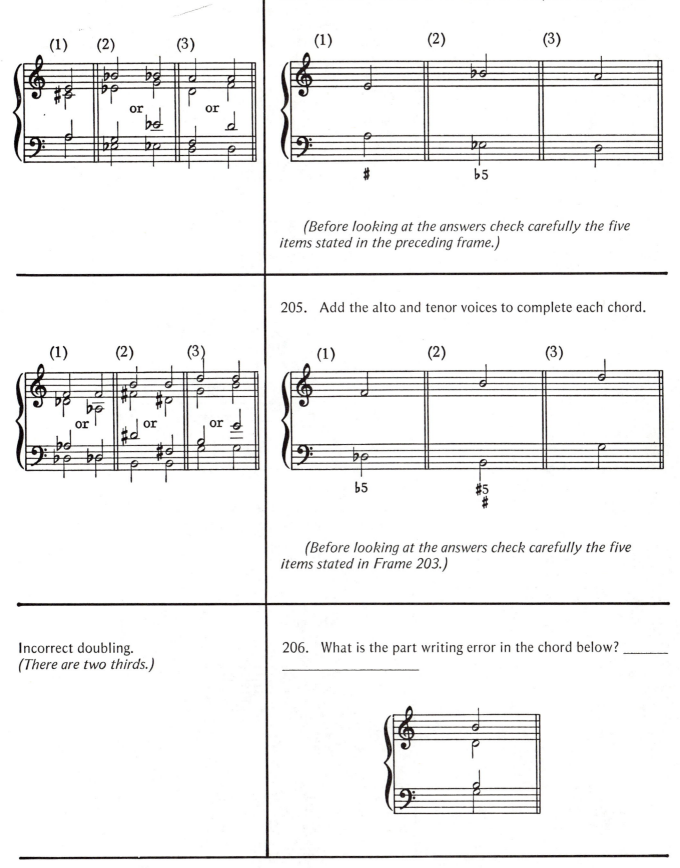

204. Add the alto and tenor voices to complete each chord.

(1)   (2)   (3)

(Before looking at the answers check carefully the five items stated in the preceding frame.)

205. Add the alto and tenor voices to complete each chord.

(1)   (2)   (3)

(Before looking at the answers check carefully the five items stated in Frame 203.)

Incorrect doubling.
(There are two thirds.)

206. What is the part writing error in the chord below? _____

_____

The soprano and alto are more than an octave apart.

207. What is the part writing error in the chord below? _____

_____

_____

Incorrect doubling.
(There is no fifth in the chord.)

208. What is the part writing error in the chord below? _____

_____

---

209. In the example below, the tones of the C major triad have been spaced two different ways.

(1)   (2)

close (and) open
(Any order.)

The spacing in (1) is called CLOSE STRUCTURE, and the spacing in (2) is called OPEN STRUCTURE.

Close and *open* structure concern the way the three upper voices are spaced. The spacing of triad tones results in two kinds of structures; these are called _____ and _____ _____ structure.

210. Observe in (1) of the preceding frame that the upper voices are as *close* together as they can be. Reading down from the soprano each successive voice takes the next available chord tone.

Soprano - C
Alto   - G
Tenor   - E

There are no vacant triad tones between the upper voices when a triad is in _____ structure.

close

---

211. When a triad is in *open* structure there is a vacant triad tone between the soprano and alto, and between the alto and tenor voices. This causes the interval between the soprano and tenor voices to be greater than an octave.

The example below shows a chord in *open* structure. Indicate (with a black notehead) the *unoccupied* triad tone between each of the three upper voices.

THE A MINOR TRIAD

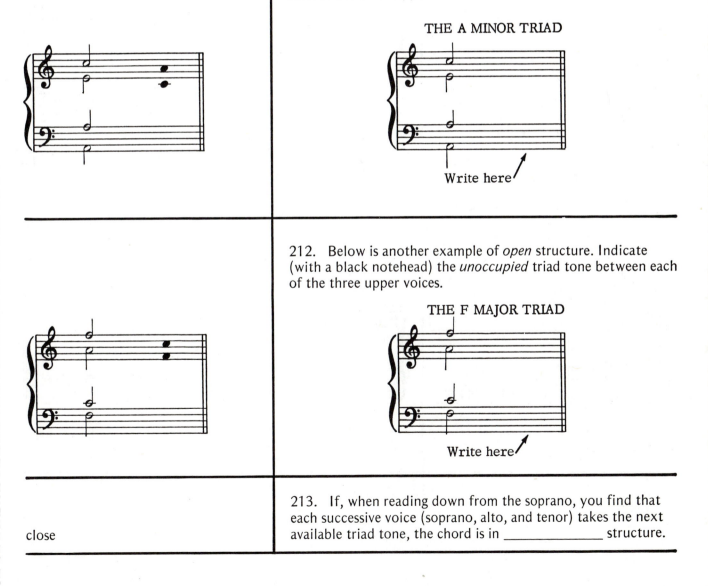

Write here

---

212. Below is another example of *open* structure. Indicate (with a black notehead) the *unoccupied* triad tone between each of the three upper voices.

THE F MAJOR TRIAD

Write here

---

213. If, when reading down from the soprano, you find that each successive voice (soprano, alto, and tenor) takes the next available triad tone, the chord is in _____ structure.

close

(1) and (4).

214. Which of the chords below are in *close* structure? _____ _____

(2) and (4).

215. Which of the chords below are in *close* structure? _____ _____

216. Write the alto and tenor voices so that each chord is in *close* structure.

217. Write the alto and tenor voices so that each chord is in *close* structure.

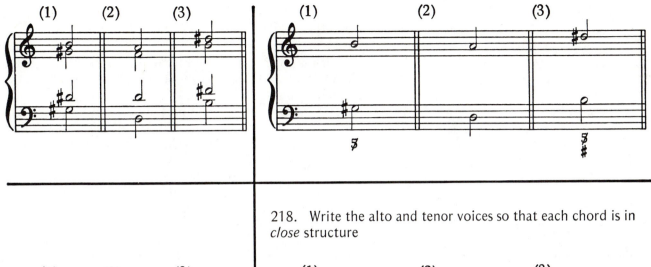

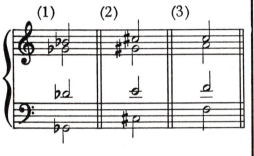

218. Write the alto and tenor voices so that each chord is in *close* structure

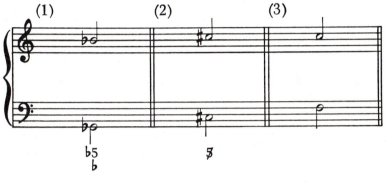

219. Write the alto and tenor voices so that each chord is in *close* structure.

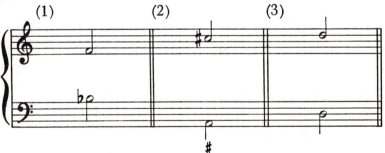

(If you have made no more than four errors in the last six frames you may skip to Frame 228.)

220. If you have made mistakes in translating the figured bass symbols, you should review Frames 160-177.

Review, also, the principles of doubling and spacing stated below:

1. When a triad is in root position double the bass (root).
2. A triad in root position should have two roots, one third and one fifth.
3. The voices should be distributed normally (the highest tone given to the soprano, the next highest to the alto, the next to the tenor, and the lowest to the bass).
4. There should not be more than an octave between any of the upper voices.
5. *Close* structure means that the three upper voices take successive triad tones. These voices are as close together as the triad permits.

(No response.)

---

(4).

221. Which of the chords is in *close* structure? _____

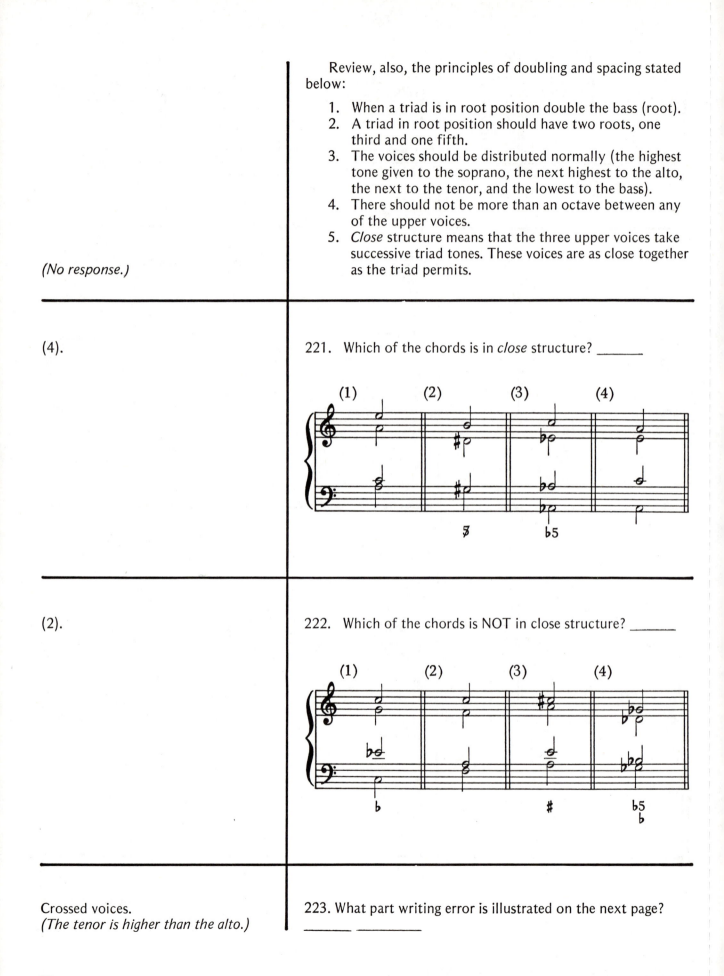

---

(2).

222. Which of the chords is NOT in close structure? _____

Crossed voices.
(The tenor is higher than the alto.)

223. What part writing error is illustrated on the next page? _____ _____

The interval between the alto and tenor is larger than an octave.

224. What part writing error is illustrated below? _____
_____

The figured bass symbol 6 has not been realized *(F-sharp is needed)*.

225. What part writing error is illustrated below? _____
_____

226. Write the alto and tenor voices so that each chord is in *close* structure.

(1)   (2)   (3)

(1)   (2)   (3)

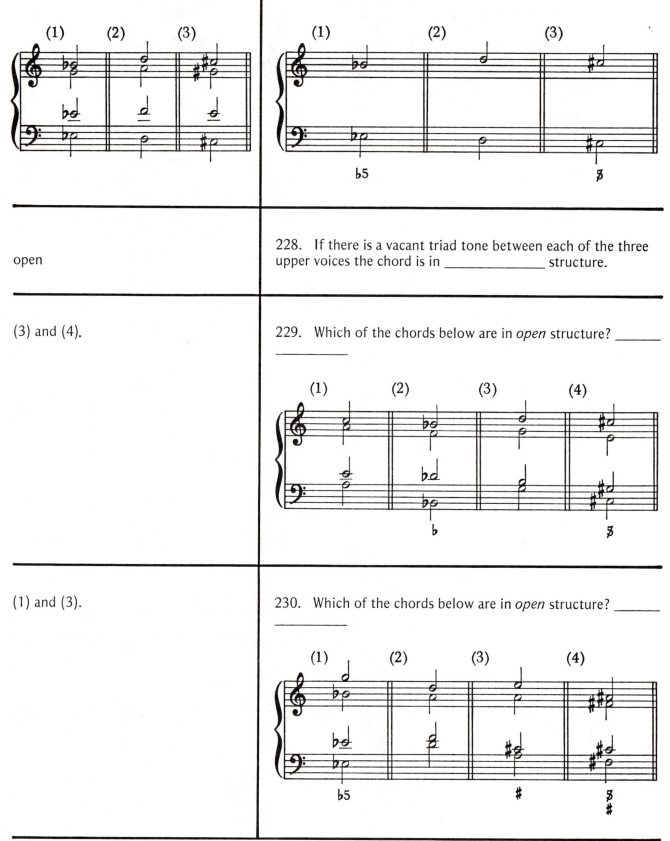

227. Write the alto and tenor voices so that each chord is in *close* structure.

(1)   (2)   (3)

open

228. If there is a vacant triad tone between each of the three upper voices the chord is in _____ structure.

(3) and (4).

229. Which of the chords below are in *open* structure? _____ _____

(1) and (3).

230. Which of the chords below are in *open* structure? _____ _____

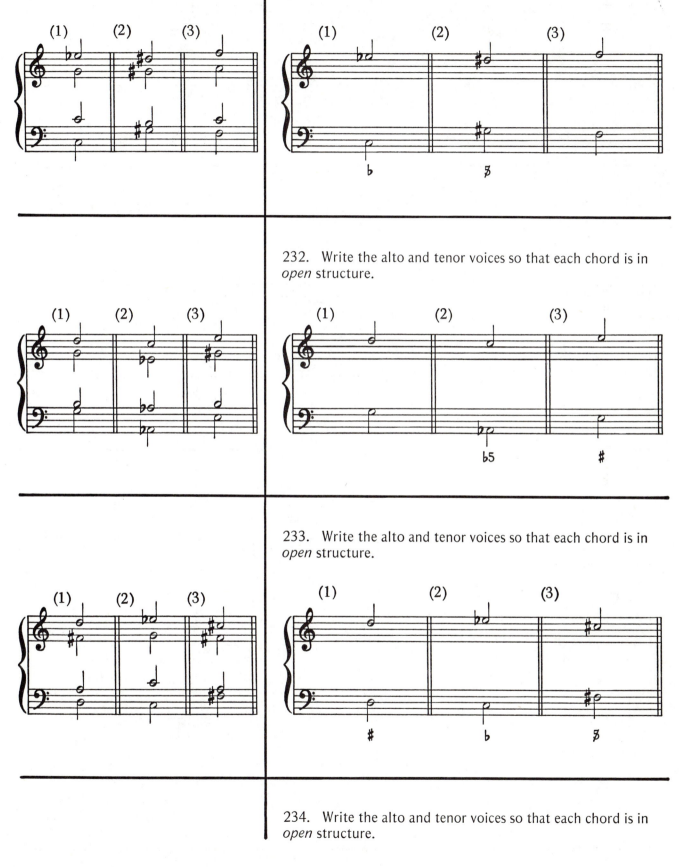

231. Write the alto and tenor voices so that each chord is in *open* structure.

232. Write the alto and tenor voices so that each chord is in *open* structure.

233. Write the alto and tenor voices so that each chord is in *open* structure.

234. Write the alto and tenor voices so that each chord is in *open* structure.

TRIADS IN ROOT POSITION: DOUBLING AND SPACING

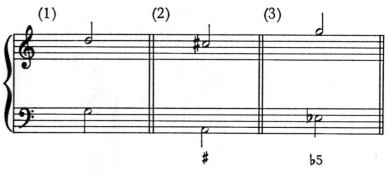

235. Write the alto and tenor voices so that each chord is in *open* structure.

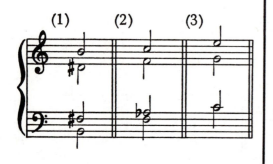

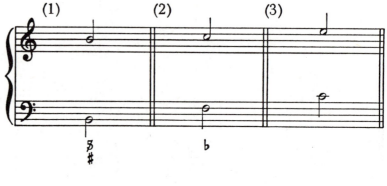

236. Due to the location of the given notes, each of the chords below can be written only one way without producing irregularities in part writing.

Write the alto and tenor voices choosing the structure (close or open) which is correct in each case.

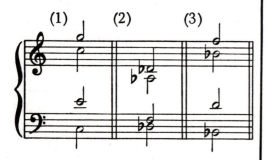

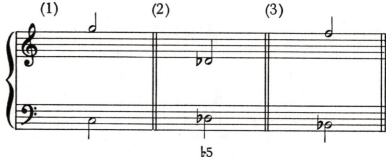

(If your solutions do not agree with the ones given, examine your work to find the errors, and consult your instructor if necessary.)

CHAPTER THREE

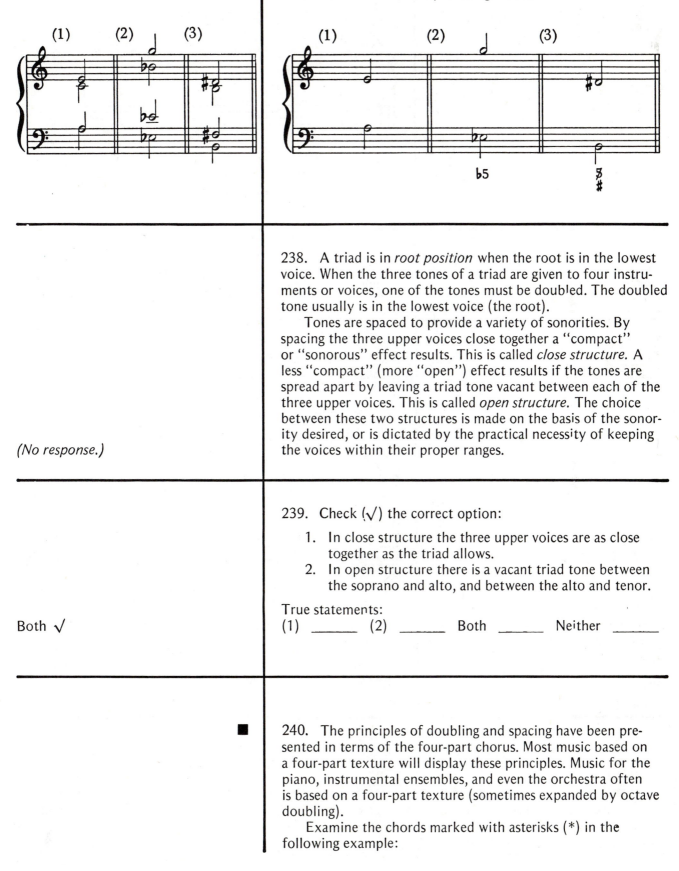

237. Continue as in the preceding frame.

(No response.)

238. A triad is in *root position* when the root is in the lowest voice. When the three tones of a triad are given to four instruments or voices, one of the tones must be doubled. The doubled tone usually is in the lowest voice (the root).

    Tones are spaced to provide a variety of sonorities. By spacing the three upper voices close together a "compact" or "sonorous" effect results. This is called *close structure.* A less "compact" (more "open") effect results if the tones are spread apart by leaving a triad tone vacant between each of the three upper voices. This is called *open structure.* The choice between these two structures is made on the basis of the sonority desired, or is dictated by the practical necessity of keeping the voices within their proper ranges.

Both √

239. Check (√) the correct option:

  1. In close structure the three upper voices are as close together as the triad allows.
  2. In open structure there is a vacant triad tone between the soprano and alto, and between the alto and tenor.

True statements:
(1) _____ (2) _____ Both _____ Neither _____

240. The principles of doubling and spacing have been presented in terms of the four-part chorus. Most music based on a four-part texture will display these principles. Music for the piano, instrumental ensembles, and even the orchestra often is based on a four-part texture (sometimes expanded by octave doubling).

    Examine the chords marked with asterisks (*) in the following example:

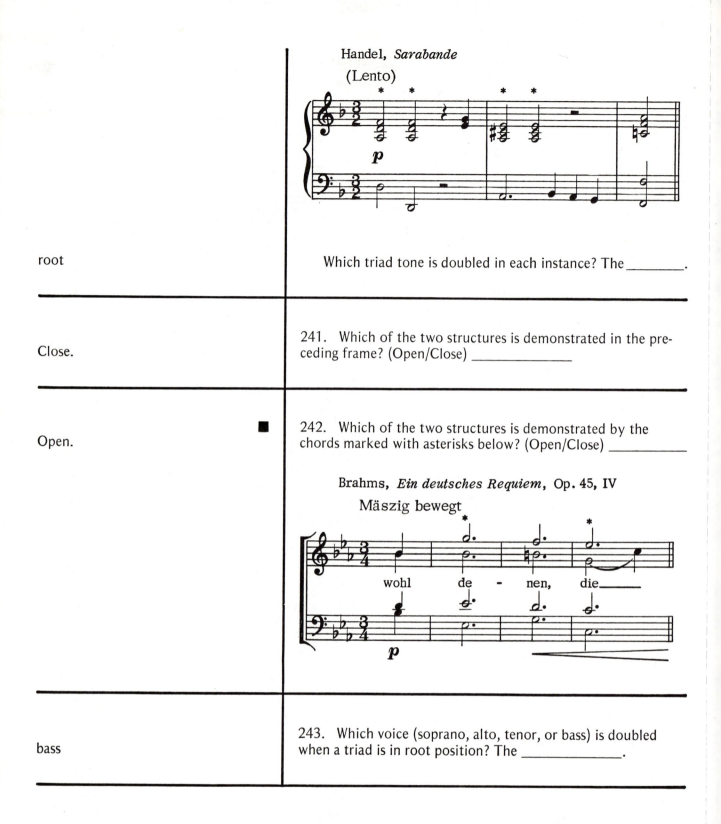

Handel, *Sarabande*

(Lento)

root

Which triad tone is doubled in each instance? The _____.

Close.

241. Which of the two structures is demonstrated in the preceding frame? (Open/Close) _____

Open.

242. Which of the two structures is demonstrated by the chords marked with asterisks below? (Open/Close) _____

Brahms, *Ein deutsches Requiem*, Op. 45, IV

Mäszig bewegt

wohl   de - nen,   die_____

---

bass

243. Which voice (soprano, alto, tenor, or bass) is doubled when a triad is in root position? The _____.

SUMMARY

If the three upper voices are spaced as close together as possible the chord is in *close* structure. *Open* structure results when there is a vacant chord tone between the soprano and alto, and the alto and tenor voices. In this case the interval between the soprano and tenor voices is greater than an octave. Close structure produces a more "compact" sound than open structure.

The basic principles which govern the doubling and spacing of triads in root position are listed below:

1. The voices should be kept within their practical ranges.
2. The voices should be in normal distribution (avoid crossed voices).
3. The interval between any two adjacent upper voices should not exceed an octave.
4. Double the bass in four-part writing.

Figured bass symbols are used to quickly convey certain musical facts about chordal structures. They may also be used to indicate melodic movement. The symbols consist mainly of numbers, accidentals, and other signs. Used for whatever purpose, they actually indicate nothing more than intervals above the lowest sounding note.

The figured bass symbols introduced in this chapter are summarized below:

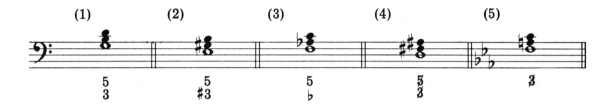

(1) The numbers 5 and 3 indicate a 5th and a 3rd above the note G. The result is a triad in root position.
(2) The figure ♯3 indicates the note G-sharp. The result is an E major triad.
(3) Used as a figured bass symbol, an accidental that stands alone (and is not associated with a number) affects the note that is a third above the bass, in this case A-flat. The result is an F minor triad.
(4) A slash (/) through a number causes the note represented by the number to be raised a half-step. In this case both the fifth and third above the bass are raised a half-step by the use of sharps.
(5) Here a natural is used to raise the third above the bass. (The natural cancels the A-flat in the key signature.)

Mastery Frames

root   (156–159)

3–1. When the root of a triad is in the lowest voice, the triad is in _____ position.

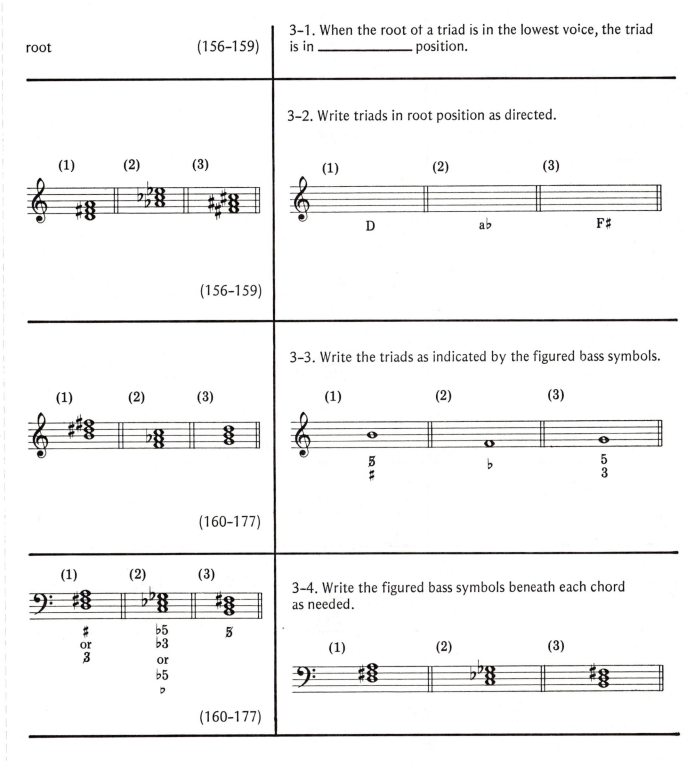

3–2. Write triads in root position as directed.

(1)   (2)   (3)

D   ab   F♯

(156–159)

3–3. Write the triads as indicated by the figured bass symbols.

(160–177)

3–4. Write the figured bass symbols beneath each chord as needed.

(160–177)

3-5. Write the figured bass symbols beneath each chord as needed.

(1)   (2)   (3)

(160-177)

---

root   (199-200)

3-6. In four-part writing, a triad in root position will usually have the _____ doubled.

---

(1), (3).

3-7. Which chords have *incorrect* doubling?_____

(1)   (2)   (3)   (4)

(199-202)

---

(4).   (209-212)

3-8. List the chord(s) in the preceding frame that is in *close* structure._____

---

fifth   (194)

3-9. Adjacent upper voices normally should not be spaced more than the interval of a(n)_____ apart.

Supplementary Assignments

ASSIGNMENT 3-1

Name_____

1. Which of the triads are in root position?_____

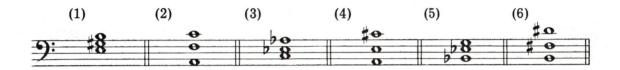

2. Write triads in root position as directed. (Capital letter = major; lower case letter = minor.)

3. Write the chords indicated by the figured bass symbols.

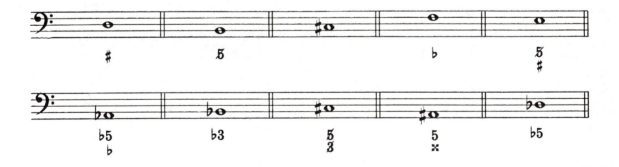

4. Supply the figured bass symbols where needed.

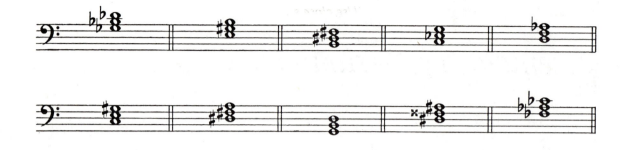

5. Indicate the approximate range for each voice of the four-part chorus.

Soprano   Alto

Tenor   Bass

6. Which chords are in *close* structure?_____

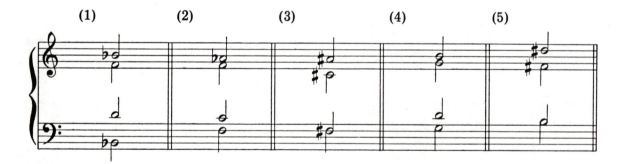

7. What interval should not be exceeded when spacing adjacent upper voices?_____

Name_____

1. Write the missing two voices for each chord. *(Use close structure.)*

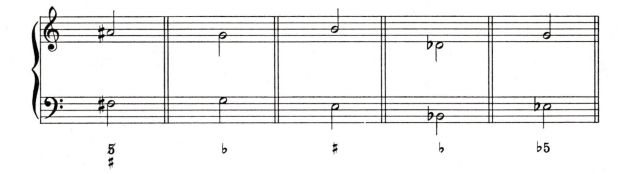

2. Write the missing two voices for each chord. *(Use open structure.)*

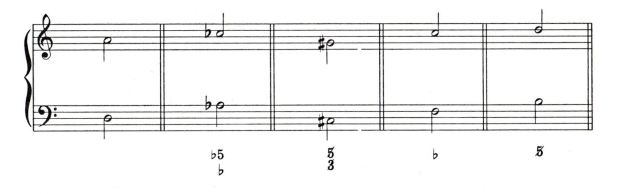

3. Choose one or more of the options for each example.

(A)_____ (B)_____ (C)_____ (D)_____ (E)_____

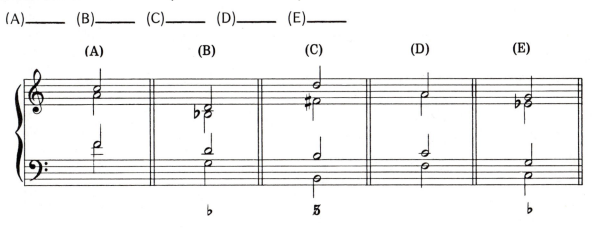

(1) Crossed voices
(2) Incorrect spacing
(3) Incorrect doubling
(4) Voice out of normal range
(5) No error

4. Supply the figured bass symbols for each chord.

5. Write the three upper voices using either open or close structure. Observe all rules of doubling and spacing.

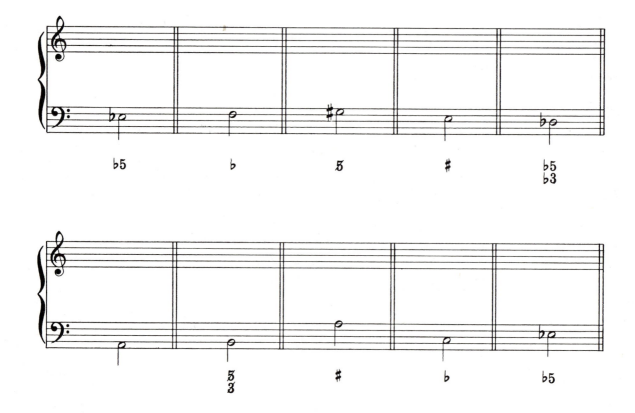

CHAPTER THREE

chapter four

Triads in Root Position: Voice Leading

Chords are the result of several voices sounding simultaneously. When several chords occur in succession it is desirable that each voice produce an agreeable melodic line. With reference to tonal harmony in the traditional styles of the eighteenth and nineteenth centuries this means that the voices should lead smoothly (with few leaps) from one chord to the next. The principles of voice leading presented in this chapter will serve as guide lines for the effective movement of voices.

244. Since harmony consists of several melodic lines sounding together to produce chords, it is important to know how voices relate to one another in terms of relative motion. There are four kinds of relative motion: *similar, parallel, oblique,* and *contrary.* We shall examine each of these separately.

Below are three examples of SIMILAR motion:

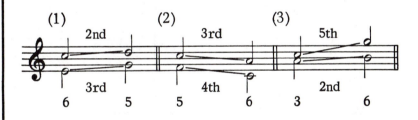

Voices which move in similar motion move in the same direction (up or down), but *not by the same interval.* In (1), for example, the upper voice ascends a second while the lower voice ascends a third. This is reflected by the harmonic intervals produced by the two voices (a sixth followed by a fifth).

In *similar* motion the voices move in the same direction but not by the same _____.

interval

245. Write the notes indicated by the figured bass symbols.

(1)   (2)   (3)

3   5   3   6   6   5

similar

---

246. Each of the examples in the preceding frame demonstrates _____ motion.

---

247. Write the notes indicated by the figured bass symbols.

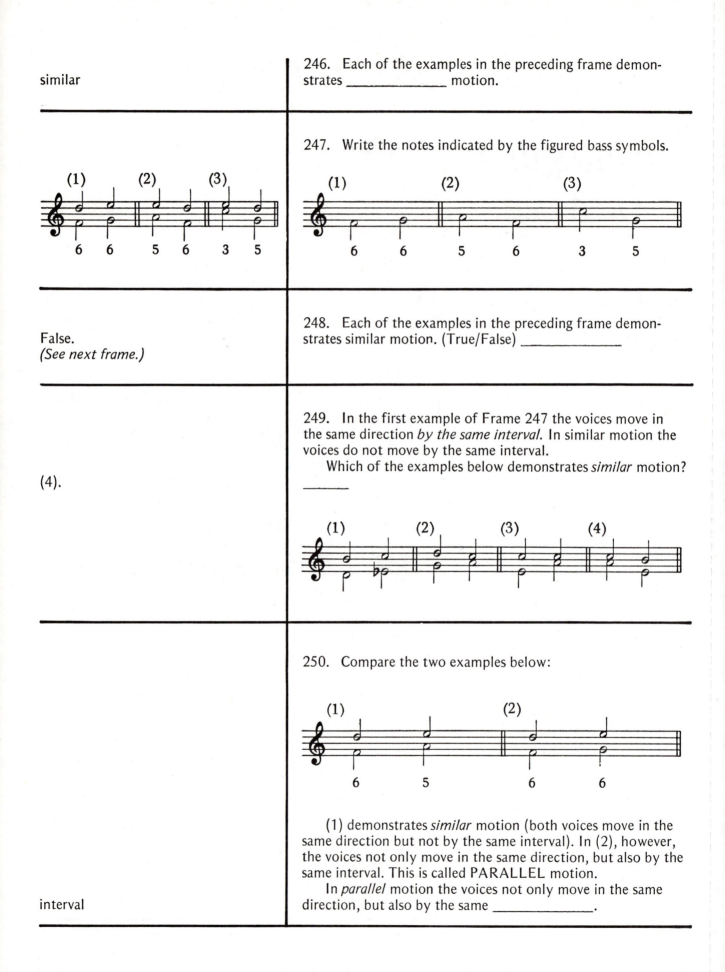

False.
(See next frame.)

248. Each of the examples in the preceding frame demonstrates similar motion. (True/False) _____

---

(4).

249. In the first example of Frame 247 the voices move in the same direction *by the same interval.* In similar motion the voices do not move by the same interval.
　　Which of the examples below demonstrates *similar* motion? _____

---

250. Compare the two examples below:

interval

　　(1) demonstrates *similar* motion (both voices move in the same direction but not by the same interval). In (2), however, the voices not only move in the same direction, but also by the same interval. This is called PARALLEL motion.
　　In *parallel* motion the voices not only move in the same direction, but also by the same _____.

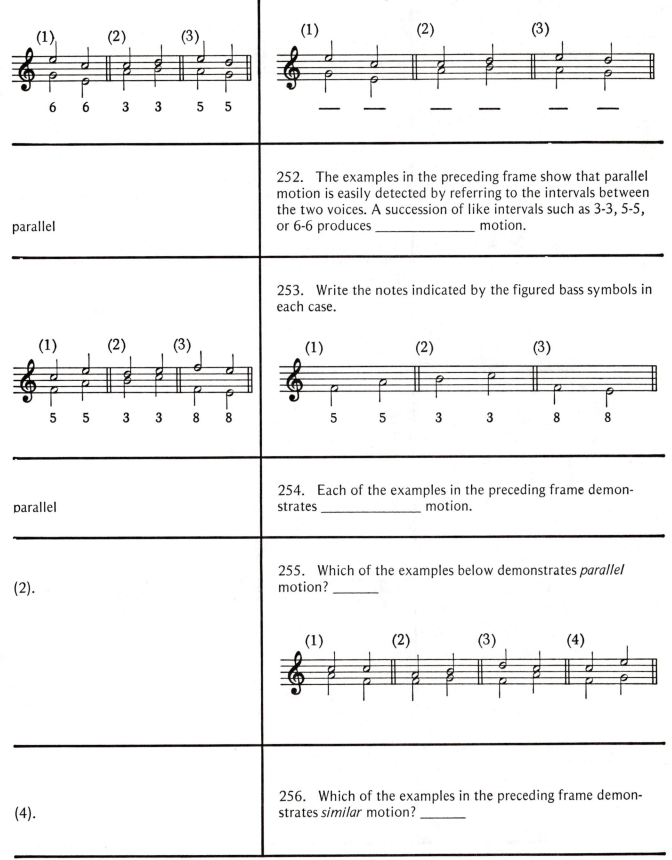

251. Write the figured bass symbol for each interval.

(1)   (2)   (3)

6   6   3   3   5   5

---

parallel

252. The examples in the preceding frame show that parallel motion is easily detected by referring to the intervals between the two voices. A succession of like intervals such as 3-3, 5-5, or 6-6 produces _____ motion.

---

253. Write the notes indicated by the figured bass symbols in each case.

(1)   (2)   (3)

5   5   3   3   8   8

---

parallel

254. Each of the examples in the preceding frame demonstrates _____ motion.

---

(2).

255. Which of the examples below demonstrates *parallel* motion? _____

(1)   (2)   (3)   (4)

---

(4).

256. Which of the examples in the preceding frame demonstrates *similar* motion? _____

257. Compare the two examples below:

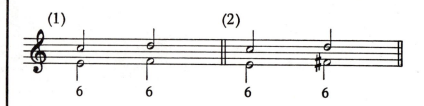

Both (1) and (2) demonstrate parallel motion, yet there *is* a difference: in (1) a minor sixth is followed by a major sixth, whereas both intervals are minor sixths in (2).

From this you can see that the term *parallel motion* does not always refer to absolutely parallel voices. We refer to voices as moving in parallel motion when the basic intervals are the same (third to third, or sixth to sixth, etc.) without consideration of the specific quality of each interval.

Both (1) and (2) are examples of parallel motion; but (2), illogically, is "more parallel" than (1).

The term parallel motion does not usually take into account the precise quality of the _____.

intervals

258. When it is necessary to identify absolutely parallel motion, phrases such as "parallel major thirds," "perfect fifths," or "minor sixths" may be used.

Some parallel intervals are forbidden in traditional writing. These are parallel perfect unisons, perfect fifths, and perfect octaves.

Perfect unisons, perfect fifths, and perfect octaves are such pure consonances that voices moving parallel by these intervals tend to lose their individuality.

List the intervals which should not occur in parallel motion:

(1) Perfect unison
(2) Perfect fifth
(3) Perfect octave
(Any order.)

(1) _____
(2) _____
(3) _____

(4).

259. Which example illustrates incorrect parallel motion? *(Look for consecutive perfect unisons, fifths, or octaves.)* _____

(1)   (2)   (3)   (4)

---

(2).

260. Which example illustrates incorrect parallel motion? _____

(1)   (2)   (3)   (4)

---

(3).

261. Which example illustrates incorrect parallel motion? _____

(1)   (2)   (3)   (4)

No.
(Both (2) and (3) are diminished fifths.)

262. Are all of the intervals in the example below perfect fifths? _____

(1)   (2)   (3)

No.
(The second interval is a diminished fifth.)

263. Parallel fifths are incorrect only if both are *perfect.* Does the example below illustrate incorrect use of parallel motion? _____

(4).

(2).

(3).

264. The preceding frame demonstrates that parallel fifths are incorrect only if both are *perfect*.
    Which of the examples below illustrates *incorrect* parallel motion? _____

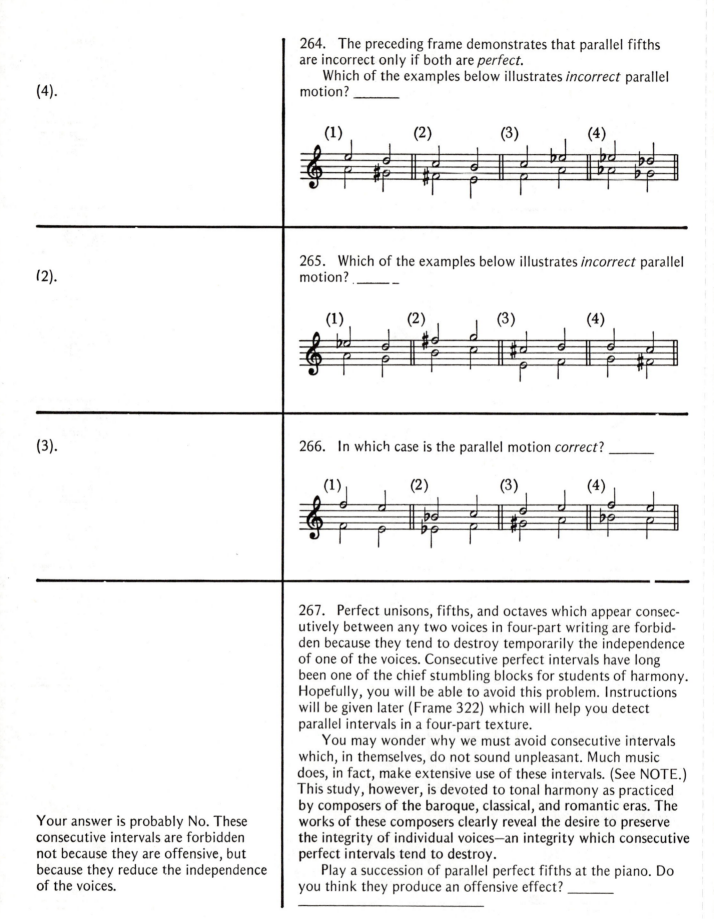

265. Which of the examples below illustrates *incorrect* parallel motion? _____

266. In which case is the parallel motion *correct*? _____

267. Perfect unisons, fifths, and octaves which appear consecutively between any two voices in four-part writing are forbidden because they tend to destroy temporarily the independence of one of the voices. Consecutive perfect intervals have long been one of the chief stumbling blocks for students of harmony. Hopefully, you will be able to avoid this problem. Instructions will be given later (Frame 322) which will help you detect parallel intervals in a four-part texture.
    You may wonder why we must avoid consecutive intervals which, in themselves, do not sound unpleasant. Much music does, in fact, make extensive use of these intervals. (See NOTE.) This study, however, is devoted to tonal harmony as practiced by composers of the baroque, classical, and romantic eras. The works of these composers clearly reveal the desire to preserve the integrity of individual voices—an integrity which consecutive perfect intervals tend to destroy.
    Play a succession of parallel perfect fifths at the piano. Do you think they produce an offensive effect? _____

Your answer is probably No. These consecutive intervals are forbidden not because they are offensive, but because they reduce the independence of the voices.

NOTE: Parallel triads as well as seventh and ninth chords occur frequently in the music of the impressionist composers Debussy and Ravel. Melodic doubling at all intervals is a prominent feature in much twentieth-century music.

268. Check (√) the correct option:
1. In both similar and parallel motion the voices move in the same direction.
2. In parallel motion the voices move in the same direction and by the same basic interval.

True statements:
(1) _____ (2) _____ Both _____ Neither _____

Both √

269. OBLIQUE motion is demonstrated in the example below:

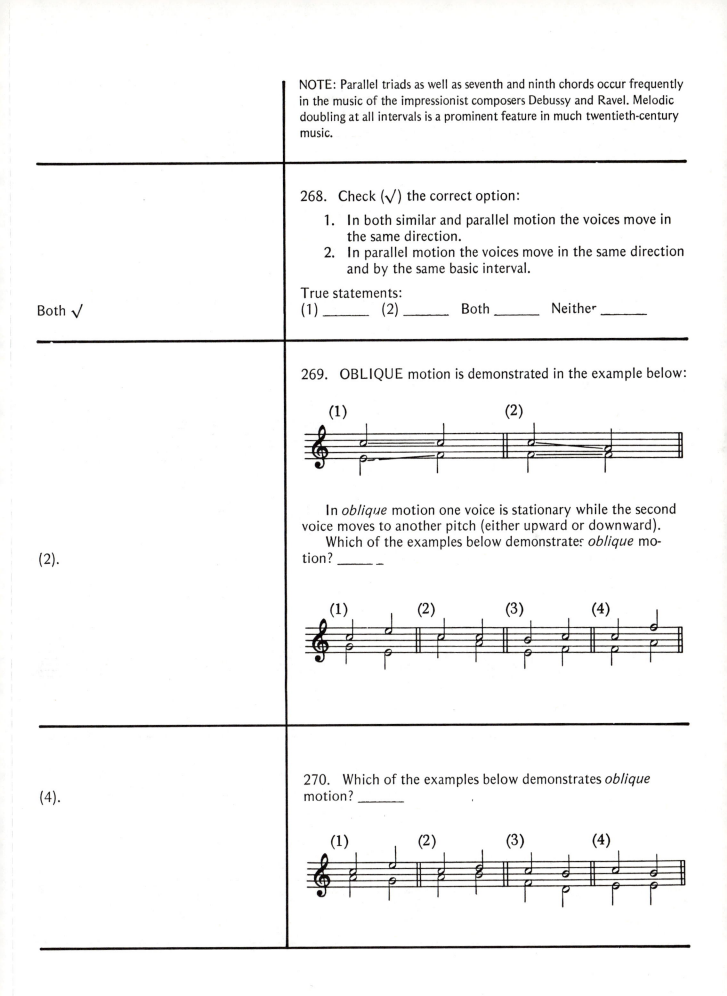

In *oblique* motion one voice is stationary while the second voice moves to another pitch (either upward or downward).
Which of the examples below demonstrates *oblique* motion? _____

(2).

270. Which of the examples below demonstrates *oblique* motion? _____

(4).

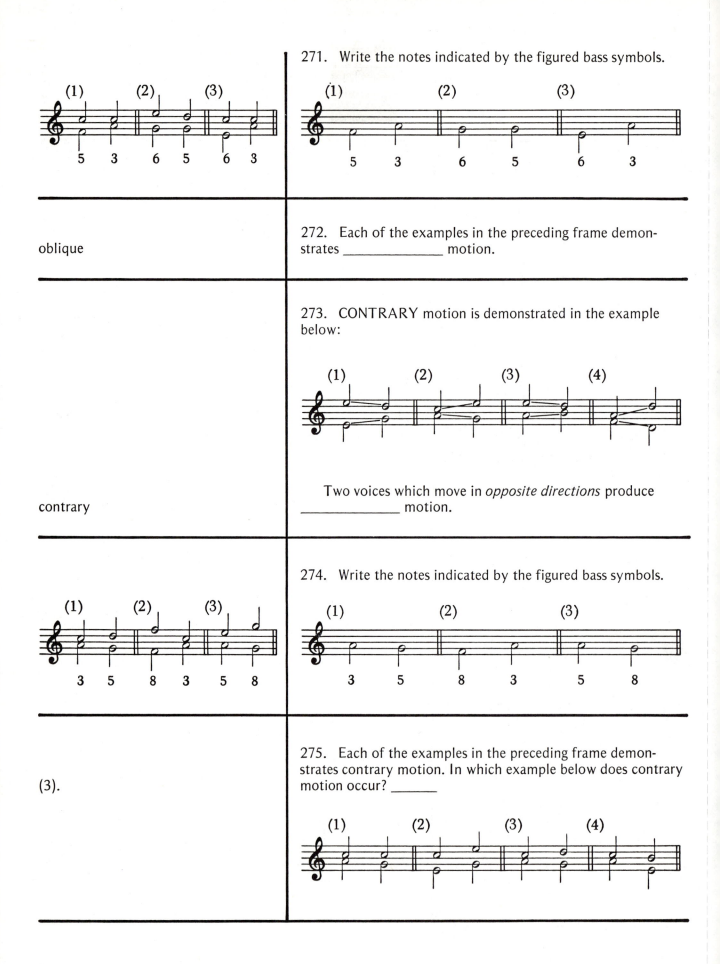

271. Write the notes indicated by the figured bass symbols.

(1)   (2)   (3)

5   3   6   5   6   3

oblique

272. Each of the examples in the preceding frame demonstrates _____ motion.

273. CONTRARY motion is demonstrated in the example below:

(1)   (2)   (3)   (4)

Two voices which move in *opposite directions* produce _____ motion.

contrary

274. Write the notes indicated by the figured bass symbols.

(1)   (2)   (3)

3   5   8   3   5   8

(3).

275. Each of the examples in the preceding frame demonstrates contrary motion. In which example below does contrary motion occur? _____

(1)   (2)   (3)   (4)

276. List the type of motion in eacn example.

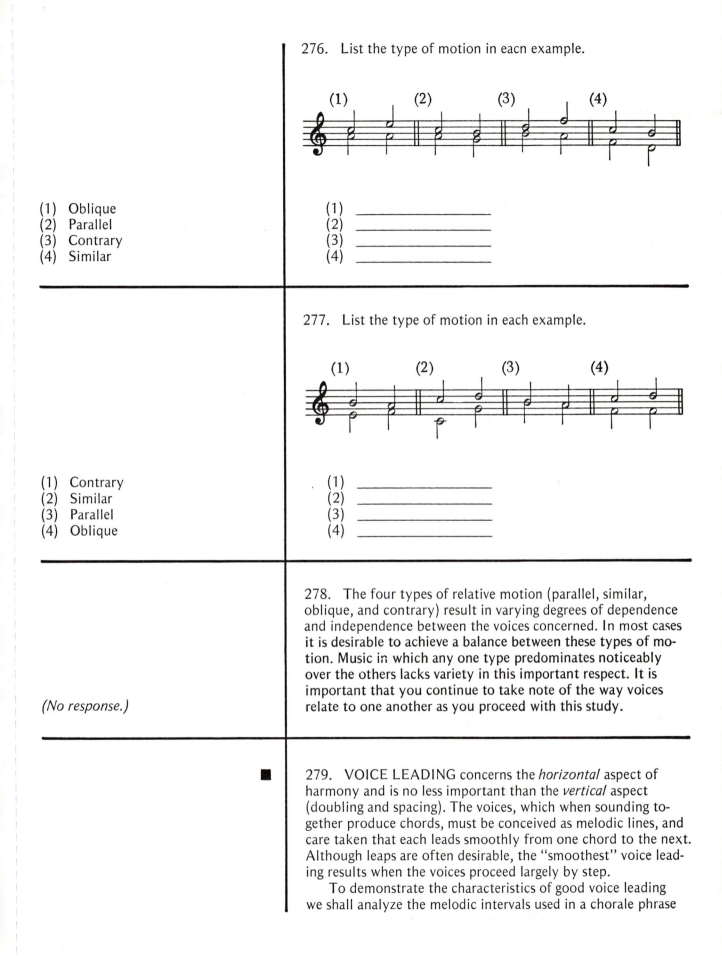

(1) Oblique
(2) Parallel
(3) Contrary
(4) Similar

(1) _____
(2) _____
(3) _____
(4) _____

277. List the type of motion in each example.

(1) Contrary
(2) Similar
(3) Parallel
(4) Oblique

(1) _____
(2) _____
(3) _____
(4) _____

278. The four types of relative motion (parallel, similar, oblique, and contrary) result in varying degrees of dependence and independence between the voices concerned. In most cases it is desirable to achieve a balance between these types of motion. Music in which any one type predominates noticeably over the others lacks variety in this important respect. It is important that you continue to take note of the way voices relate to one another as you proceed with this study.

(No response.)

279. VOICE LEADING concerns the *horizontal* aspect of harmony and is no less important than the *vertical* aspect (doubling and spacing). The voices, which when sounding together produce chords, must be conceived as melodic lines, and care taken that each leads smoothly from one chord to the next. Although leaps are often desirable, the "smoothest" voice leading results when the voices proceed largely by step.
　　To demonstrate the characteristics of good voice leading we shall analyze the melodic intervals used in a chorale phrase

harmonized by J. S. Bach. You are to scan each of the voices separately and count the number of times a tone is followed by the same tone (repetition), the number of times seconds occur, and the number of times leaps of a third occur. Complete the tabulations, and indicate the total for each category. (The soprano has been analyzed as an example.)

Bach, Chorale: *Befiel du deine Wege*

	Rep.	2nd	3rd
S:	0	8	0
A:	2	7	0
T:	2	6	1
B:	2	8	1
T:	6	29	2

	Repetition	2nd	3rd
SOPRANO:	0	8	0
ALTO:	____	____	____
TENOR:	____	____	____
BASS:	____	____	____
TOTAL:	____	____	____

---

step

280.   Of the total melodic intervals in the preceding example 78% are major or minor seconds. Not all music displays such notable smoothness of voice leading. Indeed, melodic leaps of a fourth or more occasionally are used for their expressive value. The example above does serve, however, to demonstrate the smoothness which results when step-wise motion predominates.

You should strive for smooth voice leading. This is accomplished by having a predominance of _____-wise motion.

---

(4).

281.   The augmented second and the augmented fourth should be avoided as melodic intervals when writing vocal music. These intervals are awkward to sing, and composers of the baroque and classical eras took pains to avoid their use.

Which of the examples below is incorrect (in terms of the above statement)? _____

augmented second	282. What interval is demonstrated in (4) of the preceding frame? The _____ _____.
(3).	283. Which example demonstrates awkward melodic movement? _____
augmented second	284. What interval is demonstrated in (3) of the preceding frame? The _____ _____.
(2).	285. Which example demonstrates awkward melodic movement? _____
augmented fourth	286. What interval is demonstrated in (2) of the preceding frame? The _____ _____.
(1) M2 (2) A2 (3) P4 (4) A4	287. Name the melodic interval of each example (use abbreviations).
(2) A2; (4) A4.	288. Which of the examples in the preceding frame demonstrate intervals which should be avoided when writing vocal music? _____

289. The augmented second and the augmented fourth sometimes occur as melodic intervals in instrumental music. This is due to the fact that instrumentalists do not have the problem of finding their pitch as do vocalists. Even in instrumental music, however, these intervals often are avoided for the sake of smooth melodic writing. In addition, instrumental music of the eighteenth and early nineteenth centuries was strongly influenced by vocal music. Thus it is natural that vocal melodic concepts should be reflected in instrumental styles.

Melodic intervals of the augmented second and the augmented fourth are not absolutely prohibited, but they should be avoided, particularly in music intended for voices.

(No response.)

---

290. An augmented second is used as a melodic interval in the example below. Find this interval and indicate it with the sign ($\llcorner\underset{x2}{\quad}\lrcorner$).

Bach, *Well–Tempered Clavier*, Vol. 1, Prelude XII
(Andante)

---

291. An augmented fourth appears in the example below. Find this interval and indicate it with the sign ($\llcorner\underset{x4}{\quad}\lrcorner$).

Beethoven, *Sonatina in F Major*
Allegro assai

---

292. The remainder of this chapter is devoted to the mechanics of voice leading. Before proceeding, however, let us review the principles upon which this study will be based.

The two chief concerns of part writing are the doubling and spacing of triad tones to produce agreeable sonorities, and leading the voices smoothly from one chord to another so that each voice constitutes an expressive melodic line.

Keep in mind the following principles regarding the part writing of triads in root position:

1. When a triad is in root position double the bass.
2. Each chord should contain two roots, one third and one fifth.
3. The voices should be in normal distribution (from upper to lower: soprano, alto, tenor, and bass).
4. The interval between adjacent upper voices should not exceed an octave.
5. Step-wise motion should predominate in leading voices from one chord to another.
6. Melodic leaps of an augmented second or augmented fourth should be avoided.
7. Consecutive perfect unisons, fifths, or octaves are forbidden.

(No response.)

---

293. When a chord in root position is repeated it is often desirable to change the position of some (or all) of the upper voices. In the example below, the static effect of (1) is avoided in (2) by moving each of the upper voices down one triad tone; in (3) the root and third have been exchanged in the soprano and tenor voices.

Which triad tone is doubled in each chord above? The (root/3rd/5th) _____.

root

---

294. Notice that in (3) of the preceding frame there is a change from close to open structure, whereas in (2) both chords are in close structure. Change of structure occurs frequently upon chord repetition.

Write the alto and tenor voices for the second chord in each case *without change of structure.*

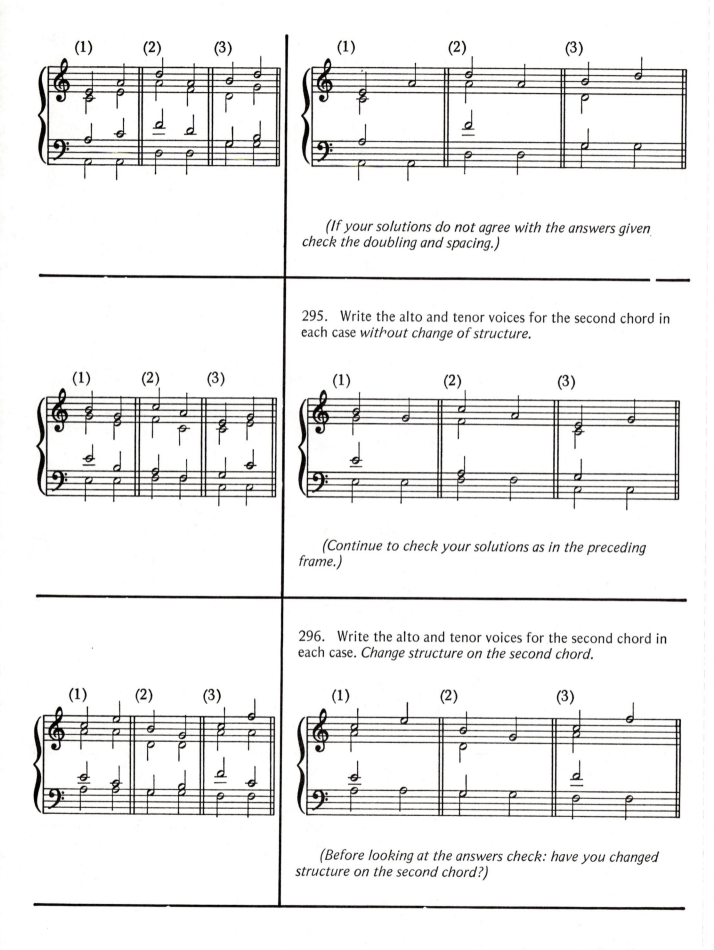

(If your solutions do not agree with the answers given check the doubling and spacing.)

295. Write the alto and tenor voices for the second chord in each case *without change of structure.*

(Continue to check your solutions as in the preceding frame.)

296. Write the alto and tenor voices for the second chord in each case. *Change structure on the second chord.*

(Before looking at the answers check: have you changed structure on the second chord?)

297. Write the alto and tenor voices for the second chord in each case. *Change structure on the second chord.*

(1)   (2)   (3)

(1)   (2)   (3)

(Have you changed structure on the second chord?)

Incorrect doubling.
(There is no fifth in the second chord.)

298. What is the part writing error in the example below?
_____ _____

In the second chord the interval between the alto and tenor is greater than an octave. *(Or equivalent.)*

299. What is the part writing error in the example below?
_____
_____

---

300. In a succession of two chords there are often tones which occur in both. These are called COMMON TONES. When a triad is repeated both chords obviously contain the same tones.

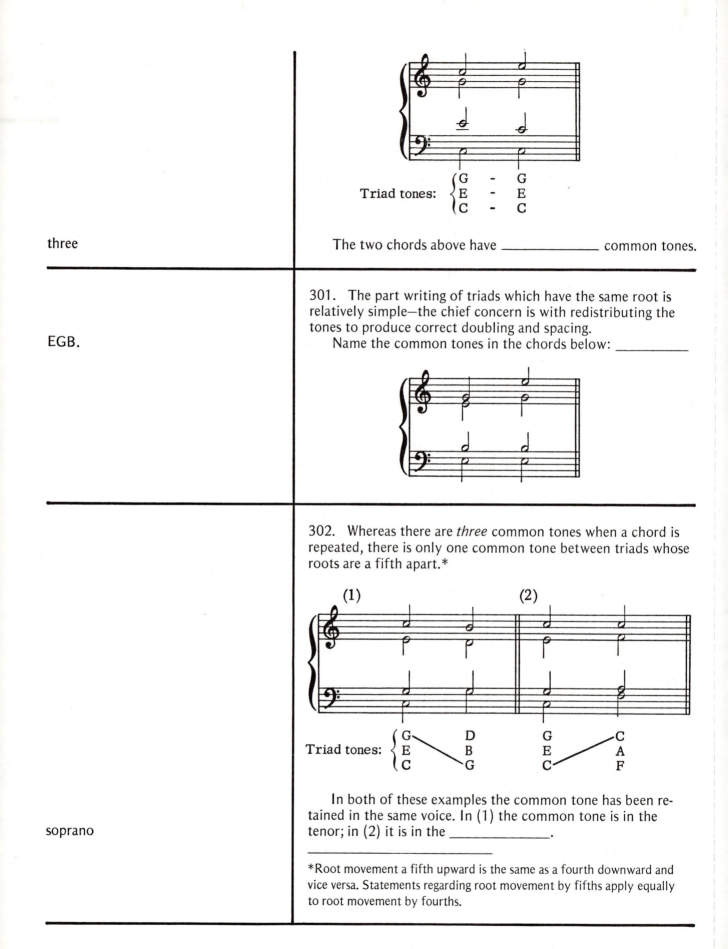

Triad tones: { G - G
               E - E
               C - C }

three

The two chords above have _____ common tones.

EGB.

301. The part writing of triads which have the same root is relatively simple—the chief concern is with redistributing the tones to produce correct doubling and spacing.

Name the common tones in the chords below: _____

---

302. Whereas there are *three* common tones when a chord is repeated, there is only one common tone between triads whose roots are a fifth apart.*

(1)   (2)

Triad tones: { G   D   G   C
               E   B   E   A
               C   G   C   F }

soprano

In both of these examples the common tone has been retained in the same voice. In (1) the common tone is in the tenor; in (2) it is in the _____.

_____

*Root movement a fifth upward is the same as a fourth downward and vice versa. Statements regarding root movement by fifths apply equally to root movement by fourths.

303. The examples in the preceding frame demonstrate the first method of part writing triads whose roots are a fifth apart. Learn this principle:

When connecting triads whose roots are a fifth (or fourth) apart, retain the common tone in the same voice and move the remaining voices to the NEAREST chord tones to achieve correct doubling and spacing.

How many tones are common to two triads whose roots are a fifth apart? _____

One.

D.

304. Name the tone which is common to the triads below: _____

Yes.
(D has been retained in the tenor.)

305. Has the common tone been retained in the same voice in the preceding frame? _____

---

306. Write the alto and tenor voices for the second chord in each case. *Retain the common tone in the same voice.*

(1)   (2)   (3)

(1)   (2)   (3)

---

307. Write the alto and tenor voices for the second chord in each case. *Retain the common tone in the same voice.*

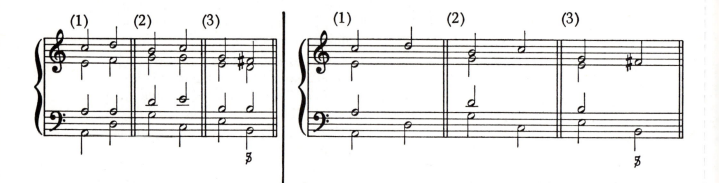

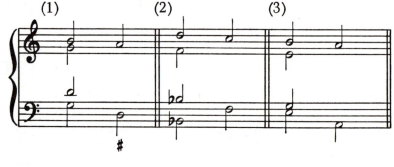

308. Write the alto and tenor voices for the second chord in each case. *Retain the common tone in the same voice.*

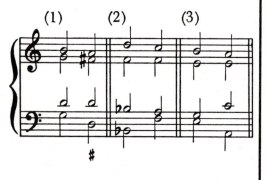

309. Notice in (3) of the preceding frame that the tenor was forced to leap a fourth to find a triad tone which resulted in correct doubling and spacing. *This is satisfactory.* Such leaps, however, must not occur too frequently, and should enhance the expressiveness of the melodic lines.

Write the alto and tenor voices for the second chord in each case. *Retain the common tone in the same voice.*

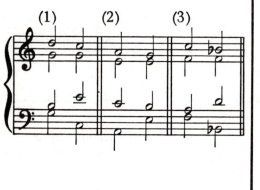

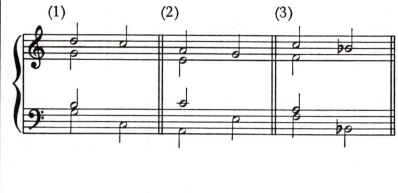

310. Examine the example below:

The common tone in this example is G. Has this tone been retained in the same voice? _____

No.

311. The preceding example demonstrates the second method of part writing triads whose roots are a fifth apart. Learn this principle:

If, when connecting triads whose roots are a fifth (or fourth) apart the common tone is NOT retained in the same voice, move all voices to the NEAREST chord tones which result in correct doubling and spacing.

In the example of the preceding frame the common tone (G) occurs in the alto of the first chord. In the second chord this tone is in the _____.

tenor

312. The key word in the principle stated in the preceding frame is "nearest." It is seldom necessary to leap more than a third in any of the upper voices. Any leap larger than a third should be examined carefully; it may be symptomatic of a part writing error.

Write the alto and tenor voices for the second chord in each case. *Do NOT retain the common tone in the same voice.*

313. Write the alto and tenor voices for the second chord in each case. *Do NOT retain the common tone in the same voice.*

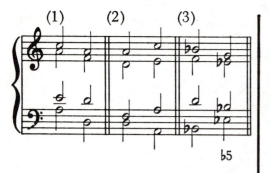

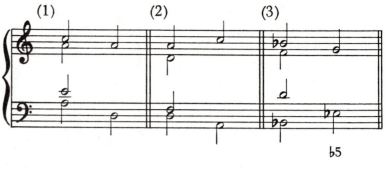

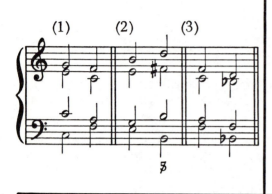

314. Write the alto and tenor voices for the second chord in each case. *Do NOT retain the common tone in the same voice.*

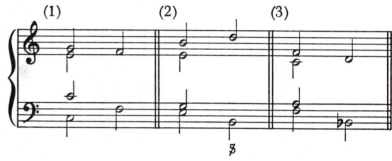

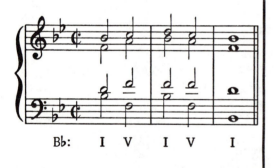

315. Write the alto and tenor voices and supply the Roman numeral analysis. *Use CLOSE structure for all chords.*

316. Write the alto and tenor voices and supply the Roman numeral analysis. *Use OPEN structure for all chords.*

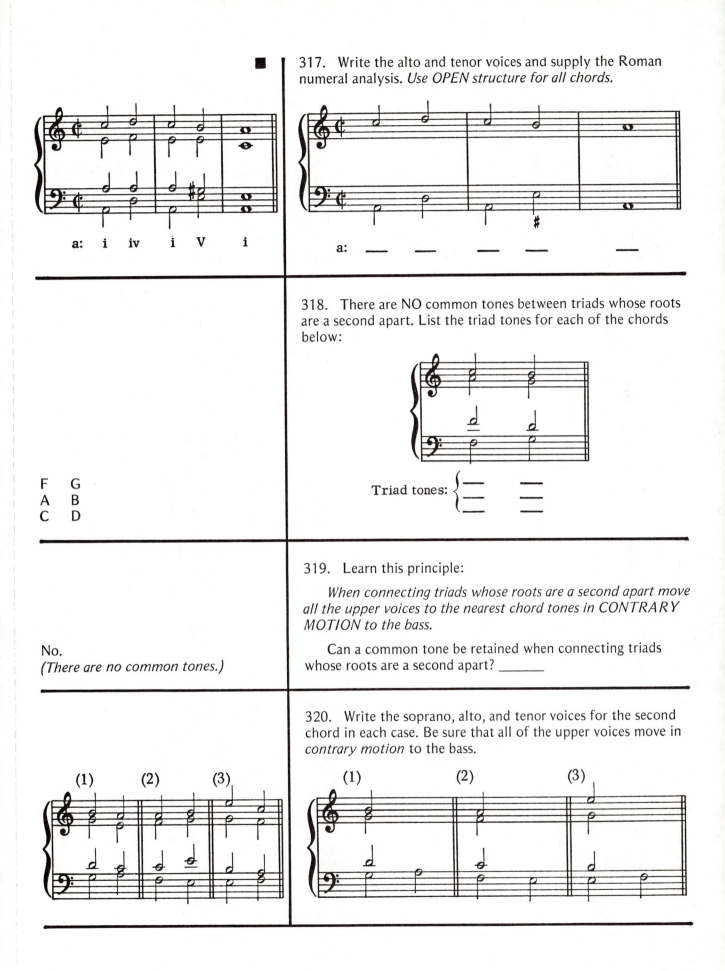

317. Write the alto and tenor voices and supply the Roman numeral analysis. *Use OPEN structure for all chords.*

a: i   iv   i   V   i

a: __ __ __ __ __

318. There are NO common tones between triads whose roots are a second apart. List the triad tones for each of the chords below:

Triad tones: { __ __
               __ __
               __ __ }

F   G
A   B
C   D

319. Learn this principle:

When connecting triads whose roots are a second apart move all the upper voices to the nearest chord tones in CONTRARY MOTION to the bass.

Can a common tone be retained when connecting triads whose roots are a second apart? _____

No.
(There are no common tones.)

320. Write the soprano, alto, and tenor voices for the second chord in each case. Be sure that all of the upper voices move in *contrary motion* to the bass.

(1)   (2)   (3)

(1)   (2)   (3)

321. Write the soprano, alto, and tenor voices for the second chord in each case. Be sure that all of the upper voices move in *contrary motion* to the bass.

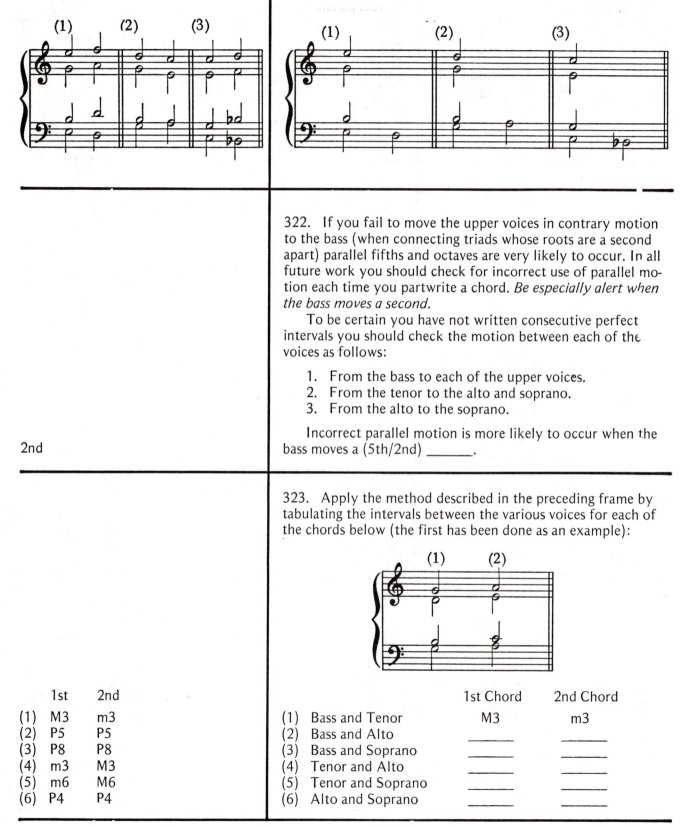

322. If you fail to move the upper voices in contrary motion to the bass (when connecting triads whose roots are a second apart) parallel fifths and octaves are very likely to occur. In all future work you should check for incorrect use of parallel motion each time you partwrite a chord. *Be especially alert when the bass moves a second.*

To be certain you have not written consecutive perfect intervals you should check the motion between each of the voices as follows:

1. From the bass to each of the upper voices.
2. From the tenor to the alto and soprano.
3. From the alto to the soprano.

Incorrect parallel motion is more likely to occur when the bass moves a (5th/2nd) _____.

2nd

323. Apply the method described in the preceding frame by tabulating the intervals between the various voices for each of the chords below (the first has been done as an example):

	1st	2nd
(1)	M3	m3
(2)	P5	P5
(3)	P8	P8
(4)	m3	M3
(5)	m6	M6
(6)	P4	P4

		1st Chord	2nd Chord
(1)	Bass and Tenor	M3	m3
(2)	Bass and Alto	_____	_____
(3)	Bass and Soprano	_____	_____
(4)	Tenor and Alto	_____	_____
(5)	Tenor and Soprano	_____	_____
(6)	Alto and Soprano	_____	_____

bass (and) alto

324. In a check such as that of the preceding frame incorrect parallel motion shows up as a succession of perfect unisons, fifths, or octaves *between the same two voices.* In this case incorrect parallel motion occurs not only between the bass and soprano, but also between the _____ and _____.

---

325. For additional practice in detecting incorrect parallel motion tabulate the intervals between the various voices in each of the chords below:

(Note: The first chord is not in root position.)

	1st	2nd
(1)	m3	M3
(2)	m6	P8
(3)	m3	P5
(4)	P4	m6
(5)	P8	m3
(6)	P5	P5

		1st Chord	2rd Chord
(1)	Bass and Tenor	_____	_____
(2)	Bass and Alto	_____	_____
(3)	Bass and Soprano	_____	_____
(4)	Tenor and Alto	_____	_____
(5)	Tenor and Soprano	_____	_____
(6)	Alto and Soprano	_____	_____

---

alto (and) soprano

326. Between which voices does incorrect parallel motion occur in the preceding frame? Between the _____ and _____.

---

bass (and) alto

327. The method of checking for incorrect parallel motion described in Frame 322 seems at first to be laborious. There is no other way, however, to be certain that you have made no mistakes, and you will soon find ways to speed the process. By using this method each time you partwrite a chord, many careless mistakes will be avoided.

Between which voices does incorrect parallel motion occur in the example on the next page? Between the _____ and _____.

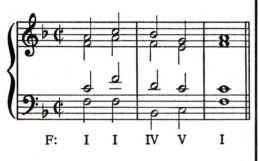

328. Write the alto and tenor voices and supply the Roman numeral analysis. *Use CLOSE structure for all chords.*

F: __ __ __ __ __ __

F: I I IV V I

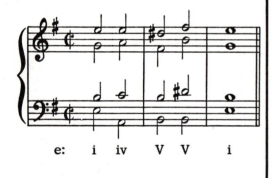

329. Write the alto and tenor voices and supply the Roman numeral analysis. *Use OPEN structure for all chords.*

e: __ __ __ __ __

e: i iv V V i

---

330. Examine the progression below:

The bass has not been doubled. *(There are two 3rds instead of two roots.)*

What irregularity occurs in the second chord? _____
_____
_____.

contrary

331. The preceding frame demonstrates an exception to the usual method of partwriting triads whose roots are a second apart. Learn this principle:

When the bass moves UP a second one voice may move in parallel thirds (or tenths) with the bass resulting in a doubled third in the second chord.

Except for the voice which moves in parallel thirds (or tenths) with the bass, all upper voices move normally (down in _____ motion to the bass).

---

(3).

332. Which of the examples below demonstrates the principle stated in the preceding frame? *(Look for a doubled third in the second chord.)* _____

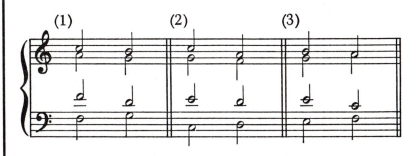

---

333. Note in (3) of the preceding frame that all of the upper voices move normally (in contrary motion to the bass) except the one which moves up in parallel tenths.

Write the soprano, alto, and tenor voices for the second chord applying the principle stated in Frame 331. *(Remember: the third must be doubled in the second chord.)*

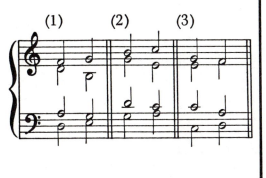

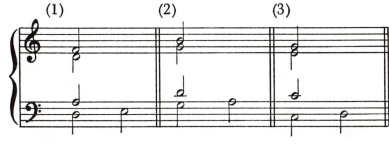

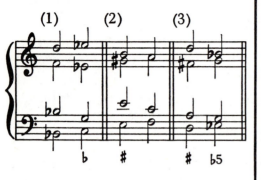

334. Continue as in the preceding frame.

335. The irregularity of doubling described in Frame 331 is used most often as a means of avoiding the augmented second which otherwise occurs when progressing from V to VI in harmonic minor.

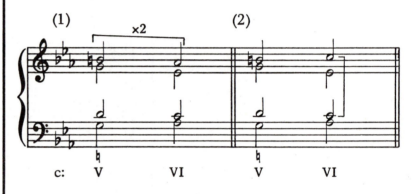

If all voices move in contrary motion to the bass an augmented second results as is shown in (1). The usual solution to this problem is shown in (2). The irregular doubling in the second example is less offensive than the augmented second in the first.

When progressing from V to VI in harmonic minor, the second chord will usually contain a doubled _____.

third

■

336. Write the alto and tenor voices and supply the Roman numeral analysis. *(Irregular doubling must occur in the final chord.)*

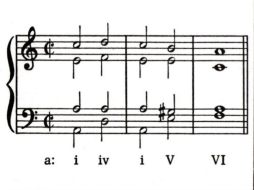

337. Write the alto and tenor voices and supply the Roman numeral analysis.

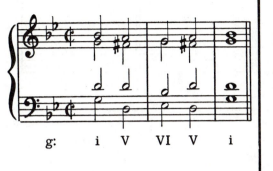

g: i   V   VI   V   i

g: ___ ___ ___ ___ ___

338. There are *two* common tones between triads whose roots are a third apart.

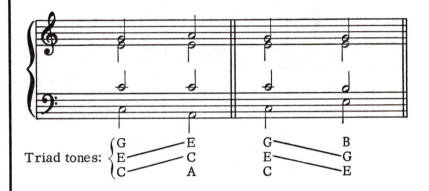

Triad tones: $\begin{cases} G \\ E \\ C \end{cases}$ — E — C — A   G — E — C   B — G — E

The above example demonstrates the usual method of partwriting triads whose roots are a third apart. Learn this principle:

When connecting triads whose roots are a third apart retain two common tones and move the remaining voice to the nearest chord tone.

In applying the principle stated above, how many of the upper voices will move? _____

One.

339. Write the soprano, alto, and tenor voices for the second chord in each case. *Retain TWO common tones in the same voices.*

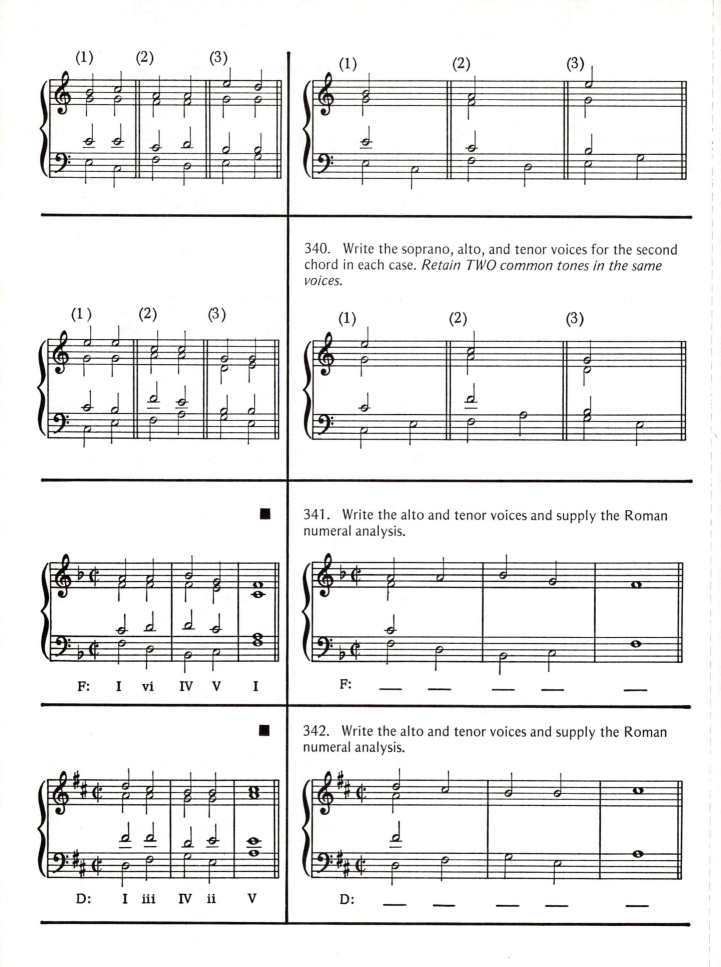

340. Write the soprano, alto, and tenor voices for the second chord in each case. *Retain TWO common tones in the same voices.*

341. Write the alto and tenor voices and supply the Roman numeral analysis.

F: I   vi   IV   V   I

F: ___ ___ ___ ___ ___

342. Write the alto and tenor voices and supply the Roman numeral analysis.

D: I   iii   IV   ii   V

D: ___ ___ ___ ___ ___

a: i   VI   iv   V   VI

343. Write the alto and tenor voices and supply the Roman numeral analysis. *(Take care to avoid having an augmented second in any voice between the last two chords.)*

a: ___   ___   ___   ___   ___

344. Compare the two examples below:

(1)   (2)

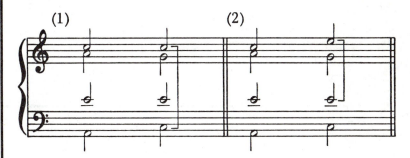

third

In (1) the usual method of part writing is used. In (2), however, the soprano note "C" is not retained even though it is a common tone. This results in a doubled _____ in the second chord.

345. Example (2) in the preceding frame demonstrates an exception to the usual method of part writing triads whose roots are a third apart. Learn this principle:

When the bass moves UP a third, one voice may move in parallel thirds (or tenths) with the bass resulting in a doubled third in the second chord.

The usual doubling for triads in root position is two roots, one third, and one fifth. In order to produce more interesting melodic lines or to avoid more serious errors, sometimes instead of doubling the root, we may double the _____.

third

346. Write the soprano, alto, and tenor voices for the second chord in each case applying the principle stated in the preceding frame. *(Remember: the third must be doubled in the second chord.)*

TRIADS IN ROOT POSITION: VOICE LEADING

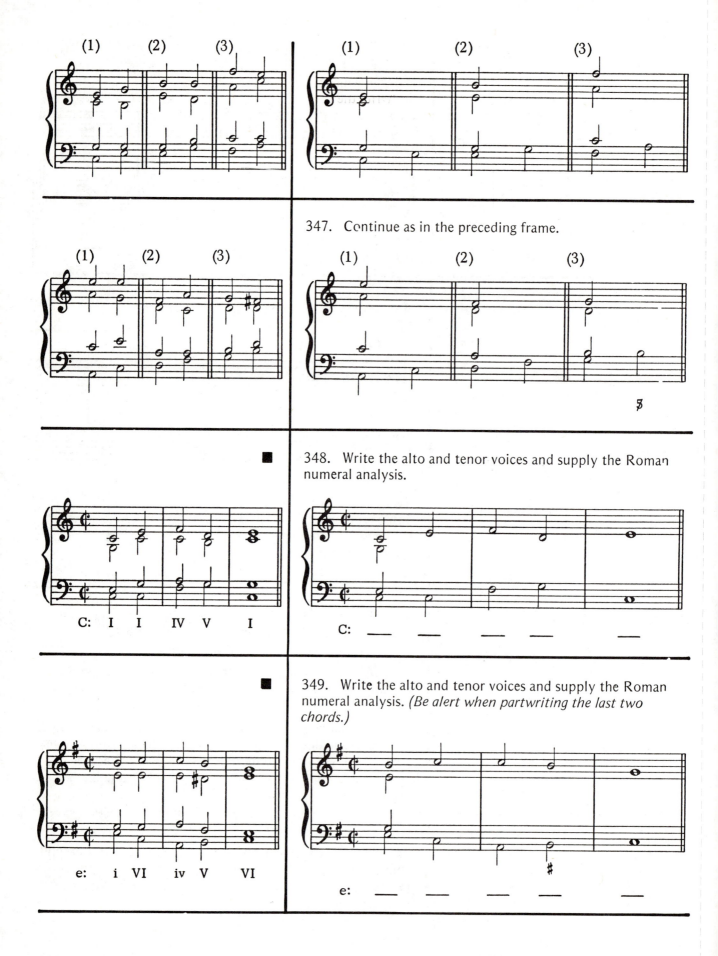

347. Continue as in the preceding frame.

348. Write the alto and tenor voices and supply the Roman numeral analysis.

C: I   I   IV   V   I

C: ___ ___ ___ ___ ___

349. Write the alto and tenor voices and supply the Roman numeral analysis. *(Be alert when partwriting the last two chords.)*

e: i   VI   iv   V   VI

e: ___ ___ ___ ___ ___

350. Irregular doubling should not occur in several chords in succession. Return immediately to normal doubling after a chord in which irregular doubling occurs.

Write the alto and tenor voices and supply the Roman numeral analysis. Irregular doubling will occur at the asterisk. Take care that the doubled tones are left in *contrary* motion.

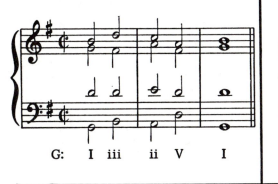

G: I iii ii V I

G: __ __ __ __ __

351. Write the alto and tenor voices and supply the Roman numeral analysis. Irregular doubling will occur at the asterisk. Return to normal doubling immediately.

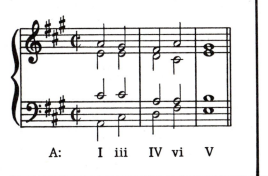

A: I iii IV vi V

A: __ __ __ __ __

SUMMARY

Part writing is not an exact science. No absolute rules can be established to guarantee good musical effects. As we progress further into this study it will become increasingly necessary to allow your musical instincts to influence your decisions. Principles governing doubling, spacing, and voice leading have been established, but all of these are tempered by practical necessities. The nearest thing to a "rule" is the prohibition against parallel perfect unisons, fifths, and octaves. For the present, these should be avoided, even at the expense of normal doubling, spacing, or voice leading.

The most important principle: The smoothest voice leading results if voices always move to the nearest possible chord tones. Retain common tones in the same voice(s) when possible. Leaps in any of the upper voices beyond the nearest chord tones should be carefully scrutinized. You must be able to justify such leaps as being necessary to avoid more serious flaws such as undesirable melodic intervals (augmented seconds and fourths), or parallel unisons, fifths, or octaves. Of course leaps sometimes contribute to more effective melodic lines, or are necessary to produce desirable doublings. But for now you should use mostly seconds and thirds—and occasionally fourths—as melodic intervals in the soprano, alto, and tenor voices. More frequent use of larger intervals is to be expected in the bass.

Mastery Frames

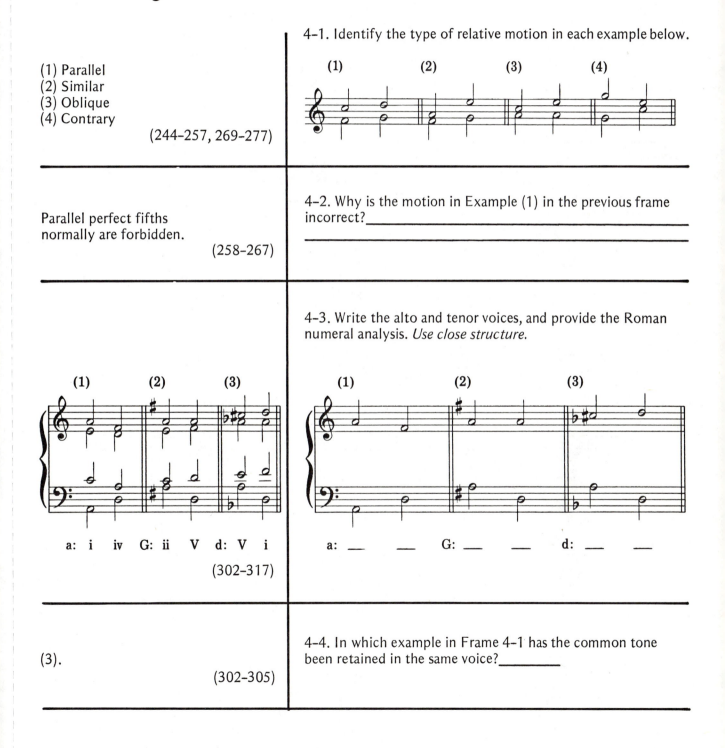

(1) Parallel
(2) Similar
(3) Oblique
(4) Contrary

(244-257, 269-277)

4-1. Identify the type of relative motion in each example below.

(1)　　　(2)　　　(3)　　　(4)

Parallel perfect fifths normally are forbidden.

(258-267)

4-2. Why is the motion in Example (1) in the previous frame incorrect?_____

_____

(1)　　(2)　　(3)

a: i　iv　G: ii　V　d: V　i

(302-317)

4-3. Write the alto and tenor voices, and provide the Roman numeral analysis. *Use close structure.*

(1)　　　(2)　　　(3)

a: __ __　G: __ __　d: __ __

(3).

(302-305)

4-4. In which example in Frame 4-1 has the common tone been retained in the same voice?_____

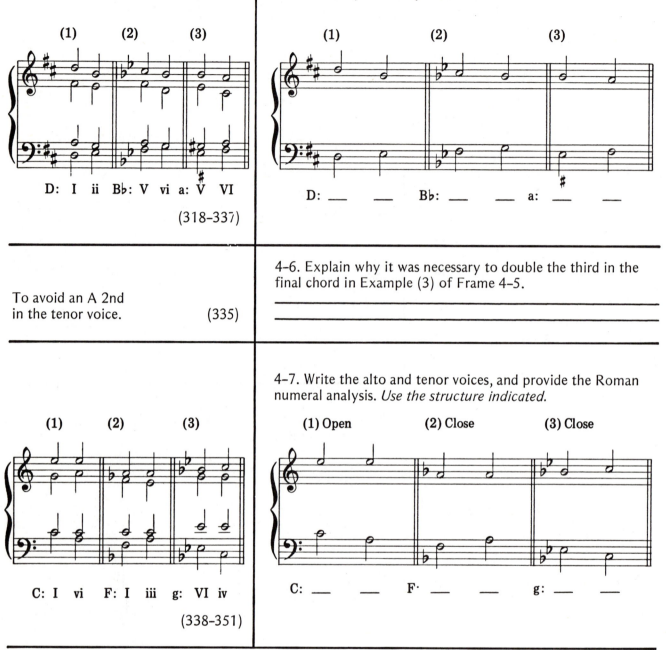

4-5. Write the alto and tenor voices, and provide the Roman numeral analysis. *Use open structure.*

(1) **(2)** **(3)**

D: __ __ Bb: __ __ a: __ __

D: I ii Bb: V vi a: V VI

(318-337)

To avoid an A 2nd in the tenor voice. (335)

4-6. Explain why it was necessary to double the third in the final chord in Example (3) of Frame 4-5.

_____

_____

(1) **(2)** **(3)**

C: I vi F: I iii g: VI iv

(338-351)

4-7. Write the alto and tenor voices, and provide the Roman numeral analysis. *Use the structure indicated.*

(1) Open **(2) Close** **(3) Close**

C: __ __ F: __ __ g: __ __

Supplementary Assignments

ASSIGNMENT 4-1   Name_____ _____ _____

1 Write an example in two voices of each type of relative motion as indicated.

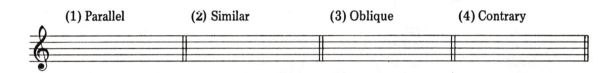

2 Which examples show *incorrect* parallel motion?_____

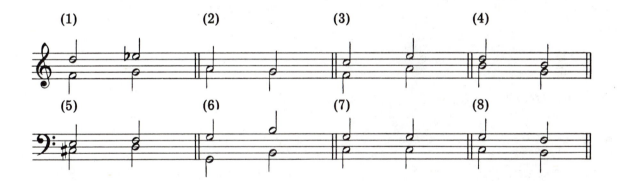

3. Which type of relative motion results in the greatest independence between two voices?_____
   (1) Similar
   (2) Parallel
   (3) Contrary
   (4) Oblique

4. Select the preferred version.____

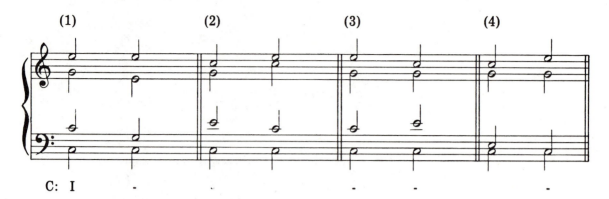

C: I   -   .   -   -   -

5. Select the preferred version.____

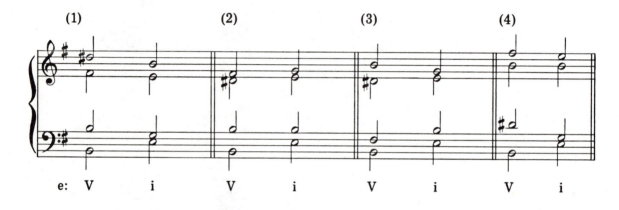

e: V   i   V   i   V   i   V   i

6. Select the preferred version.____

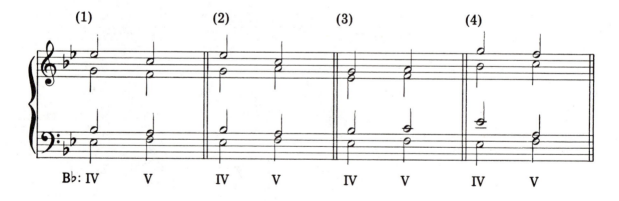

B♭: IV   V   IV   V   IV   V   IV   V

1. Write the alto and tenor voices. *(Observe the rules of doubling and spacing.)*

　　　　b:　V　　VI　　Eb:　I　　iii　　G:　I　　I　　d:　iv

2. Write the alto and tenor voices. *(Observe the rules of doubling and spacing.)*

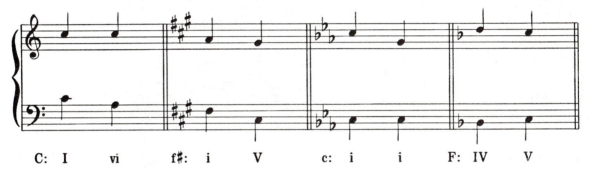

　　　　C:　I　　vi　　f#:　i　　V　　c:　i　　i　　F:　IV　　V

3. Choose one or more of the options below for each example.

(A)_____　　(B)_____　　(C)_____

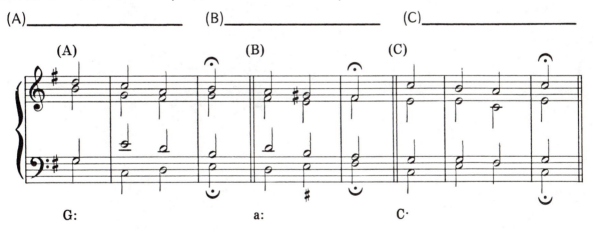

　　　　G:　　　　　　　　　　　　a:　　　　　　　　C:

(1) Incorrect doubling
(2) Incorrect spacing
(3) Incorrect melodic interval
(4) Incorrect parallel motion
(5) No error

4. Write the alto and tenor voices, and analyze with Roman numerals.

(A)

A:

(B)

d:

(C)

D.

Triads in First and Second Inversion

Depending upon whether the root, third, or fifth is in the bass, triads are said to be in root position, first inversion, or second inversion. Inversions are used to produce a variety of chordal effects and enhance the melodic character of the bass line. The principles which govern the partwriting of triads in first and second inversion are presented in this chapter.

	352. A triad is in *root position* when the lowest tone is the root. If the tones of a triad are arranged so that the root is *not* in the lowest voice, the triad is INVERTED. A triad is inverted by placing the third or fifth in the _____ voice.
lowest *(or bass)*	
	353. Compare the three chords below: 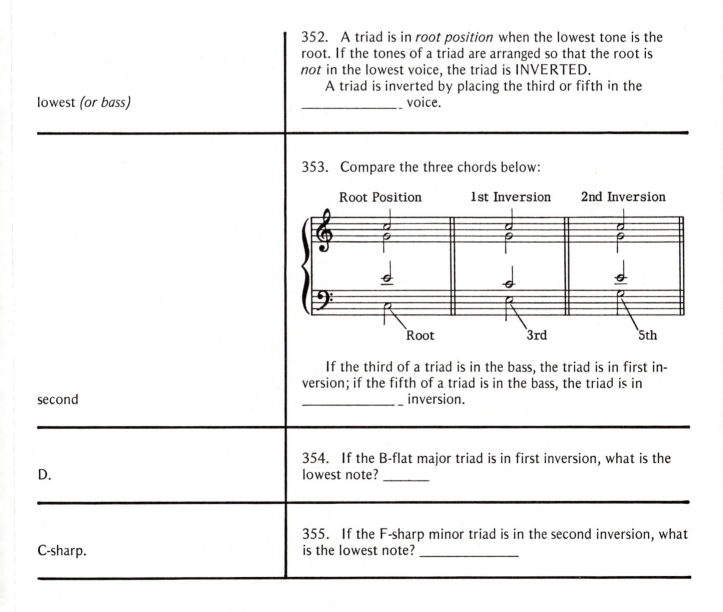 If the third of a triad is in the bass, the triad is in first inversion; if the fifth of a triad is in the bass, the triad is in _____ inversion.
second	
D.	**354.** If the B-flat major triad is in first inversion, what is the lowest note? _____
C-sharp.	**355.** If the F-sharp minor triad is in the second inversion, what is the lowest note? _____

G.	356. If the G major triad is in root position, what is the lowest note? _____
A.	357. If the D minor triad is in second inversion, what is the lowest note? _____
A-flat.	358. If the F diminished triad is in first inversion, what is the lowest note? _____
bass *(or lowest)*	359. It is important to know which tone is the root of each chord. This is no problem when all chords are in root position. But when some of the chords are inverted, you must rearrange the tones mentally in order to locate the root. In progressions which include inversions, the root will not always be in the _____ voice.
first (or) second	360. When analyzing a chord which may or may not be an inversion it is a good idea to notice first if the notes can be arranged in thirds above the bass. This is because many triads are in root position. If the notes of a triad *cannot* be arranged in thirds above the bass it means that the triad is in either _____ or _____ inversion.
	361. To find the root of an inverted triad you must mentally rearrange the notes to produce a succession of thirds. The root, of course, will be the lowest note when they are arranged in this manner. Try each successive note until you find the one upon which thirds can be built. We shall demonstrate this process. Notice in the example below that the notes arranged above the bass as in (a) are CEA. The interval E to A is a fourth, so C is not the root. Arranged above the tenor as in (b), however, the notes are ACE. The notes now are arranged in thirds, so the lowest note (A) is the root.

thirds

The root of a triad is always the lowest note when the notes are arranged in _____.

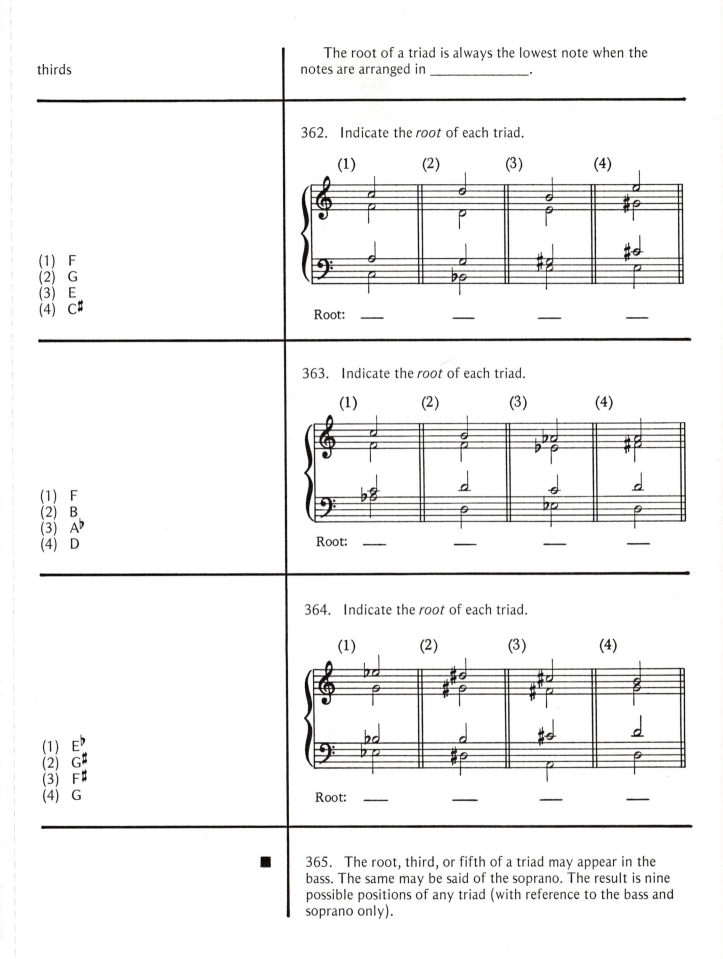

362. Indicate the *root* of each triad.

(1) (2) (3) (4)

Root: ___   ___   ___   ___

(1) F
(2) G
(3) E
(4) C♯

363. Indicate the *root* of each triad.

(1) (2) (3) (4)

Root: ___   ___   ___   ___

(1) F
(2) B
(3) A♭
(4) D

364. Indicate the *root* of each triad.

(1) (2) (3) (4)

Root: ___   ___   ___   ___

(1) E♭
(2) G♯
(3) F♯
(4) G

365. The root, third, or fifth of a triad may appear in the bass. The same may be said of the soprano. The result is nine possible positions of any triad (with reference to the bass and soprano only).

THE G MAJOR TRIAD

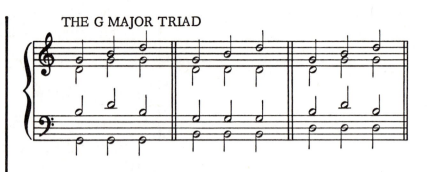

(Play the nine positions of the G major triad as illustrated above. Listen to the different sonority of each position.)

All triads in root position sound alike. (True/False) _____

False.
(The note in the soprano and the spacing of the tones affect the sound of a triad.)

---

366.   A triad in *first inversion* has the intervals of a sixth and a third above the lowest note.

The figured bass symbol $\frac{6}{3}$ indicates a triad in _____ inversion.

first

---

367.   The number 6 is sufficient to indicate a triad in first inversion. The complete figuration $\frac{6}{3}$ is used only if needed to show alterations.

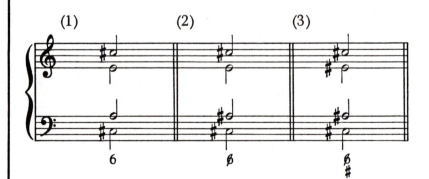

In the example above, merely the number 6 is adequate in (1) as neither the third nor the sixth is altered; in (2) the A-sharp is shown by the slash through the 6; a sharp is added to the figured bass in (3) to show the alteration of E to E-sharp.

3rd

The number 6 in the figured bass means that the note in the bass is the (root/3rd/5th) _____ of the chord.

---

368. Spell the triads indicated by the figured bass symbols.

(1)   (2)   (3)

6   ⌀6   6
                        ♭

(1) EGB
(2) G♯BD
(3) ACE♭

(1) _____   (2) _____   (3) _____

---

369   Spell the triads indicated by the figured bass symbols.

(1)   (2)   (3)

6   6   ♭6
♯

(1) BDF♯
(2) DFA
(3) B♭DF

(1) _____   (2) _____   (3) _____

---

370. Spell the triads indicated by the figured bass symbols.

(1)   (2)   (3)

⌀6   6   ♭6
♯   ♯   ♭

(1) E♯G♯B♯
(2) DF♯A♯
(3) A♭CE♭

(1) _____   (2) _____   (3) _____

---

371. Check (√) the correct option:

1. The figured bass symbol "6" represents a triad in first inversion.
2. The figured bass symbol "6" means that the bass note is the root of the triad.

True statements:
(1) _____   (2) _____   Both _____   Neither _____

(1) √

---

372. A triad in *second inversion* has intervals of a sixth and fourth above the lowest note.

A triad in second inversion is indicated by the figured bass symbol $\frac{6}{4}$. In second inversion the tone in the bass is the (root/3rd/5th) _____ of the triad.

5th

---

373. Neither the 6 nor the 4 can be omitted from the figured bass in the case of a triad in second inversion.

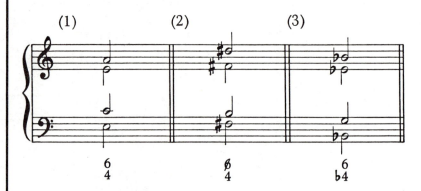

Notice that in (1) both the number 6 and the number 4 are used even though the notes represented by these numbers are not altered.

Write the figured bass symbol which indicates a triad in second inversion. _____

$\frac{6}{4}$

---

374. Spell the triads indicated by the figured bass symbols.

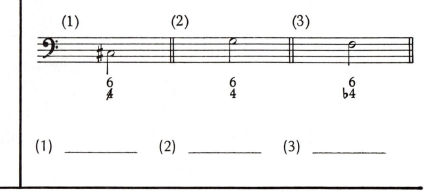

(1) _____   (2) _____   (3) _____

(1) F♯ A C♯
(2) C E G
(3) B♭ D F

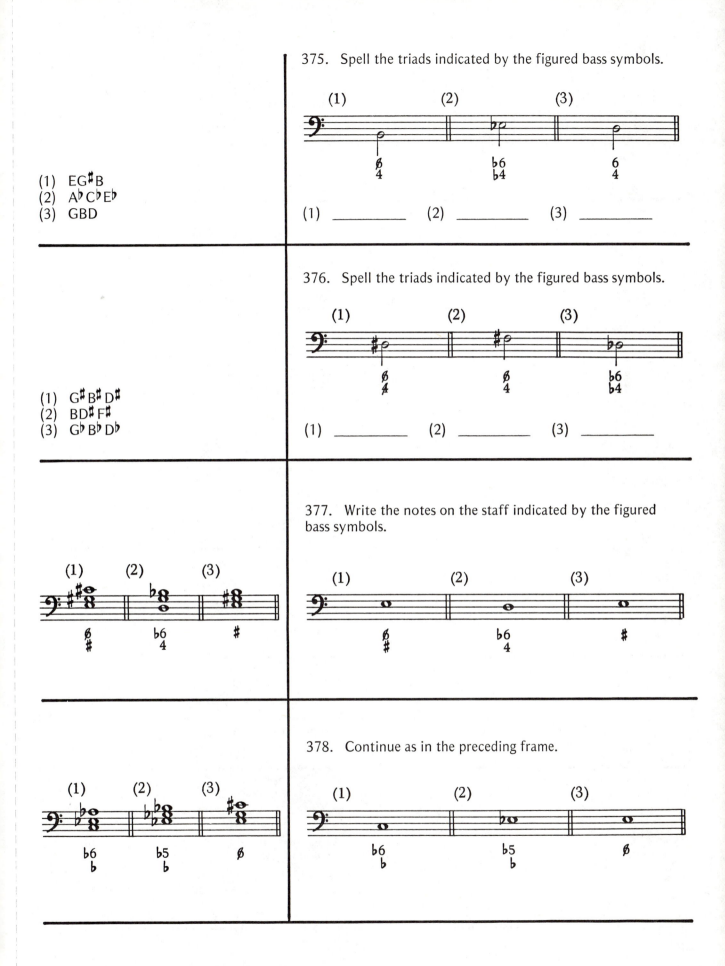

375. Spell the triads indicated by the figured bass symbols.

(1)   (2)   (3)

(1) EG♯B
(2) A♭C♭E♭
(3) GBD

(1) _____ (2) _____ (3) _____

376. Spell the triads indicated by the figured bass symbols.

(1)   (2)   (3)

(1) G♯B♯D♯
(2) BD♯F♯
(3) G♭B♭D♭

(1) _____ (2) _____ (3) _____

377. Write the notes on the staff indicated by the figured bass symbols.

(1)   (2)   (3)

(1)   (2)   (3)

378. Continue as in the preceding frame.

(1)   (2)   (3)

(1)   (2)   (3)

(1)　　　(2)　　　(3)

b　　　　　ø
　　　　　4

379. Continue as in the preceding frame.

(1)　　　　　(2)　　　　　(3)

♮　　　　　　　ø
　　　　　　　4

■

380. Play and compare the two examples below:

(1)

(2)

6　　　6　　　6

Which of these examples has the "smoother" bass line?

_____

(2).
(There are fewer and smaller leaps.)

---

381. The use of inversions permits the bass line to flow more smoothly, thereby producing a better melodic line. This is an important reason for using inversions.

A more melodic bass line results from the use of _____ _____.

inversions

---

382. Play again the two examples of Frame 380. As all of the chords of (1) are in root position, there is a uniformity of sonority. The contrast in sonority provided by inversions in (2) adds greatly to the musical interest. This is the second reason for using inversions.

Inversions contribute to the musical interest in two ways: the bass line may become more melodic, and there can be greater variety of sonorities.

(No response.)

(No response.)

383. The character of triads varies according to whether they are in root position, first inversion, or second inversion. You must become sensitive to these differences through listening experiences. Major and minor triads in root position provide the most stable sonorities. Triads in first inversion, however, are less stable; they help motivate the harmony by demanding resolution into more stable sonorities. A sense of "forward motion" is imparted by the use of first inversions.

Triads in second inversion are still less stable than those in first inversion. Because of the relatively weak sonority of triads in second inversion, they are used sparingly.

---

second

384. First and second inversions are shown when analyzing with Roman numerals by including the appropriate figured bass symbol as part of the chord symbol.

The numbers $\frac{6}{4}$ added to a Roman numeral indicate that the chord is in _____ inversion.

3rd

385. The chord symbol I^6 indicates that the (root/3rd/5th) _____ of the tonic triad is in the bass.

---

386. Write the appropriate chord symbol in each case. *(Be sure to show the inversion.)*

(1) A: I^6
(2) d: iv^6
(3) c: V

---

387. Continue as in the preceding frame.

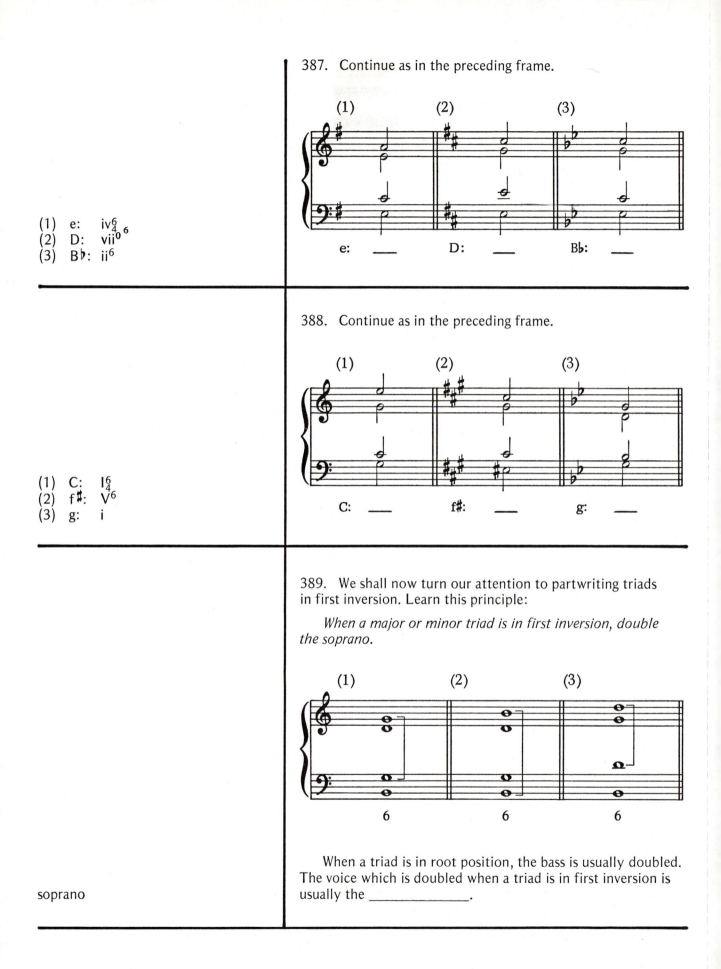

(1)   e: iv$_4^6$
(2)   D: vii^{o6}
(3)   B♭:   ii^6

e: ___   D: ___   B♭: ___

---

388. Continue as in the preceding frame.

(1)   C: I$_4^6$
(2)   f♯:   V^6
(3)   g: i

C: ___   f♯: ___   g: ___

---

389. We shall now turn our attention to partwriting triads in first inversion. Learn this principle:

When a major or minor triad is in first inversion, double the soprano.

6   6   6

When a triad is in root position, the bass is usually doubled. The voice which is doubled when a triad is in first inversion is usually the _____.

soprano

390. Write the alto and tenor voices for each triad. *(Be sure the soprano is doubled.)*

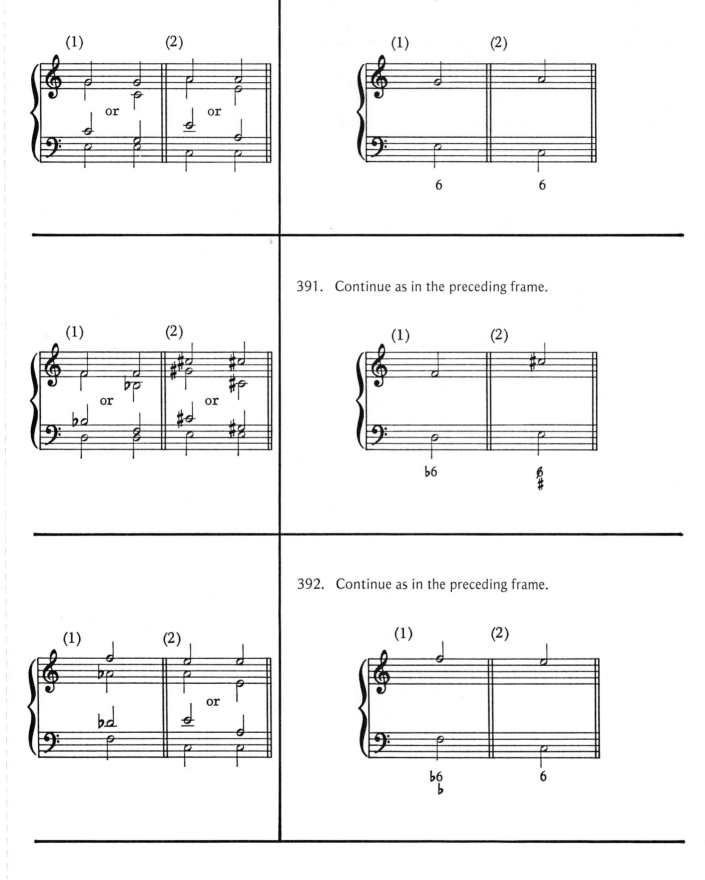

391. Continue as in the preceding frame.

392. Continue as in the preceding frame.

(1) ✓

(3).
(There is more than an octave between the alto and tenor voices.)

(1) ✓

---

393. Continue as in the preceding frame.

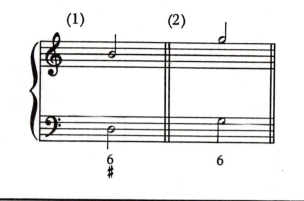

---

394. The preceding four frames have shown that first inversions often give rise to several possibilities of spacing. Take care that the interval between adjacent upper voices is not larger than an octave, and do not use notes which are outside the normal range of each voice. (See Frame 181).

When triads are in first inversion the doubled tone varies. It is the root, third, or fifth depending on which of these is in the soprano.

Which of the triads below contains a part writing error?

_____

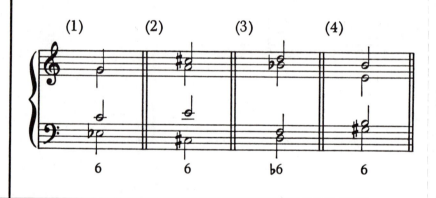

---

395. Considerable freedom is exercised by composers regarding the doubling of triads in first inversion. Doubling usually is determined by the necessity of avoiding a part writing error, or in order to produce a more desirable melodic line in one or more parts. But in spite of this, it is advisable to try the normal doubling *first*, as this usually provides the most satisfactory solution.

Check (√) the correct option:

1. Triads in root position usually have a doubled root.
2. Triads in first inversion usually have a doubled 3rd.

True statements:
(1) _____ (2) _____ Both _____ Neither _____

396. When moving from a triad in first inversion to one in root position, follow the steps outlined below:

1. Move the doubled tones in contrary, oblique or (rarely) similar motion to the nearest chord tones possible.
2. Move the remaining voice* to the tone which will complete the triad or which provides correct doubling.

The example below illustrates step one:

The doubled voices have moved to the nearest chord tones possible in _____ motion.

*If the soprano is doubled by the bass, there will be two remaining voices.

contrary

---

397. With reference to the example in the preceding frame why is it undesirable to leave the doubled tones as below?

_____

_____

Doubled tones must not be left in parallel motion. *(Or equivalent.)*

---

398. Step two of the process described in Frame 396 is illustrated in (b) below:

    (a) Step One   (b) Step Two

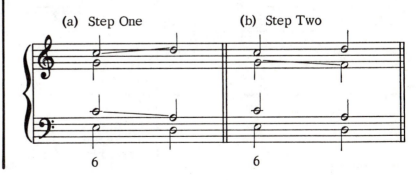

The triad tone which was needed to complete the chord was the third (F). The voice which moves to complete the triad (as above) rarely moves more than a second. A larger leap may indicate an error.

Check especially for parallel perfect intervals.

The voice which remains after the doubled voices have found their place in the next chord moves to a tone which completes the triad, or which provides correct _____.

doubling

---

399.   In the example below, perform step one (move the doubled tones in contrary, oblique, or similar motion to the nearest chord tones possible).

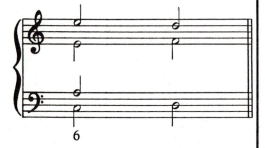

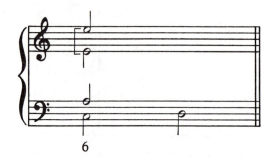

There is only one correct answer. If your solution does not agree with the one given, try to find your mistake. Consult your instructor if necessary.

---

400.   In the example below, perform step two (move the remaining voice to the tone which will complete the triad or which provides correct doubling):

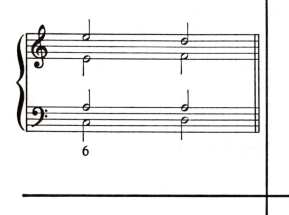

---

401.   Partwrite the second chord applying the method presented in Frame 396.

402. Partwrite the second chord.

403. Partwrite the second chord. Note that, because the soprano is doubled by the bass, *two* voices will remain after the doubled tones have moved. You must fit these remaining voices into the chord in order to achieve correct doubling and spacing.

404. Partwrite the second chord.

405. Continue as in the preceding frame.

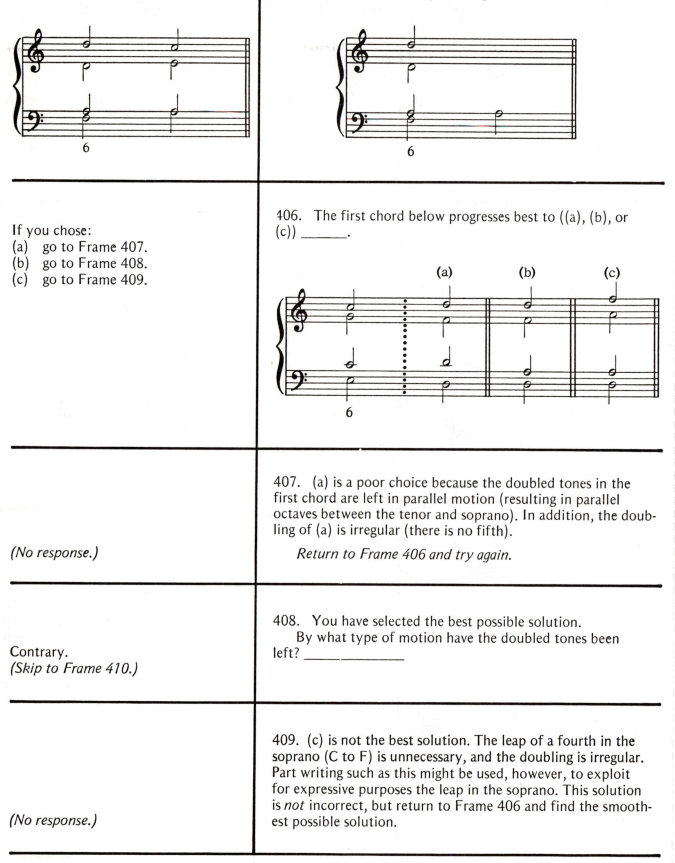

If you chose:
(a) go to Frame 407.
(b) go to Frame 408.
(c) go to Frame 409.

406. The first chord below progresses best to ((a), (b), or (c)) _____.

407. (a) is a poor choice because the doubled tones in the first chord are left in parallel motion (resulting in parallel octaves between the tenor and soprano). In addition, the doubling of (a) is irregular (there is no fifth).

Return to Frame 406 and try again.

(No response.)

408. You have selected the best possible solution.
By what type of motion have the doubled tones been left? _____

Contrary.
(Skip to Frame 410.)

409. (c) is not the best solution. The leap of a fourth in the soprano (C to F) is unnecessary, and the doubling is irregular. Part writing such as this might be used, however, to exploit for expressive purposes the leap in the soprano. This solution is *not* incorrect, but return to Frame 406 and find the smoothest possible solution.

(No response.)

410. When moving from a triad in root position to one in first inversion, follow the steps outlined below:

1. Move *into* the doubled tones in contrary, oblique, or (rarely) similar motion. *Move all voices by the smallest possible intervals.*
2. Move the remaining voice(s) to the nearest tone(s) which completes the triad or provides correct doubling.

You will avoid many errors if the doubled tones are written first.

The voice which usually is doubled in first inversion triads is the _____.

soprano

---

411. The example below illustrates step one of the process described in the preceding frame:

The soprano note is doubled by retaining the common tone in the tenor. Movement into the doubled tones is by _____ motion.

oblique

---

412. Step two is illustrated in (b) below:

The triad tone needed to complete the chord is the fifth (G). The alto is able to move to this tone without producing incorrect parallel motion.

What type of motion occurs between the bass and alto in (b)? _____

Contrary.

413. Write the alto and tenor voices for the second chord in each case, applying the method presented in Frame 410.

414. Continue as in the preceding frame.

415. Continue as in the preceding frame.

416. Write the alto and tenor voices. *(Use normal doubling in all chords; check carefully for incorrect parallel motion.)*

417. Continue as in the preceding frame.

418. Continue as in the preceding frame. *(There should be irregular doubling at the asterisk.)*

An augmented 2nd used as a melodic interval. *(Or equivalent.)*

419. What part writing error would have occurred in the preceding frame if the tenor had doubled the bass on B-flat in the final chord? _____

420. Write the alto and tenor voices.

(No response.)

---

421. The soprano is usually doubled when major or minor triads are in first inversion. But irregular doubling may occur to avoid incorrect parallel motion or undesirable melodic intervals (particularly the augmented second between V and VI in harmonic minor). *The first step when moving into or out of a first inversion should be to write the voices which are doubled.*

---

422. Unlike major and minor triads, the diminished triad is seldom used in either root position or second inversion. This is due to the interval of the diminished fifth which appears between the root and fifth. Compare the three examples below:

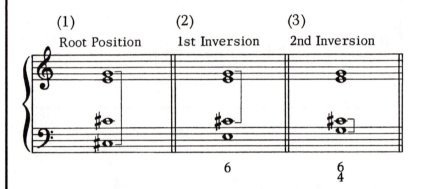

In both (1) and (3), the interval of the diminished fifth (or its enharmonic equivalent, the augmented fourth) appears above the *lowest* voice. In (2), however, the diminished fifth appears not above the bass, but above the tenor. In this case the dissonant effect of the diminished fifth is minimized because all the intervals above the bass are consonant (3rd, 6th, and octave).

The diminished triad is rarely used in _____ position or _____ inversion.

root (position or) second (inversion.)

---

423. Play diminished triads in various positions to see if you agree that the first inversion provides the most agreeable sonority. At any rate, most of the composers of the eighteenth and nineteenth centuries must have thought so, for they used this inversion more frequently than second inversion, and especially more so than root position which is the least-used of the three possible positions.

According to the statements above, which chord following provides the most agreeable sonority? _____

(2).

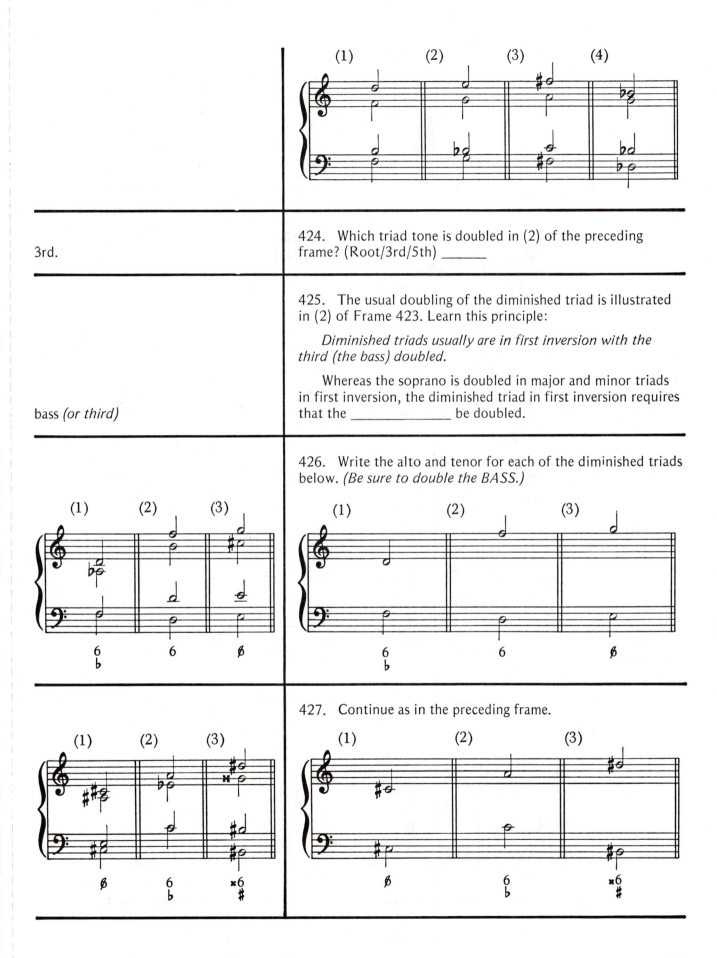

424. Which triad tone is doubled in (2) of the preceding frame? (Root/3rd/5th) _____

3rd.

425. The usual doubling of the diminished triad is illustrated in (2) of Frame 423. Learn this principle:

Diminished triads usually are in first inversion with the third (the bass) doubled.

Whereas the soprano is doubled in major and minor triads in first inversion, the diminished triad in first inversion requires that the _____ be doubled.

bass *(or third)*

426. Write the alto and tenor for each of the diminished triads below. *(Be sure to double the BASS.)*

427. Continue as in the preceding frame.

428. Let us review briefly the principles of doubling presented to this point.

1. When a major or minor triad is in *root* position, double the BASS.
2. When a major or minor triad is in *first inversion,* double the SOPRANO.
3. Diminished triads should be used in *first inversion* with the bass (or third) doubled.

(No response.)

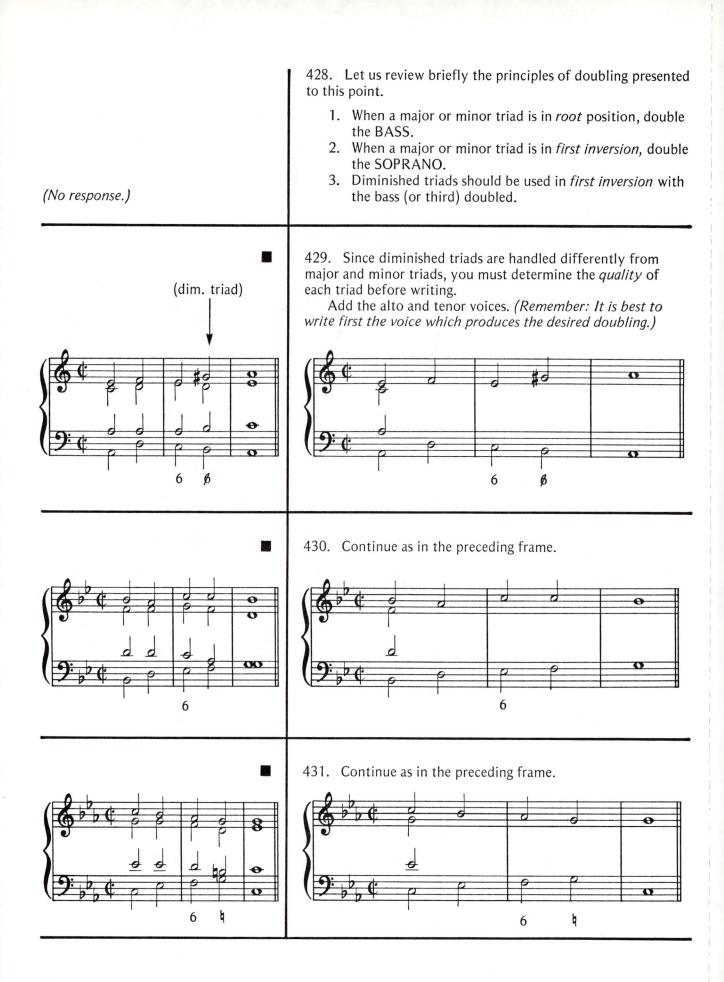

429. Since diminished triads are handled differently from major and minor triads, you must determine the *quality* of each triad before writing.

Add the alto and tenor voices. *(Remember: It is best to write first the voice which produces the desired doubling.)*

430. Continue as in the preceding frame.

431. Continue as in the preceding frame.

The descending form of the melodic minor scale *(or natural minor)*.

432. Refer, again, to the example in the preceding frame. What type of minor scale is used in the soprano voice? _____
_____
_____

433. The melodic minor scale provides alternate sixth and seventh scale degrees.

THE C MELODIC MINOR SCALE

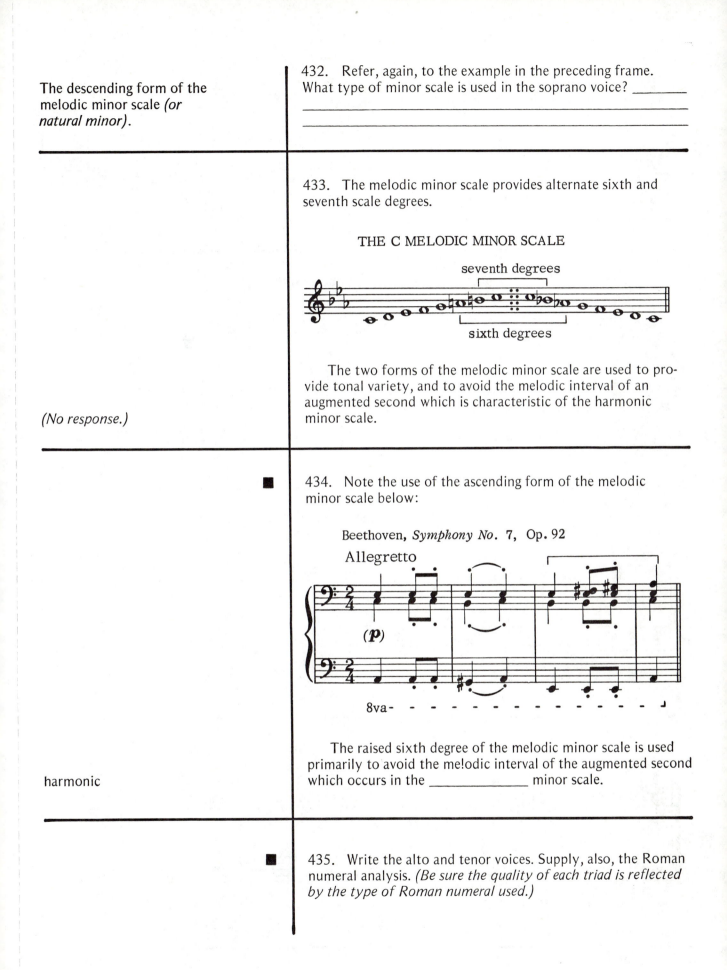

The two forms of the melodic minor scale are used to provide tonal variety, and to avoid the melodic interval of an augmented second which is characteristic of the harmonic minor scale.

(No response.)

434. Note the use of the ascending form of the melodic minor scale below:

Beethoven, *Symphony No.* 7, Op. 92

Allegretto

The raised sixth degree of the melodic minor scale is used primarily to avoid the melodic interval of the augmented second which occurs in the _____ minor scale.

harmonic

435. Write the alto and tenor voices. Supply, also, the Roman numeral analysis. *(Be sure the quality of each triad is reflected by the type of Roman numeral used.)*

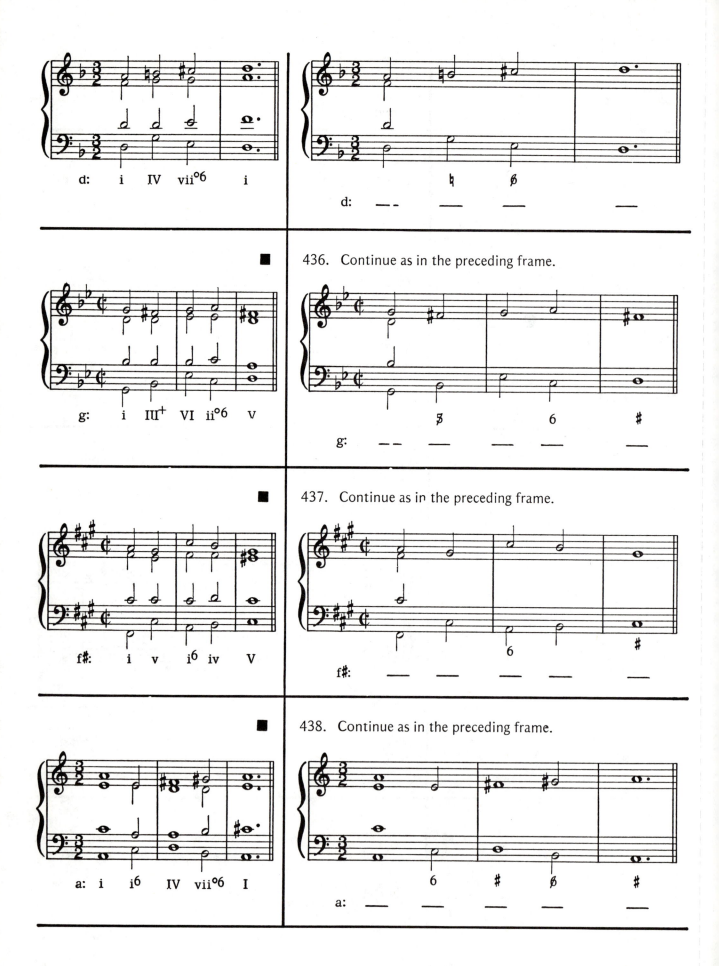

d: i   IV   vii°6   i

d:

436. Continue as in the preceding frame.

g: i   III⁺   VI   ii°6   v

g:

437. Continue as in the preceding frame.

f#:   i   v   i6   iv   V

f#:

438. Continue as in the preceding frame.

a: i   i6   IV   vii°6   I

a:

439. When two or more triads in first inversion occur in succession, it often is impossible to use normal doubling in each chord. Notice the parallel fifths and octaves in the example below:

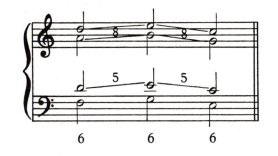

Successive first inversions often lead to the part writing error of _____.

incorrect parallel motion
(Or equivalent.)

---

440. Normal doubling sometimes can be achieved by doubling the soprano in various voices.

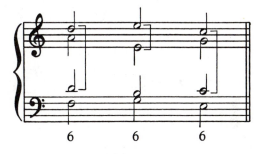

The choice of doubling in such a case is determined by expediency. Irregularities of doubling are acceptable if they contribute to smooth part writing, or are necessary to avoid incorrect parallel motion. Judged by the above statements, which is the least objectionable, parallel octaves or irregular doubling?

_____

Irregular doubling.

---

441. Notice in the example below that various pairs of voices are doubled.

Bach, Chorale: *O Herre Gott, dein göttlich Wort*

(1) Third
(2) Root
(3) Fifth

List the triad tone (root, third, fifth) which is doubled in each chord.

Doubled tone
(1) _____
(2) _____
(3) _____

---

442. For the sake of effective melodic lines in each voice and to avoid incorrect use of parallel motion, irregular doubling often occurs when several chords in first inversion are used in succession. Active tones, however, should not be doubled. An active tone is one which has a strong tendency to resolve in one specific direction. The leading tone, for example, tends to resolve up a half-step to the tonic. Notes which are inflected chromatically are active in the direction of the inflection.

In the key of F major, which tone is more active, A or E? _____

E.
(E is the leading tone in the key of F major.)

---

443. Write the alto and tenor voices. Supply, also, the Roman numeral analysis.

e: i   i⁶   vii°⁶   i

e: ___ ___ ___ ___

6   6

---

444. Write the alto and tenor voices. Supply, also, the Roman numeral analysis.

D: I   iii⁶   ii⁶   I⁶   V

(see next page)

D: ___ ___ ___ ___

6   6   6

or

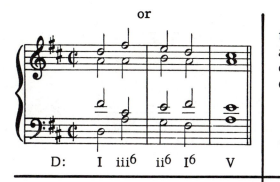

D: I iii6 ii6 I6 V

There are several possible solutions to this exercise. For this reason two answers are given. If your solution does not agree with either of these, check carefully for parallel fifths or octaves, and also for awkward leaps. If free from these errors, your answer may be as good as the ones given.

■

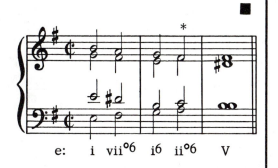

e: i vii°6 i6 ii°6 V

Irregular doubling is necessary to avoid Aug 2nd.

445. Write the alto and tenor voices and supply the Roman numeral analysis.

e: — — — — —

■

C: I I6 IV6 V6 I

446. Write the alto and tenor voices and supply the Roman numeral analysis.

C: — — — — —

There are parallel fifths between the alto and tenor, and parallel octaves between the tenor and soprano in the second and third chords. There are also parallel octaves between the soprano and bass in the last two chords.

447. What part writing errors can you find in the following example? _____
_____
_____
_____

TRIADS IN FIRST AND SECOND INVERSION

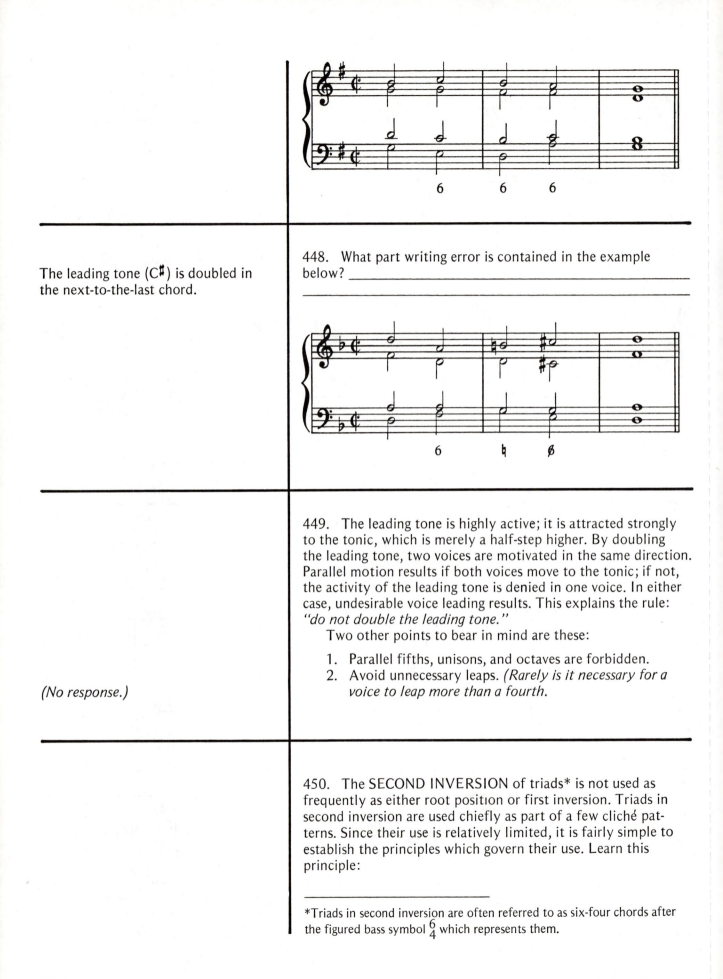

The leading tone (C♯) is doubled in the next-to-the-last chord.

448. What part writing error is contained in the example below? _____

449. The leading tone is highly active; it is attracted strongly to the tonic, which is merely a half-step higher. By doubling the leading tone, two voices are motivated in the same direction. Parallel motion results if both voices move to the tonic; if not, the activity of the leading tone is denied in one voice. In either case, undesirable voice leading results. This explains the rule: *"do not double the leading tone."*
    Two other points to bear in mind are these:

1. Parallel fifths, unisons, and octaves are forbidden.
2. Avoid unnecessary leaps. *(Rarely is it necessary for a voice to leap more than a fourth.*

(No response.)

450. The SECOND INVERSION of triads* is not used as frequently as either root position or first inversion. Triads in second inversion are used chiefly as part of a few cliché patterns. Since their use is relatively limited, it is fairly simple to establish the principles which govern their use. Learn this principle:

_____

*Triads in second inversion are often referred to as six-four chords after the figured bass symbol $\frac{6}{4}$ which represents them.

When a triad is in second inversion, double the bass.

(1) (2) (3) (4)

Which triad tone is doubled in each case above? The (root/3rd/5th) _____.

5th

451. Write the alto and tenor voices. Use *close structure* for each chord.

(1) (2) (3)

452. Write the alto and tenor voices. Use *close structure* for each chord.

(1) (2) (3)

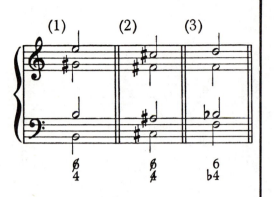

(1)   (2)   (3)

453. Write the alto and tenor voices. Use *open structure* for each chord.

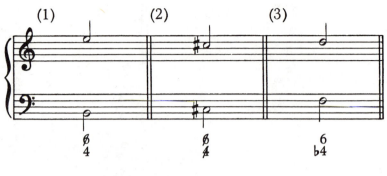

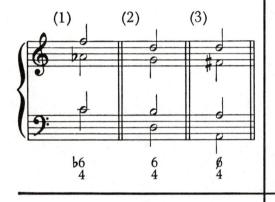

(1)   (2)   (3)

454. Write the alto and tenor voices. Use *open structure* for each chord.

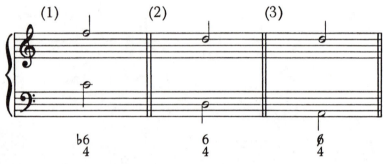

■

455. Most second inversions fall into four patterns. From these patterns second inversion triads derive their names: CADENTIAL SIX-FOUR, PASSING SIX-FOUR, PEDAL SIX-FOUR, and ARPEGGIO SIX-FOUR.

As the name implies, the CADENTIAL SIX-FOUR chord most often occurs at or near a cadence. (See NOTE.)

The example which begins below and continues on the following page includes a cadential six-four chord. Supply the Roman numeral analysis for the last two chords.

Mozart, *Sonata*, K. 331

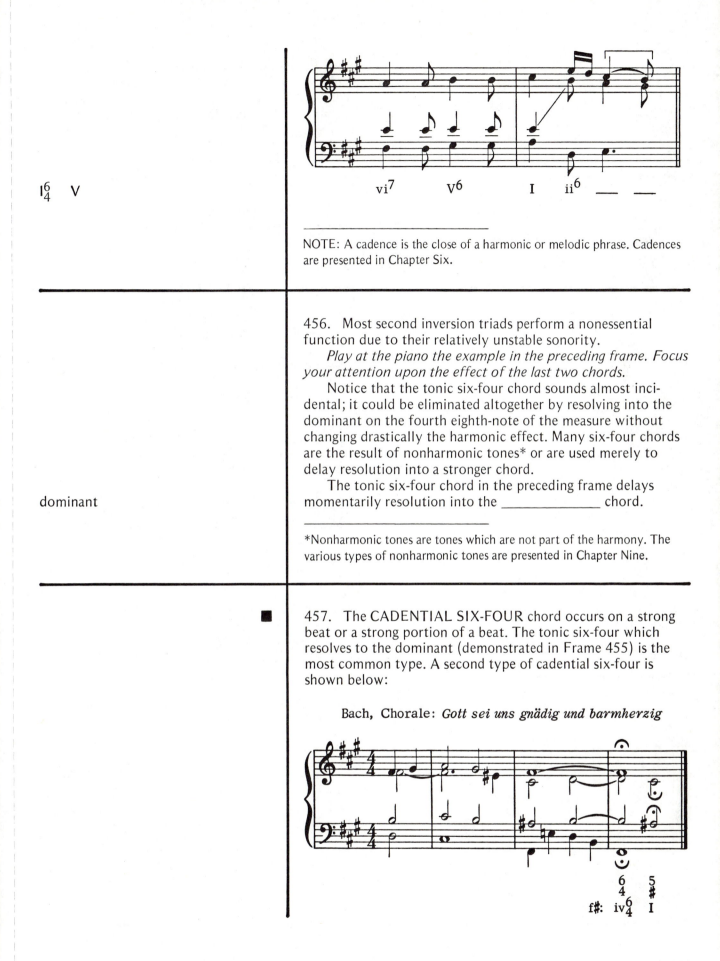

I_4^6 V

vi^7 V^6 I   ii^6 ___ ___

NOTE: A cadence is the close of a harmonic or melodic phrase. Cadences are presented in Chapter Six.

456. Most second inversion triads perform a nonessential function due to their relatively unstable sonority.

Play at the piano the example in the preceding frame. Focus your attention upon the effect of the last two chords.

Notice that the tonic six-four chord sounds almost incidental; it could be eliminated altogether by resolving into the dominant on the fourth eighth-note of the measure without changing drastically the harmonic effect. Many six-four chords are the result of nonharmonic tones* or are used merely to delay resolution into a stronger chord.

dominant

The tonic six-four chord in the preceding frame delays momentarily resolution into the _____ chord.

*Nonharmonic tones are tones which are not part of the harmony. The various types of nonharmonic tones are presented in Chapter Nine.

457. The CADENTIAL SIX-FOUR chord occurs on a strong beat or a strong portion of a beat. The tonic six-four which resolves to the dominant (demonstrated in Frame 455) is the most common type. A second type of cadential six-four is shown below:

Bach, Chorale: *Gott sei uns gnädig und barmherzig*

$\begin{matrix} 6 & 5 \\ 4 & \# \end{matrix}$

f#: iv$_4^6$ I

tonic	In this case the subdominant six-four chord causes the ultimate resolution to the tonic chord to be delayed. With respect to harmonic function, the cadential six-four chord is "unessential." It is used to sustain harmonic activity by delaying resolution to either the dominant or the _____ chord.
False. *(Cadential six-four chords occur only on strong beats.)*	458. Cadential six-four chords may occur on any beat regardless of the meter. (True/False) _____
third	459. The examples of cadential six-four chords which are shown in Frames 455 and 457 demonstrate the voice leading which is normally used. Two of the upper voices move DOWN BY STEP. THE CADENTIAL SIX-FOUR In the example above, the usual resolution of the cadential six-four chord is reflected by the figured bass symbols: the sixth above the bass moves to the fifth, and the fourth above the bass moves to the _____.
■ 	460. Write the alto and tenor voices. Supply, also, the Roman numeral analysis.

461. Write the alto and tenor voices. Supply, also, the Roman numeral analysis.

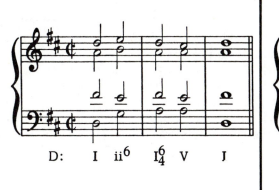

D: I   ii⁶   I⁶₄   V   I

D: ___   ___   ___   ___   ___

462. Write the alto and tenor voices. Supply, also, the Roman numeral analysis.

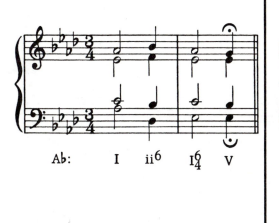

A♭:   I   ii⁶   I⁶₄   V

A♭: ___   ___   ___   ___

463. Write the alto and tenor voices. Supply, also, the Roman numeral analysis. *(Write all chords in close structure.)*

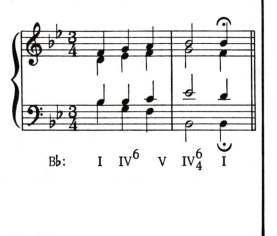

B♭:   I   IV⁶   V   IV⁶₄   I

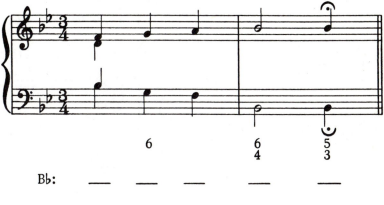

B♭: ___   ___   ___   ___

464. *Summary of principles governing the use of cadential six-four chords:*

1. The cadential six-four chord occurs in a pattern of two chords over the same bass note. There are two patterns:
   (a) over the dominant (I_4^6 - V)
   (b) over the tonic (IV_4^6 - I)
2. The cadential six-four occurs on a *strong beat* of the measure or on a *strong portion of a beat.* The resolution occupies a relatively weak position.
3. The upper voices which move upon the resolution of a cadential six-four usually move *down by step.*

In a typical cadential six-four pattern, is the six-four chord as stable a sonority as the chord which follows it? _____

No.

---

465. In terms of principles stated in the preceding frame, the cadential six-four chord in the example below is used incorrectly for two reasons. What are these errors?

(1) _____
_____
(2) _____
_____

(1) The upper voices resolve upward rather than downward;
(2) The six-four chord should occur on a strong beat.
(In your own words.)

---

466. Irregularities in the resolution of cadential six-four chords sometimes are caused by melodic considerations.

Mozart, *Quartet,* K. 387

Molto allegro

No.	
	In the preceding example, do any of the upper voices resolve "normally" (down by step)? _____
down	467. The "irregularities" in the resolution of the cadential six-four shown in the preceding frame are justified by the more emphatic effect which results. You see demonstrated here (as often is the case) that melodic requirements take precedence over such considerations as doubling, spacing, and normal resolution. Principles have been established to guide you in such matters, but they are not absolute rules, and practical necessity or the desire to produce more effective melodic lines occasionally will cause you to ignore them. In the "normal" resolution of the cadential six-four chord, the upper voices which move usually move (up/down) _____ by step.
root	468. Below is an example of a PASSING SIX-FOUR chord. Brahms, *Ein deutsches Requiem*, Op. 45, IV Mäszig bewegt S. dei - ne A. dei - ne T. lich___ sind B. dei - ne 6 6 4 In this example the passing six-four chord is used to connect a triad in first inversion with the same triad in _____ position.

469. Most passing six-four chords occur on a weak beat and connect either a triad in first inversion with the same triad in root position (as in the preceding frame), or the reverse. Both of these patterns are shown below:

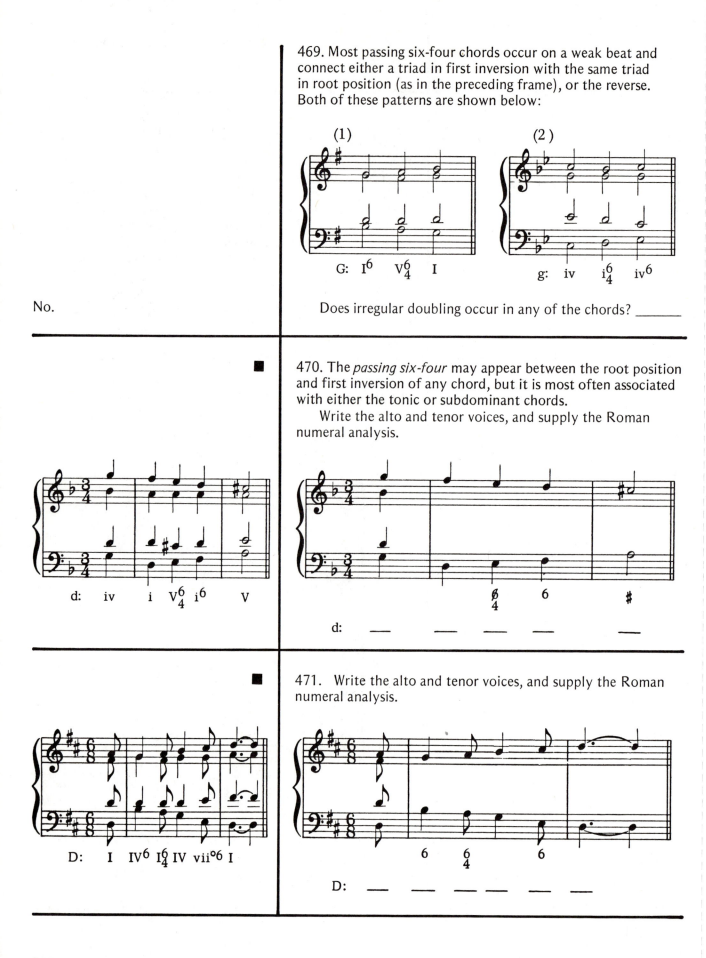

(1)

G: I⁶ V⁶₄ I

(2)

g: iv i⁶₄ iv⁶

No.

Does irregular doubling occur in any of the chords? _____

470. The *passing six-four* may appear between the root position and first inversion of any chord, but it is most often associated with either the tonic or subdominant chords.

Write the alto and tenor voices, and supply the Roman numeral analysis.

d: iv i V⁶₄ i⁶ V

d: ___ ___ ___ ___ ___

471. Write the alto and tenor voices, and supply the Roman numeral analysis.

D: I IV⁶ I⁶₄ IV vii°⁶ I

D: ___ ___ ___ ___

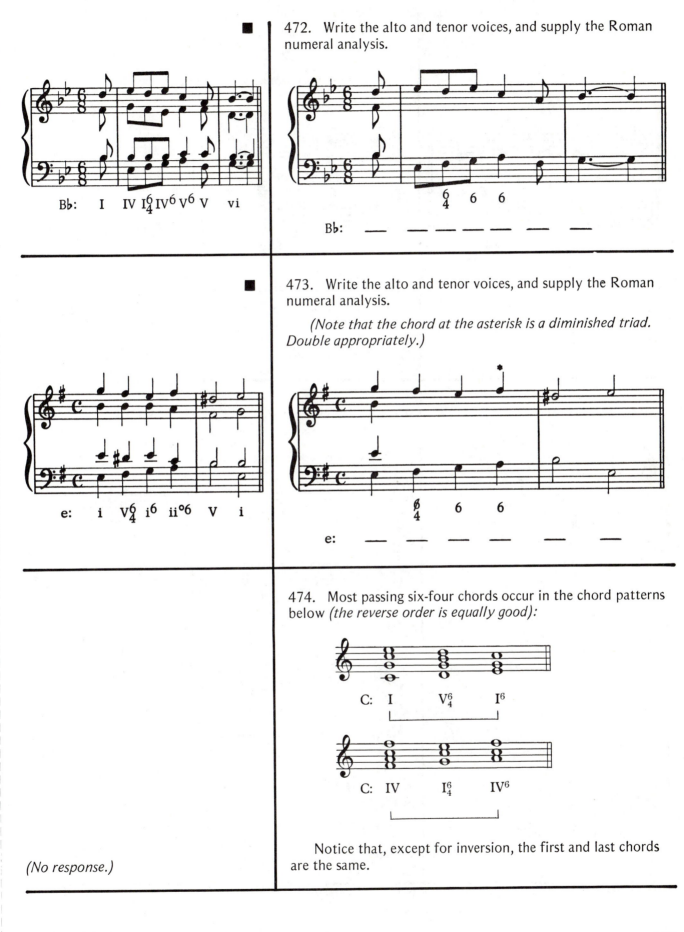

472. Write the alto and tenor voices, and supply the Roman numeral analysis.

Bb: I   IV I$^6_4$ IV^6 V^6 V   vi

Bb: __ __ __ __ __ __

473. Write the alto and tenor voices, and supply the Roman numeral analysis.

(Note that the chord at the asterisk is a diminished triad. Double appropriately.)

e: i   V$^6_4$ i^6 ii$^{\circ 6}$ V   i

e: __ __ __ __ __ __

474. Most passing six-four chords occur in the chord patterns below *(the reverse order is equally good)*:

C: I   V$^6_4$ I^6

C: IV   I$^6_4$ IV^6

Notice that, except for inversion, the first and last chords are the same.

(No response.)

a:　i　　iv$^6_4$ i　iv$^6_4$ i　V^7 i

475. The PEDAL SIX-FOUR chord* is demonstrated twice in the example below. Supply the Roman numeral analysis of the first five chords.

Schumann, *Album for the Young*, Op. 68, No. 11

(Allegretto)

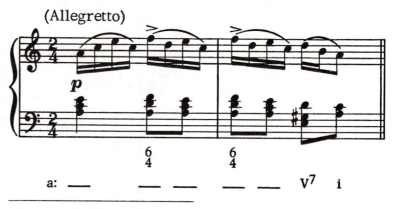

　　　　　$^6_4$　　　$^6_4$

a: __　　__ __　　__ __　　V^7　i

_____

*The pedal six-four chord is related to a nonharmonic tone device called *pedal*, or *pedal point*. This is presented in Chapter Nine (Frames 808-813). Other terms for the pedal six-four chord used by some writers are *embellishing* six-four, *auxiliary* six-four, and *stationary* six-four.

476. Another example of the pedal six-four chord is shown at the asterisk below:

Mozart, *Sonata*, K. 545

Allegro

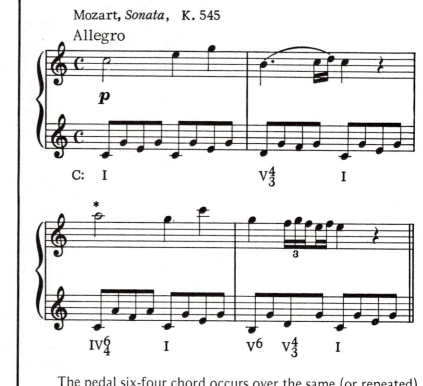

C:　I　　　　V$^4_3$　　I

　IV$^6_4$　　I　　　V^6　V$^4_3$　I

The pedal six-four chord occurs over the same (or repeated) bass note. It rarely is used except over the tonic, so the chords usually involved are the tonic-_____-tonic.

subdominant

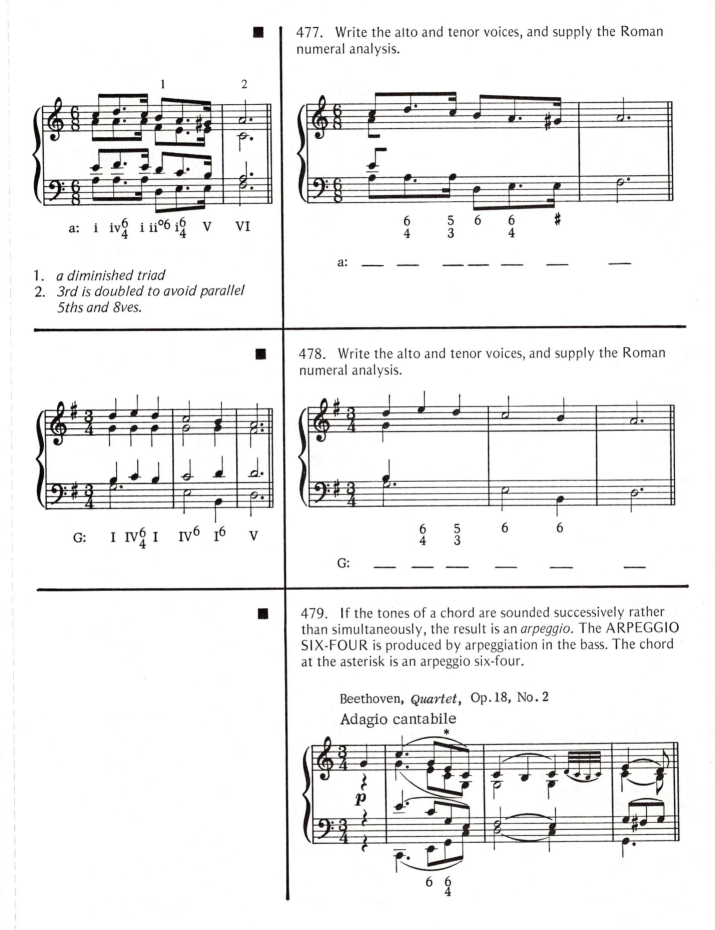

477. Write the alto and tenor voices, and supply the Roman numeral analysis.

a: ___ ___ ___ ___ ___ ___ ___

1. *a diminished triad*
2. *3rd is doubled to avoid parallel 5ths and 8ves.*

a: i iv⁶₄ i ii°⁶ i⁶₄ V VI

478. Write the alto and tenor voices, and supply the Roman numeral analysis.

G: I IV⁶₄ I IV⁶ I⁶ V

G: ___ ___ ___ ___ ___ ___ ___

479. If the tones of a chord are sounded successively rather than simultaneously, the result is an *arpeggio*. The ARPEGGIO SIX-FOUR is produced by arpeggiation in the bass. The chord at the asterisk is an arpeggio six-four.

Beethoven, *Quartet*, Op.18, No. 2
Adagio cantabile

(No response.)

The arpeggio six-four usually falls on a weak beat or weak portion of a beat and is preceded by the same chord in either root position or first inversion.

---

480. Arpeggiation is a prominent feature in piano music of the nineteenth century. It results in rich sonorous effects due to the large number of strings which can be caused to vibrate, and rhythmic animation. The arpeggio six-four, particularly in piano music, is often merely an illusion. When the damper pedal is depressed, all the strings are permitted to vibrate; thus the lowest tone continues to supply the foundation for the chord. Such a case is illustrated below:

Chopin, *Prelude*, Op. 28, No. 6

The arpeggio six-four occurs frequently in music for the

_____.

piano

---

481. Write the alto and tenor voices, and supply the Roman numeral analysis.

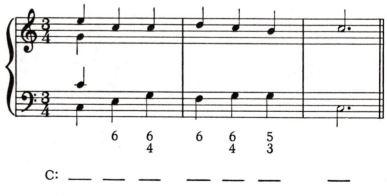

C: ___ ___ ___ ___ ___ ___ ___ ___

C: I I⁶ I⁶₄ ii⁶ I⁶₄ V I

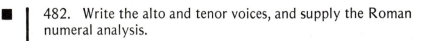

482. Write the alto and tenor voices, and supply the Roman numeral analysis.

(Use the same quarter-note rhythm as in the soprano voice.)

d: i i$^6_4$ v$^6_4$ v i^6 i$^6_4$ ii$^{\circ 6}$ V

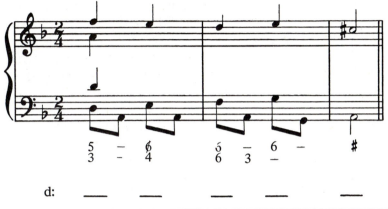

d: __ __ __ __ __ __

483. Write the alto and tenor voices, and supply the Roman numeral analysis.

(Use regular doubling for each chord.)

A: I I^6 I$^6_4$ v^{6}v$^6_4$ V I

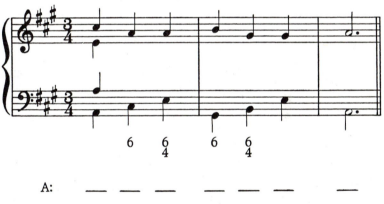

A: __ __ __ __ __ __ __

484. Write the alto and tenor voices, and supply the Roman numeral analysis.

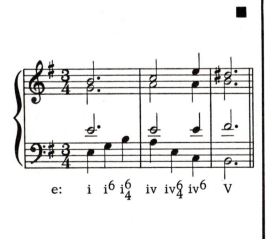

e: i i^6 i$^6_4$ iv iv$^6_4$ iv^6 V

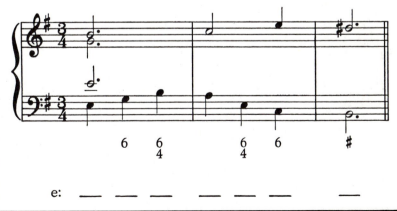

e: __ __ __ __ __ __

TRIADS IN FIRST AND SECOND INVERSION

161

SUMMARY

When all or most of the chords are in root position, the bass line tends to be angular. Inversions help smooth out the bass and thus enhance its melodic character. Inversions also provide variety with respect to chordal sonority. The interplay of sonorities that results from chords in various positions and inversions contributes significantly to the musical effect.

Care should be taken not to use chords in second inversion too frequently. Because they have a relatively weak sonority, their use is limited mainly to the four standard types presented in this chapter (cadential, passing, pedal, and arpeggio). Six-four chords were used more frequently and with greater freedom as the nineteenth century progressed; they nevertheless constitute only a small percentage of the total. First inversions, however, occur frequently. Their slightly unstable effect gives a sense of forward motion to the harmony.

Principles of Doubling for Triads in First and Second Inversion:
1. When a major or minor triad is in first inversion, double the *soprano.*
2. When a diminished triad is in first inversion, double the *bass.*
3. When a triad is in second inversion, double the *bass.*

THE FOUR TYPES OF SIX-FOUR CHORDS

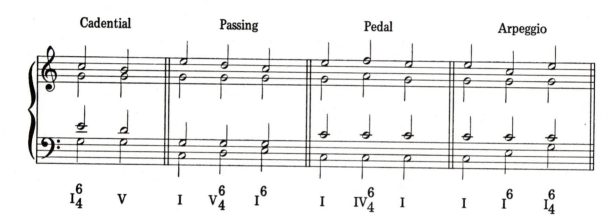

Mastery Frames

(1) First inversion

(2) Second inversion

(3) Root position

(352-379)

5-1. Identify the triad position indicated by each of the following figured bass symbols.

(1) 6_____

(2) $\begin{matrix}6\\4\end{matrix}$_____

(3) $\begin{matrix}5\\3\end{matrix}$_____

5-2. Complete the triads as indicated by the figured bass symbols.

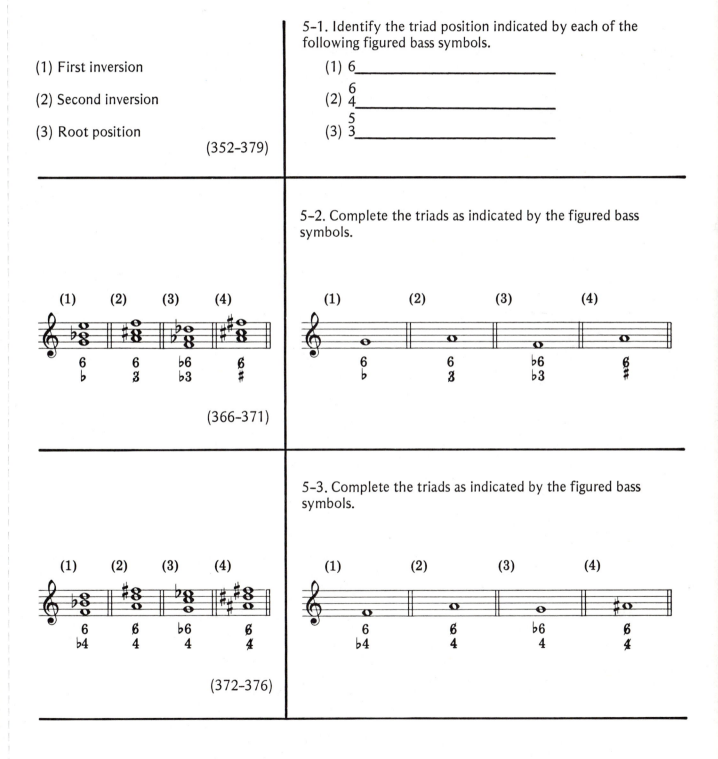

(366-371)

5-3. Complete the triads as indicated by the figured bass symbols.

(372-376)

5-4. Write the appropriate Roman numeral for each chord. *Indicate inversions.*

(1)   **(2)**   **(3)**

a: ___   B♭: ___   c: ___

(1) a: vii°⁶
(2) B♭: I⁶₄
(3) c: iv⁶

(384–388)

5-5. Write the appropriate Roman numeral for each chord. *Indicate inversions.*

(1)   **(2)**   **(3)**

D: ___   f♯: ___   d: ___

(1) D: IV⁶₄
(2) F♯: V⁶
(3) d: III⁺⁶₄

(384–388)

5-6. Write the alto and tenor voices. *Use open structure.*

                   6   6   5
                            4   ♯

(389–467)

5-7. The example in the preceding frame contains a cadential six-four chord. Name the three additional types of six-four chords.

(1)_____
(2)_____
(3)_____

(1) Passing
(2) Pedal
(3) Arpeggio
(Any order.)

(457–484)

Supplementary Assignments

ASSIGNMENT 5-1   Name_____

1. Indicate the note that will be in the lowest voice for each of the various positions of the designated triads.

TRIADS	B♭ MAJOR	C♯ MINOR	A♭ MAJOR
Root Position			
First Inversion			
Second Inversion			

2. Write the chords indicated by the figured bass symbols. *(Use correct doubling and spacing.)*

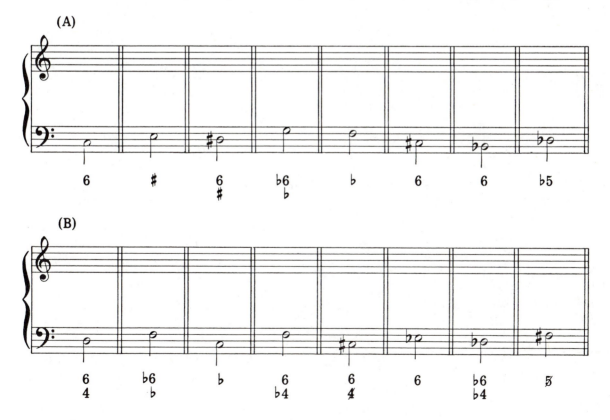

3. Supply the proper chord symbols.

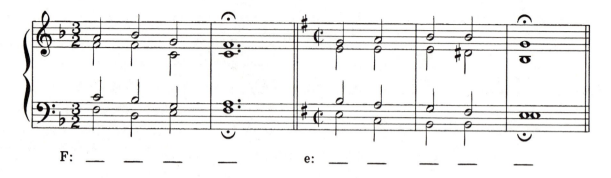

F: ___ ___ ___ ___   e: ___ ___ ___ ___ ___

4. Write the alto and tenor voices, and provide the Roman numeral analysis.

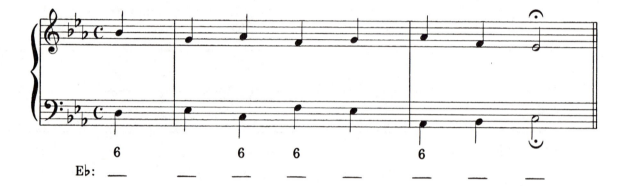

Eb: ___   6   ___   6   6   ___   6   ___   ___

Name_____

1. Name the type of second inversion illustrated in each example.

(1)_____ (2)_____
(3)_____ (4)_____

2. Which is the preferred version?_____

3. Which is the preferred version?_____

4. Write the alto and tenor voices, and provide the Roman numeral analysis.

chapter six

Phrase Structure and Cadences

The organized sounds of music elicit a variety of responses—sensual, emotional, and intellectual; thus, music may be viewed as a form of communication. Like all communication intended for human consumption, music must take into account the listener's limited attention span. This causes musical ideas to be presented in digestible portions and punctuated in a manner comparable to the chapters, paragraphs, sentences, and phrases of literature. The basic formal unit in music is the *phrase,* and phrases are set off from one another by *cadences.* Cadences provide moments of repose, as well as points of orientation.

Another elemental facet of communication in music is the use of *tension* and *relaxation* to arouse varying types and degrees of emotional response. Tension derives from harmony, rhythm, timbre, dynamics, texture, and melodic contour. In this chapter we shall focus on the contribution of melodic contour to phrase structure. The role of harmonic cadences as terminators of phrases will also be stressed.

---

485.   Music is organized into segments of various lengths, and the basic unit of organization is the PHRASE. Most phrases in traditional music are four measures long. The four-measure phrase is so prevalent (especially during the classical period), that it can be regarded as the "normal" phrase length. Nevertheless, phrases both longer and shorter occur.

One of the basic units of formal organization is the

phrase

_____.

---

486.   Another reason for the organization of music into relatively small units is the fact that, until the rise of pure instrumental music during the seventeenth and eighteenth centuries, music had a predominantly vocal orientation. Even in instrumental music the influence of vocal style continued to be felt until the end of the nineteenth century. Obviously, music which is intended for voices must provide breathing places for the performers. Since instrumental style has long been a reflection of vocal writing, it tends to have the same sort of organization. Breathing places are necessary for the comfort of the listener, too, as there is a tendency to breathe empathetically with the performer.

The phrase is a basic unit in the formal organization of music.* While phrases vary in length, their duration is usually

_____

*Rudimentary information regarding phrase structure is presented here as it is vital to the understanding of certain aspects of harmony.

vocal

about as long as a vocalist comfortably can sustain his or her breath. This is due to the predominantly _____ orientation of music during the period of tonal harmony.

---

487.   Shaping elements of the phrase include rhythm, harmony, and melodic contour. The ascending and descending intervals of a melody produce lines, most of which fall into a few simple types. These types will be introduced in the next few frames.

   The melody below ascends from a relatively low pitch to a higher level.

Tchaikovsky, *Symphony No. 4,* Op. 36

Andantino (più mosso)

Contour: _____

The "shape" of a melody—the line which is traced by its various pitches—is called melodic _____.

contour

---

488.   Another simple melodic contour is shown below:

Franck, *Symphonic Variations* (1885)

Poco Allegro (più lento)

Contour: _____

This contour is the reverse of that shown in the preceding frame. Sing or play these two melodies. Which do you feel gives the more pronounced feeling of repose? (Frame 487/Frame 488) _____

You are entitled to your own opinion, but see next frame.

489. Under most circumstances an ascending melodic line generates tension whereas a descending line provides relaxation. Ebb and flow of tension is an important element of musical expression, and one way tensions and relaxations are produced is through the contour of melodic lines.

Normally tension is produced by an _____ line, relaxation by a _____ line.

ascending
descending

490. The melody below illustrates a contour which occurs very frequently. This contour embodies the principle of tension followed by relaxation; the result is a sense of completion—a satisfying musical experience in miniature.

Mendelssohn, *Songs Without Words*, Op. 62, No. 4

Contour:

Contour:

(No response.)

491. Draw a profile beneath the melody below which illustrates its contour.

Brahms, *Symphony No. 4*, Op. 98

Contour:

492. The contour illustrated in the preceding frame is the reverse of that in Frame 490, and is not as common.

The four basic contours presented thus far are:

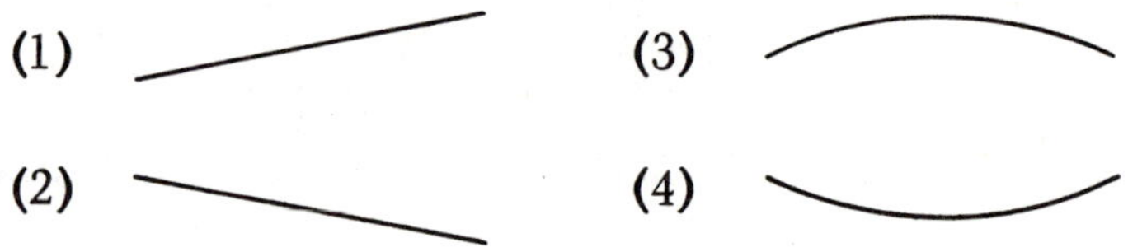

(1) _____ (3) ⌒

(2) ⌐___ ___   (4) ⌣

Which of these contours best expresses tension followed by relaxation? _____

(3).

---

493. The combination of (3) and (4) of the preceding frame produces a fifth contour.

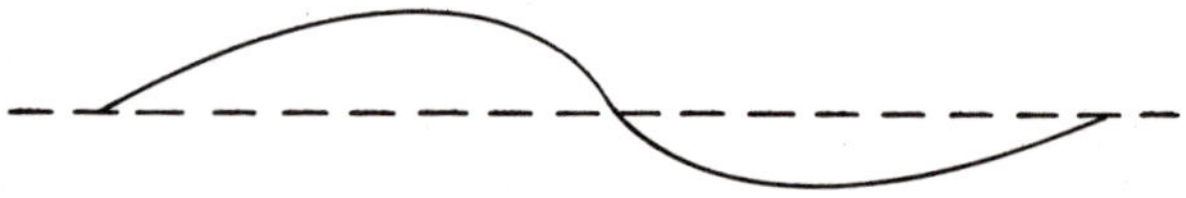

In this case, the melody extends both upward and downward from a central axis. Observe the melody below:

Haydn, *String Quartet,* Op. 3, No. 5

The note C is the axis, and both the upper and lower limit is the note _____.

F

---

494. Often rhythmic activity comes momentarily to a halt at the end of a phrase. Longer note values (and sometimes rests) are used at phrase endings to provide the desired degree of repose.

The following example consists of two phrases; the asterisks denote the end of each.

Dvořák, *Symphony No. 9*, Op. 95

Allegro molto

The desired degree of repose at the ends of phrases results from the contour of the line, but also from a lessening of the _____ activity.

rhythmic

495. We shall continue by focusing upon how phrases end. As points of repose, cadences are extremely important to the study of harmony. Because they are goals of the phrase itself, cadences have special structural significance. The ear tends to listen for these goals, and relate surrounding material to them. The ends of phrases are called CADENCES.* Learn this definition:

Cadences are melodic-harmonic formulas which bring phrases to a more or less definite close.

The points of repose which occur at the ends of phrases are called _____.

cadences

---

*The word cadence comes from the Latin root word *cadere,* to fall. The term is descriptive of the most prevalent melodic contour at the ends of phrases (especially in monophonic music such as Gregorian chant).

496. There are two types of cadences: final and non-final. Final cadences bring a phrase to a complete close. Non-final cadences point forward; they do not conclude a musical idea, but require yet another phrase to resolve their non-final effect.

List the two basic types of cadences.

(1) _____
(2) _____

(1) Final
(2) Non-final

497. There are two final cadences and two non-final cadences.

FINAL CADENCES	NON-FINAL CADENCES
Authentic	Half
Plagal	Deceptive

Authentic and plagal cadences impart a sufficient degree of finality to close an entire composition, or an important section. Half and deceptive cadences, on the other hand, lack finality;

they can be compared with the colon (:) or the question mark (?), both of which are punctuation marks which imply further elaboration.

Name the two cadences which may close an entire composition.

(1) _____

(2) _____

(1) Authentic
(2) Plagal
(Any order.)

---

498. The chords which produce each of the four cadences are shown below:

Authentic:	V or vii° - I
Plagal:	IV - I
Half:	I, IV, or ii - V
Deceptive:	V - vi

It is surprising that such a limited repertoire of cadences has sufficed for the huge mass of music which is based on tonal harmonic principles. Yet these four cadences have remained valid, and have proved their usefulness in the music of several centuries.

Perhaps the continued popularity of tonal music is due, in part, to the orientation provided the listener by only a few cadence types, whose function (final or non-final) is so easily perceived. By virtue of their common use over a long period of time, these cadences provide the listener with points of reference regarding the function of a particular phrase in relation to the musical structure as a whole.

(No response.)

---

499. The AUTHENTIC CADENCE occurs more frequently than any other. It is the strongest and most conclusive cadence. The authentic cadence consists of the chords V-I (V-i in a minor key).

Haydn, *The Creation*, No. 3

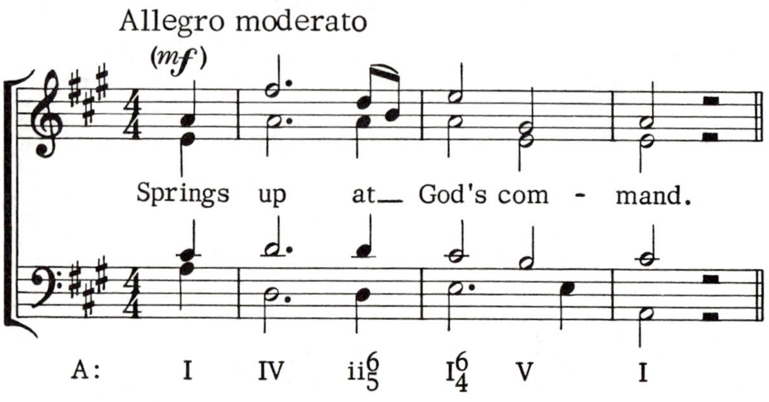

Allegro moderato

(mf)

Springs up at__ God's com - mand.

A: I IV ii$_5^6$ I$_4^6$ V I

The cadence consists of the final two chords (V-I); but, as is shown in the example above, the tonic in second inversion (the cadential six-four) often is included as part of the cadential formula.

What are the two chords which produce the authentic cadence? _____-_____

V-I
(or V-i).

---

500.   Another authentic cadence is shown below:

Beethoven, *Symphony No. 8*, Op. 93

F: V   V   I

Compare the cadence above with the one shown in the preceding frame. Both are authentic cadences, but they do not have the same degree of finality.

Which do you think produces the stronger sense of conclusion? (Frame 499/500) _____

Frame 499.
(There should be no doubt.)

---

501.   Rhythm contributes to making the cadence of Frame 499 sound more conclusive than the cadence of Frame 500 but another factor is that the root of the tonic triad is in the soprano in the first case whereas the third is in the soprano in the second.

The cadence in Frame 499 is a PERFECT authentic cadence whereas the cadence in Frame 500 is an IMPERFECT authentic cadence. The terms *perfect* and *imperfect* refer to the degree of finality imparted by a _____.

cadence

---

502.   To qualify as a PERFECT cadence, the following conditions must be met:

(1)   Both chords must be in root position.
(2)   The final tonic chord must have the root in the soprano.

Why is the example on the next page *not* a perfect authentic cadence?

_____

_____

The dominant chord is not in root position.

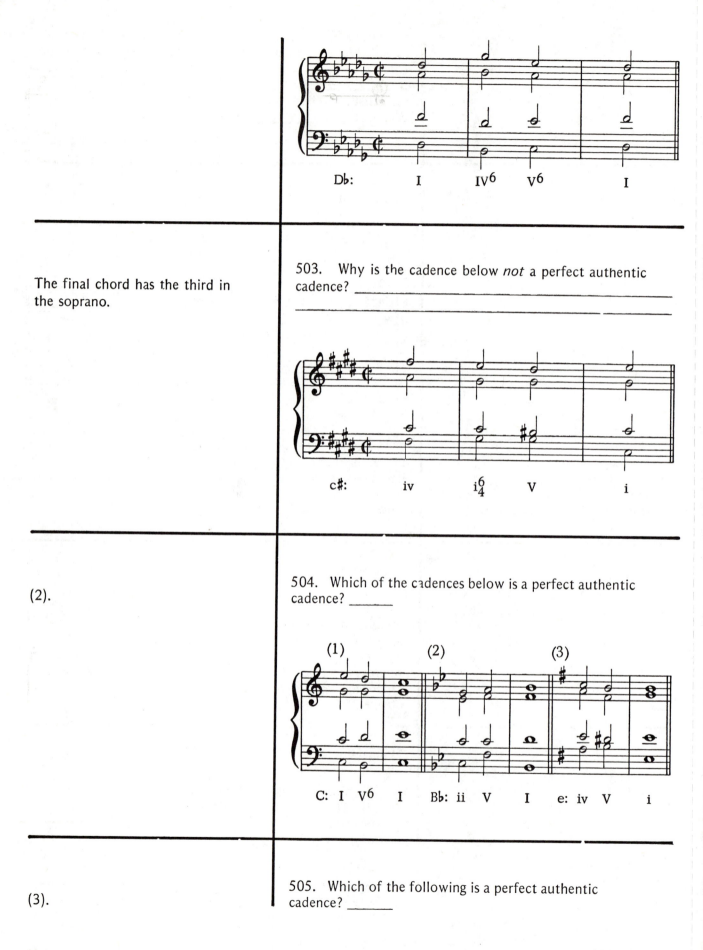

The final chord has the third in the soprano.

(2).

(3).

503.   Why is the cadence below *not* a perfect authentic cadence? _____

_____ _____

c#:   iv   i$^6_4$ V   i

504.   Which of the cadences below is a perfect authentic cadence? _____

(1)   (2)   (3)

C: I V^6 I   Bb: ii V   I   e: iv V   i

505.   Which of the following is a perfect authentic cadence? _____

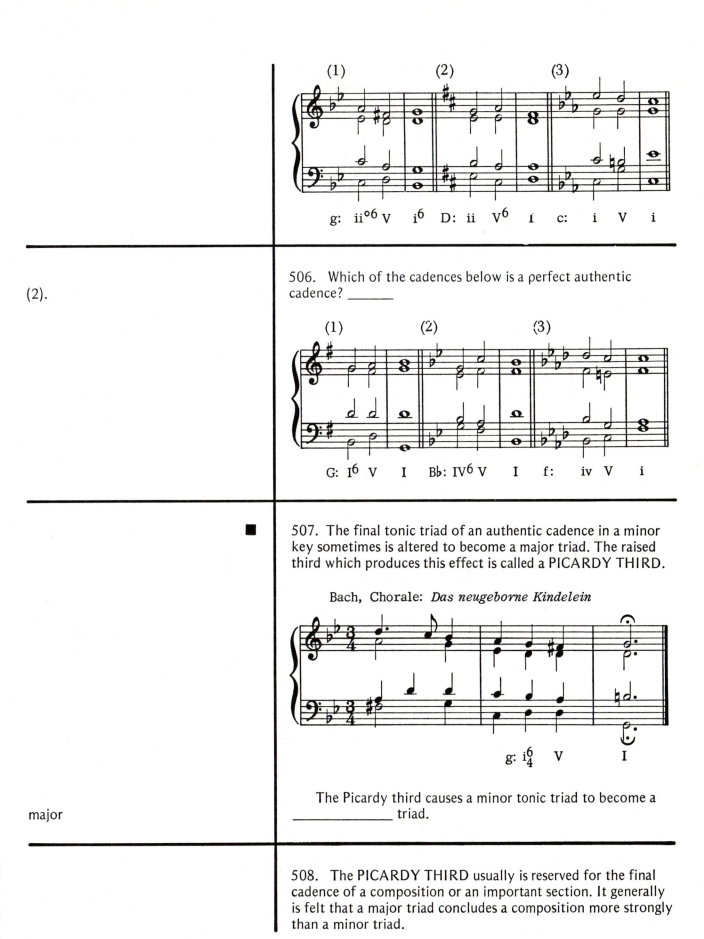

(2).

506. Which of the cadences below is a perfect authentic cadence? _____

507. The final tonic triad of an authentic cadence in a minor key sometimes is altered to become a major triad. The raised third which produces this effect is called a PICARDY THIRD.

Bach, Chorale: *Das neugeborne Kindelein*

The Picardy third causes a minor tonic triad to become a _____ triad.

major

508. The PICARDY THIRD usually is reserved for the final cadence of a composition or an important section. It generally is felt that a major triad concludes a composition more strongly than a minor triad.

You are entitled to your opinion. Certainly the B-natural produces the "brighter" sound.

Play the example in the preceding frame substituting B-flat for B-natural in the final chord. Compare the effect of this version with the original. Which do you think is the stronger? (B-flat, or B-natural) _____

■

509. Write the alto and tenor voices in accordance with the figured bass symbols. Analyze with Roman numerals.

d: ___ ___ ___ ___

True.

510. The cadence in the preceding frame is a perfect authentic cadence with a PICARDY THIRD. (True/False) _____

■

511. Write the alto and tenor voices in accordance with the figured bass symbols. Analyze with Roman numerals.

f#: ___ ___ ___ ___

False.
(There is a Picardy third, but the cadence is imperfect.)

512. The cadence in the preceding frame is a perfect authentic cadence with a PICARDY THIRD. (True/False) _____

513. Check (√) the correct option:

1. The PICARDY THIRD occurs in the authentic cadence in a minor key.

2. The PICARDY THIRD occurs only in the perfect authentic cadence.

True statements:
(1) _____   (2) _____   Both _____   Neither _____

(1) √

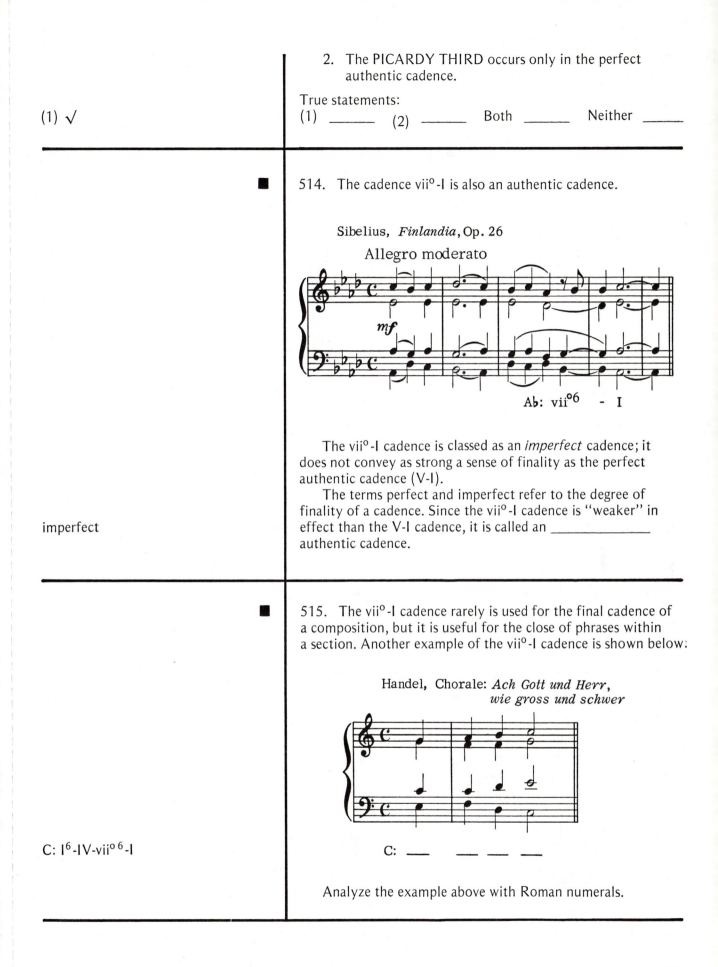

514. The cadence vii°-I is also an authentic cadence.

Sibelius, *Finlandia*, Op. 26

Allegro moderato

mf

Ab: vii°⁶ – I

The vii°-I cadence is classed as an *imperfect* cadence; it does not convey as strong a sense of finality as the perfect authentic cadence (V-I).

The terms perfect and imperfect refer to the degree of finality of a cadence. Since the vii°-I cadence is "weaker" in effect than the V-I cadence, it is called an _____ authentic cadence.

imperfect

---

515. The vii°-I cadence rarely is used for the final cadence of a composition, but it is useful for the close of phrases within a section. Another example of the vii°-I cadence is shown below:

Handel, Chorale: *Ach Gott und Herr, wie gross und schwer*

C: __ __ __ __

Analyze the example above with Roman numerals.

C: I⁶-IV-vii°⁶-I

authentic

516. The leading tone triad (vii°) has virtually the same harmonic function as the dominant (V), so it may be substituted for V to produce an imperfect _____ cadence.

517. The leading tone triad may be used to make an imperfect authentic cadence in a minor key.

Bach, Chorale: *Komm, Gott Schöpfer, heiliger Geist*

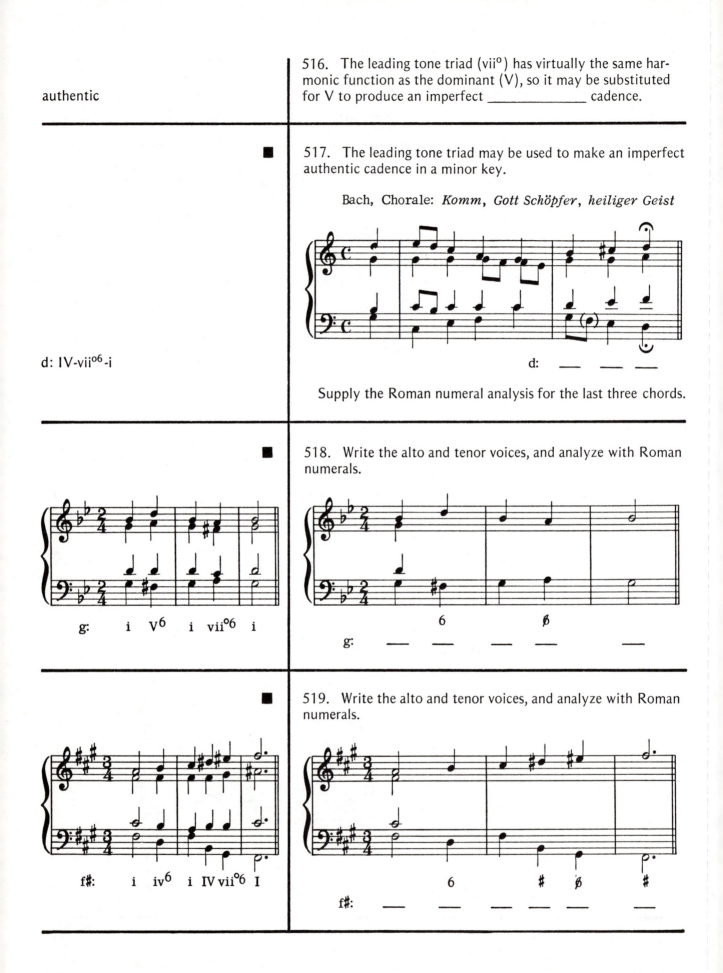

d: IV-vii°⁶-i

d: ___ ___ ___

Supply the Roman numeral analysis for the last three chords.

518. Write the alto and tenor voices, and analyze with Roman numerals.

g: i   V⁶   i   vii°⁶   i

g: ___ ___ ___ ___ ___

519. Write the alto and tenor voices, and analyze with Roman numerals.

f#:   i   iv⁶   i   IV   vii°⁶   I

f#: ___ ___ ___ ___ ___ ___

520. Notice in the preceding frame that the ascending form of the melodic minor scale is used in the soprano voice. This is to avoid the augmented second (D to E-sharp) which would have occurred if harmonic minor had been used.

This example shows that in a minor key, depending upon whether or not the sixth scale degree is raised, the quality of the subdominant triad may be either _____ or _____.

major (or) minor

---

521. Even though the example in Frame 519 is in the key of F-sharp minor, the final chord contains an A-sharp. This device is called a _____ third.

Picardy

---

522. Write the alto and tenor voices, and analyze with Roman numerals.

C: I   I^6 IV   vii^{o6} I

C: ___ ___ ___ ___ ___

---

523. Of the two "final" cadences (authentic and plagal), the authentic cadence is used much more frequently. The PLAGAL CADENCE has a "softer," less "positive" effect than the authentic cadence. The plagal cadence consists of the progression IV-I (iv-i in a minor key).

Brahms, *Symphony No.* 1, Op. 68

Più allegro

C: IV   I

(continued on next page)

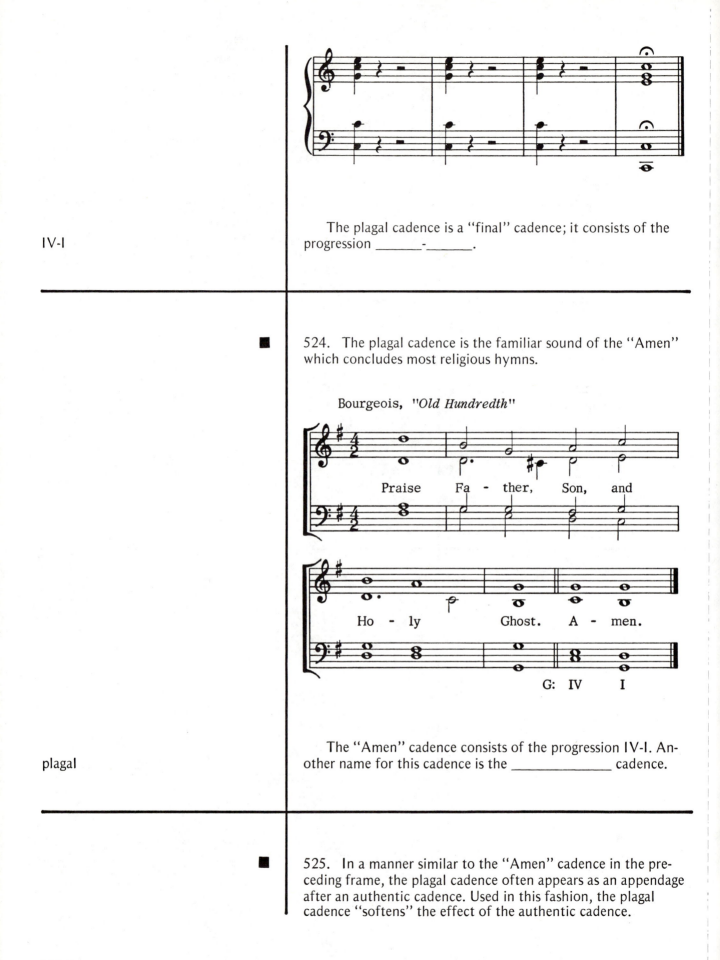

IV-I

The plagal cadence is a "final" cadence; it consists of the progression _____-_____.

524. The plagal cadence is the familiar sound of the "Amen" which concludes most religious hymns.

Bourgeois, *"Old Hundredth"*

Praise Fa - ther, Son, and

Ho - ly Ghost. A - men.

G: IV I

plagal

The "Amen" cadence consists of the progression IV-I. Another name for this cadence is the _____ cadence.

525. In a manner similar to the "Amen" cadence in the preceding frame, the plagal cadence often appears as an appendage after an authentic cadence. Used in this fashion, the plagal cadence "softens" the effect of the authentic cadence.

I-IV-I

Chopin, *Etude*, Op. 25, No. 8

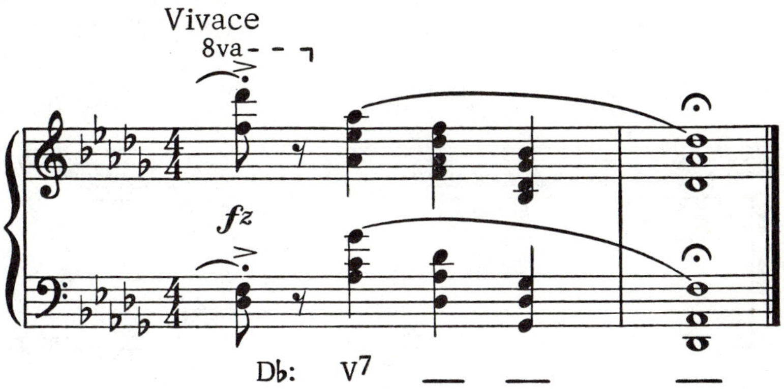

Vivace

Db: V⁷ — — —

Supply the Roman numeral analysis for the final three chords.

(3).

526. Like authentic cadences, plagal cadences are perfect or imperfect depending upon the degree of finality. A perfect plagal cadence must end with the root of the final tonic chord in the soprano, and both chords (subdominant and tonic) must be in root position.
 Which of the cadences below is a *perfect plagal cadence*? _____

Eb: IV⁶   I   IV   I   IV   I

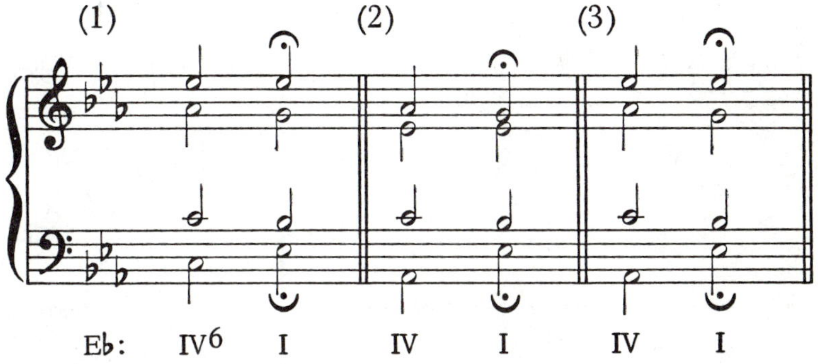

(2).

527. Which of the cadences below is NOT a *perfect plagal cadence*? _____

G: IV   I   d: iv   i   b: iv   i

PHRASE STRUCTURE AND CADENCES

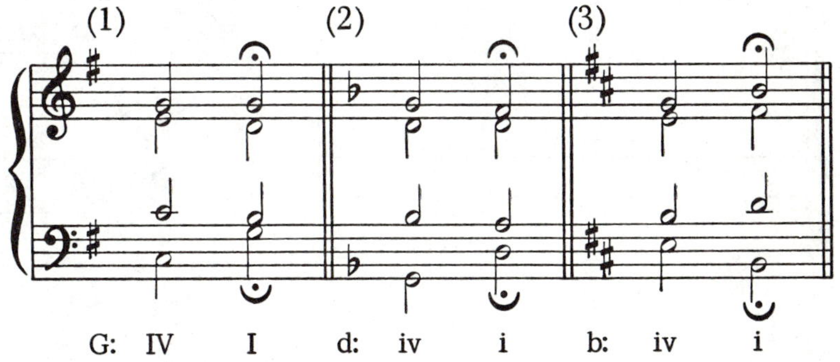

528. Write the alto and tenor voices, and analyze with Roman numerals.

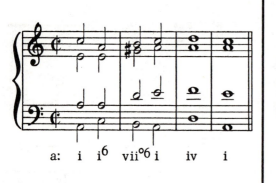

a: i   i⁶   vii°⁶ i   iv   i

Use close structure

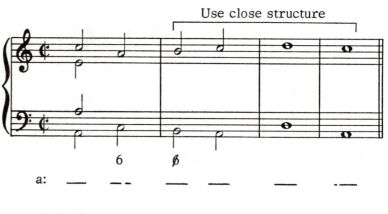

a: ___   ___   ___   ___   ___
       6   ø

529. Write the alto and tenor voices, and analyze with Roman numerals.

G: I   vi   I⁶   IV   I

G: ___   ___   ___   ___   ___
            6

530. Write the alto and tenor voices, and analyze with Roman numerals.

c: i   V⁶ i   V   iv   i

c: ___   ___   ___   ___   ___
      6   ♮

False.
(It is an imperfect plagal cadence.)

Both √

(2) √

(No response.)

531. The cadence in the preceding frame is an imperfect authentic cadence. (True/False) _____

532. Check (√) the correct option:

   1. Authentic and plagal cadences are final cadences.
   2. A composition usually ends with a perfect cadence.

True statements:
(1) _____ (2) _____ Both _____ Neither _____

533. Check (√) the correct option:

   1. The progression vii°-I produces an imperfect plagal cadence.
   2. Both authentic and plagal cadences may be either perfect or imperfect.

True statements:
(1) _____ (2) _____ Both _____ Neither _____

534. The two final cadences are *authentic* and *plagal*. These cadences are called *perfect* when the last two chords are in root position and the final tonic chord has the keynote in the highest voice. If these two conditions are not met, the effect of finality is weakened, and the term *imperfect* is used.

    The terms *perfect* and *imperfect* concern final cadences only. In the case of non-final cadences (half and deceptive), no terms are used to express the degree of finality.

535. The HALF CADENCE is a non-final cadence; it concludes a phrase which is not a complete musical idea in itself, and points forward toward yet another phrase.

Schumann, *Album for the Young*, Op. 68. No. 4

G: I   V

half

The final chord of a half cadence is usually the dominant.*
It may be preceded by the tonic (as above) or any other chord
which provides effective harmonic movement.

The progression ii-V produces a _____ cadence.

_____

*Half cadences ending on the subdominant triad, while rare, sometimes
do occur. (See Frame 537.)

■ 536. The cadential six-four often appears as part of a half
cadence.

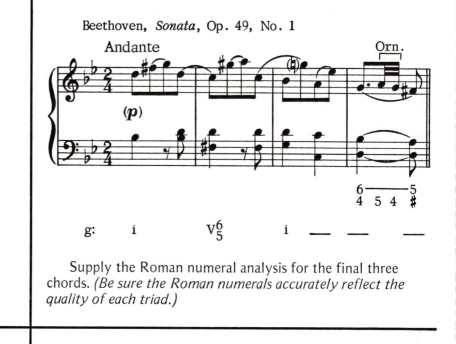

Beethoven, *Sonata*, Op. 49, No. 1

ii⁰⁶-i⁶₄-V

g: i   v⁶₅   i ___ ___ ___

Supply the Roman numeral analysis for the final three
chords. *(Be sure the Roman numerals accurately reflect the
quality of each triad.)*

■ 537. The half cadence which ends on the dominant triad is
by far the most common type. Half cadences to the subdominant, although rare, provide an interesting effect.

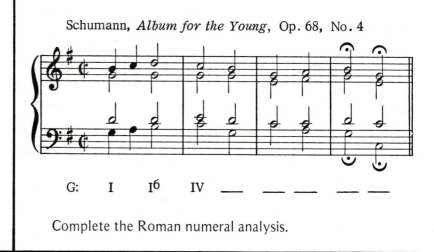

Schumann, *Album for the Young*, Op. 68, No. 4

I-IV-vii⁰⁶-I-IV

G: I   I⁶   IV ___ ___ ___ ___

Complete the Roman numeral analysis.

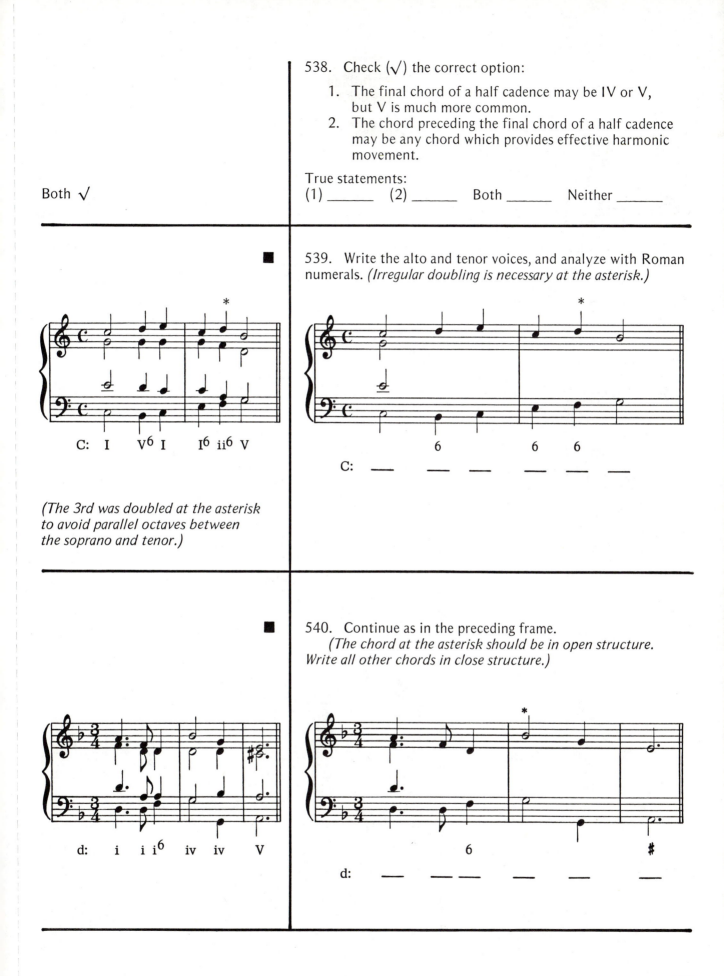

538. Check (√) the correct option:

    1. The final chord of a half cadence may be IV or V, but V is much more common.
    2. The chord preceding the final chord of a half cadence may be any chord which provides effective harmonic movement.

True statements:
(1) _____ (2) _____ Both _____ Neither _____

Both √

539. Write the alto and tenor voices, and analyze with Roman numerals. *(Irregular doubling is necessary at the asterisk.)*

C: ___ ___ ___ ___ ___ ___

C: I V⁶ I   I⁶ ii⁶ V

(The 3rd was doubled at the asterisk to avoid parallel octaves between the soprano and tenor.)

540. Continue as in the preceding frame.
    (The chord at the asterisk should be in open structure. Write all other chords in close structure.)

d: i i i⁶ iv iv V

d: ___ ___ ___ ___ ___ ___

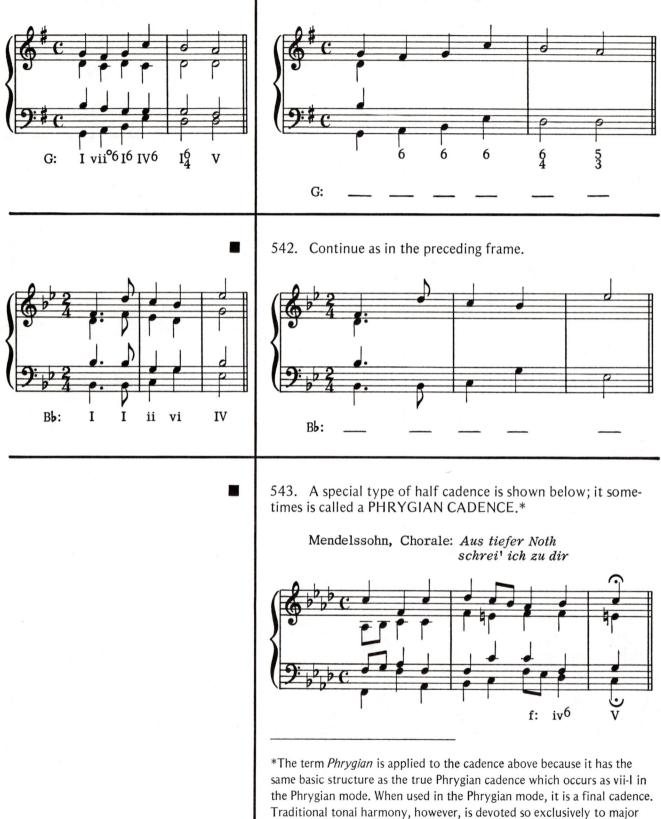

541. Continue as in the preceding frame.

G: I vii°⁶ I⁶ IV⁶ I⁶₄ V

G: ___ ___ ___ ___ ___

542. Continue as in the preceding frame.

B♭: I I ii vi IV

B♭: ___ ___ ___ ___ ___

543. A special type of half cadence is shown below; it sometimes is called a PHRYGIAN CADENCE.*

Mendelssohn, Chorale: *Aus tiefer Noth schrei' ich zu dir*

f: iv⁶ V

---

*The term *Phrygian* is applied to the cadence above because it has the same basic structure as the true Phrygian cadence which occurs as vii-I in the Phrygian mode. When used in the Phrygian mode, it is a final cadence. Traditional tonal harmony, however, is devoted so exclusively to major and minor tonalities that we shall continue to regard it as a type of half cadence.

half

first

The *Phrygian cadence* is most often a special type of
_____ cadence.

544.   The Phrygian cadence consists of the progression iv-V
in harmonic minor. There are two ways that it may be written.
These are shown below:

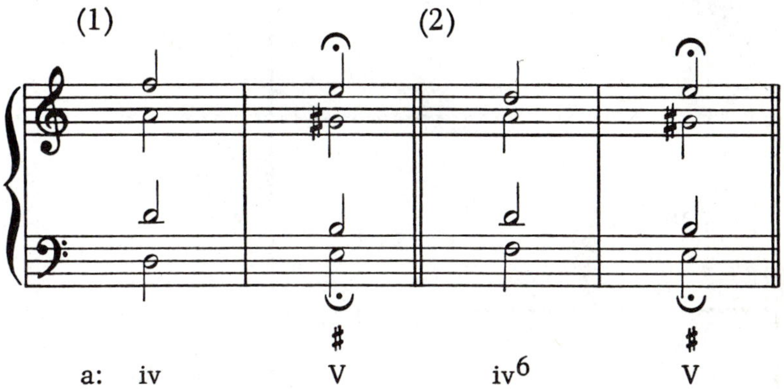

a: iv   V   iv⁶   V

The subdominant chord which precedes the final dominant
in a Phrygian cadence may be in either root position or
_____ inversion.

545.   In the Phrygian cadence the root of the dominant chord
is approached by step in contrary motion in the soprano and
bass voices.

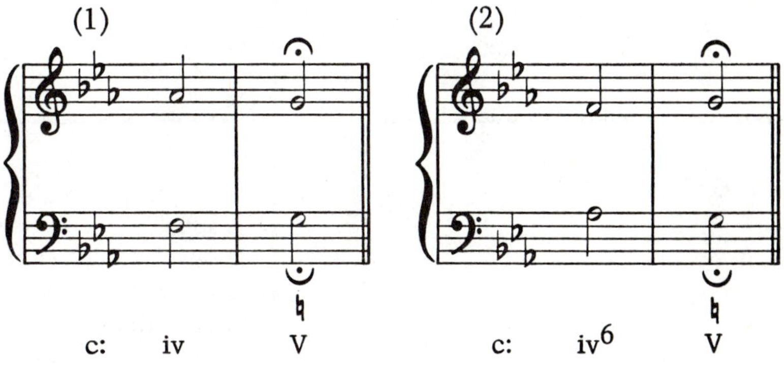

c: iv   V   c: iv⁶   V

Write the alto and tenor voices for (1) and (2) above.

546. Write the alto and tenor voices, and analyze with Roman numerals.

e: i   V⁶   i   iv⁶   V

6   6

e: ___ ___ ___ ___ ___ ___

Phrygian

547. The example in the preceding frame ends with a half cadence, but it is a special type of half cadence. It is a _____ _____ cadence.

---

548. The DECEPTIVE cadence is best understood by referring to the authentic cadence. When another chord is substituted for the final tonic, the expected resolution of the dominant is avoided.

(1) AUTHENTIC   **(2) DECEPTIVE**

G: __ __ __ __   G: __ __ __ __

Analyze each of the above examples with Roman numerals.

(1) ii   I⁶   V   I
(2) ii   I⁶   V   vi

---

submediant (vi)

549. In (2) of the preceding frame the submediant triad (vi) is substituted for the tonic. *This is by far the most common type of deceptive cadence.*

The deceptive cadence is similar to an authentic cadence except that the dominant does not resolve to the tonic as expected. Although the final chord might be any one to which the dominant could resolve, it usually is the _____.

550. Composers use the deceptive cadence for variety and to prolong harmonic interest. The deceptive cadence is not a final cadence; several additional chords (or a phrase or two) are required to give a sense of completion following a deceptive cadence.

Play the example below:

Bach, Chorale: *Es ist das Heil uns kommen her*

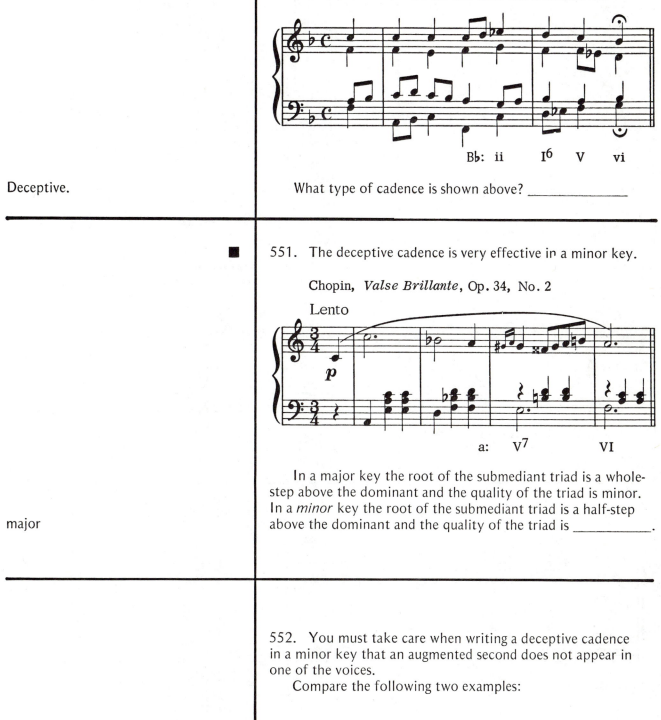

B♭: ii   I⁶   V   vi

Deceptive.

What type of cadence is shown above? _____

551. The deceptive cadence is very effective in a minor key.

Chopin, *Valse Brillante*, Op. 34, No. 2

Lento

a: V⁷   VI

In a major key the root of the submediant triad is a whole-step above the dominant and the quality of the triad is minor. In a *minor* key the root of the submediant triad is a half-step above the dominant and the quality of the triad is _____.

major

552. You must take care when writing a deceptive cadence in a minor key that an augmented second does not appear in one of the voices.

Compare the following two examples:

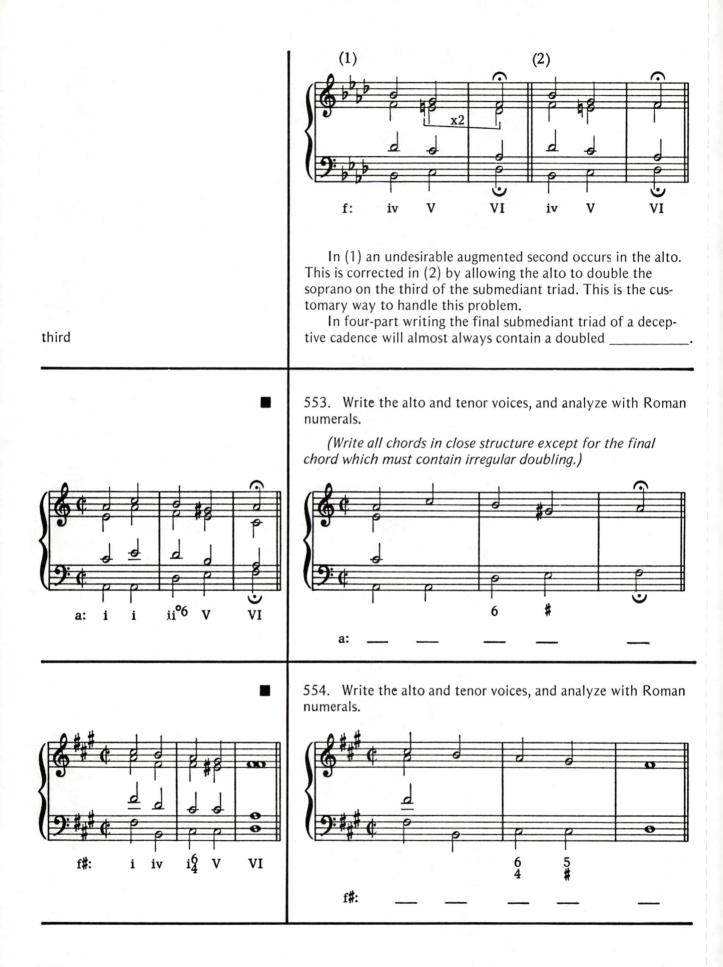

In (1) an undesirable augmented second occurs in the alto. This is corrected in (2) by allowing the alto to double the soprano on the third of the submediant triad. This is the customary way to handle this problem.

In four-part writing the final submediant triad of a deceptive cadence will almost always contain a doubled _____.

third

553. Write the alto and tenor voices, and analyze with Roman numerals.

(Write all chords in close structure except for the final chord which must contain irregular doubling.)

554. Write the alto and tenor voices, and analyze with Roman numerals.

555. Continue as in the preceding frame.

(The chords at the asterisks should contain doubled thirds.)

F:

556. Continue as in the preceding frame.

D:

557. To provide an extra element of surprise the submediant chord, which would normally appear in minor, sometimes is used in a major key.

Schubert, *Symphony No. 5 in B-flat Major*
Andante con moto

The borrowing of a chord from a minor mode for use in its parallel major is discussed in Part II, Chapter Five: BORROWED deceptive

CHORDS. The example above is presented here as it illustrates a common type of deceptive cadence.

The element of surprise is an important feature of the _____ cadence.

---

558. Write the alto and tenor voices.

(Watch for parallel fifths between the second and third chords. Remember, also, to double the final chord as if it were in the key of A minor.)

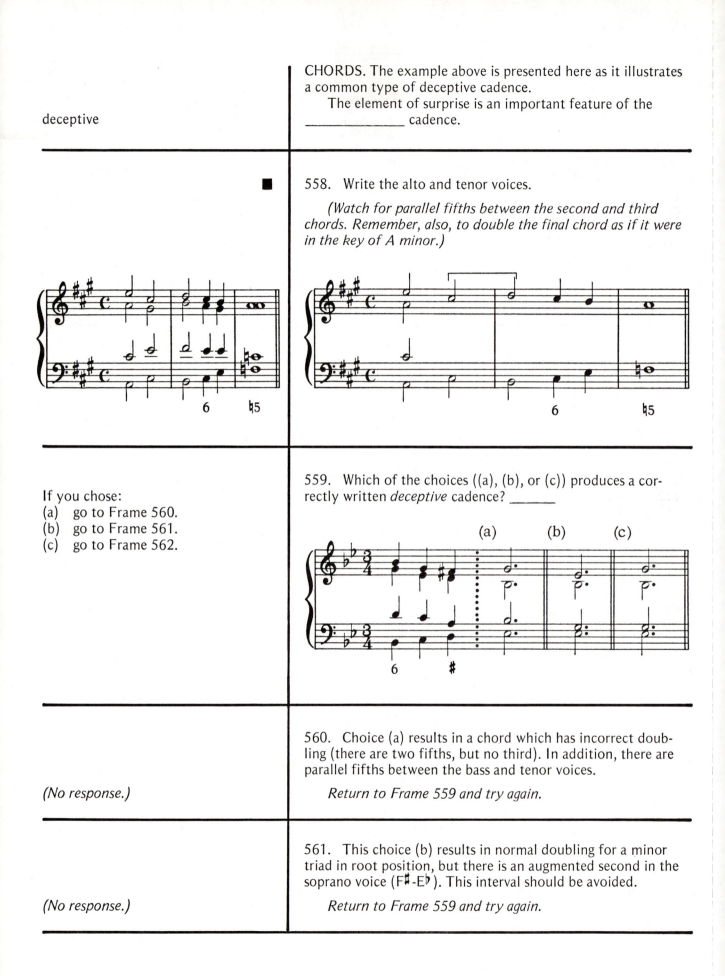

If you chose:
(a) go to Frame 560.
(b) go to Frame 561.
(c) go to Frame 562.

559. Which of the choices ((a), (b), or (c)) produces a correctly written *deceptive* cadence? _____

(a)   (b)   (c)

(No response.)

560. Choice (a) results in a chord which has incorrect doubling (there are two fifths, but no third). In addition, there are parallel fifths between the bass and tenor voices.

Return to Frame 559 and try again.

(No response.)

561. This choice (b) results in normal doubling for a minor triad in root position, but there is an augmented second in the soprano voice (F♯-E♭). This interval should be avoided.

Return to Frame 559 and try again.

---

augmented second

562. You have made the correct choice. The third of the submediant triad must be doubled in the deceptive cadence in a minor key. This is to avoid the melodic use of an undesirable interval. What is this interval? The _____ _____.

If you chose:
(a) go to Frame 564.
(b) go to Frame 565.
(c) go to Frame 566.

563. Which of the choices ((a), (b), or (c)) produces a correctly written *imperfect authentic* cadence? _____

(No response.)

564. Choice (a) results in an imperfect *plagal* cadence.

Return to Frame 563 and find the imperfect authentic cadence.

The third of the final chord is in the soprano.
(Or equivalent.)

565. You have made the correct choice. What makes this an *imperfect* cadence? _____
_____

(Skip to Frame 567.)

(No response.)

566. Choice (c) results in a *perfect* authentic cadence.

Review Frame 502 then return to Frame 563 and try again.

---

(1) Half
(2) Deceptive

567. The authentic and plagal cadences are "final" cadences. Name the two "non-final" cadences.

(1) _____
(2) _____

SUMMARY

One of the basic formal units of music is the phrase; most are four measures in length. The phrase is a segment of music that can be assimilated comfortably by the listener. The melodic aspect of a phrase is traced by the successive pitches. Rising pitches tend to create tension; falling pitches tend to relax tension.

Most melodic phrases are based on one of four basic contours; a fifth contour is a combination of the third and fourth. The basic contours are:

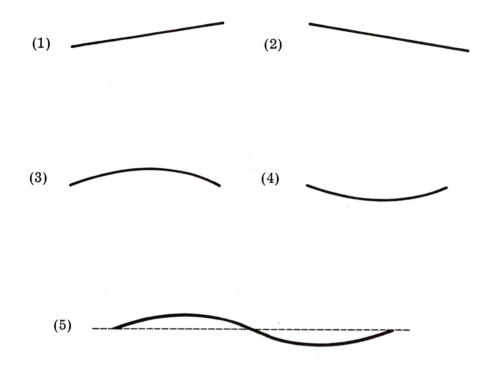

Cadences serve to punctuate the phrases which unite to build larger formal units. The four types of cadences (authentic, plagal, half, and deceptive) provide a very limited repertoire of punctuations. This is one reason why traditional music is easy for the listener to apprehend. Not only is the expressive significance of each cadence type clear, but tonal implications usually are unambiguous. Thus, frequent tonal orientations are provided the listener, and these orientations lend assurance that the path through tonal thickets is not lost.

It is useful to compare cadences with the punctuation marks used in writing.

PUNCTUATION		CADENCE
Period(.) Exclamation point (!)	=	Perfect Authentic and Perfect Plagal
Semicolon (;) Comma (,)	=	Imperfect Authentic and Imperfect Plagal
Colon (:) Question Mark (?)	=	Half and Deceptive

Of course you must regard this list as being merely suggestive. Musical expression is far too subtle to be neatly pinned down in this fashion, and the analogy between music and language should not be pressed too hard. On the other hand, you must acquire a sensitivity to the functions of the various types of cadences, and a personal reference of your own—similar to the one above—might be useful.

Mastery Frames

6-1. Identify the type of cadence represented by the Roman numerals.

(1) Deceptive
(2) Plagal
(3) Authentic
(4) Half

(498)

    (1) V–vi   _____
    (2) IV– I   _____
    (3) V or vii°–I   _____
    (4) I, IV, or ii-V   _____

---

(2) Plagal (and) (3) Authentic

(497)

6-2. List the cadences in the preceding frame that are final cadences._____ and _____ .

---

(1) Authentic
(2) Plagal

6-3. Name each of the cadences in the example below:
    (1)_____
    (2)_____

(499-534)

---

(2).

(501-506)

6-4. Which example in the preceding frame shows an imperfect cadence?_____

(1) Deceptive
(2) Half (or Phrygian)

6-5. Name each of the cadences below:

(1)_____
(2)_____

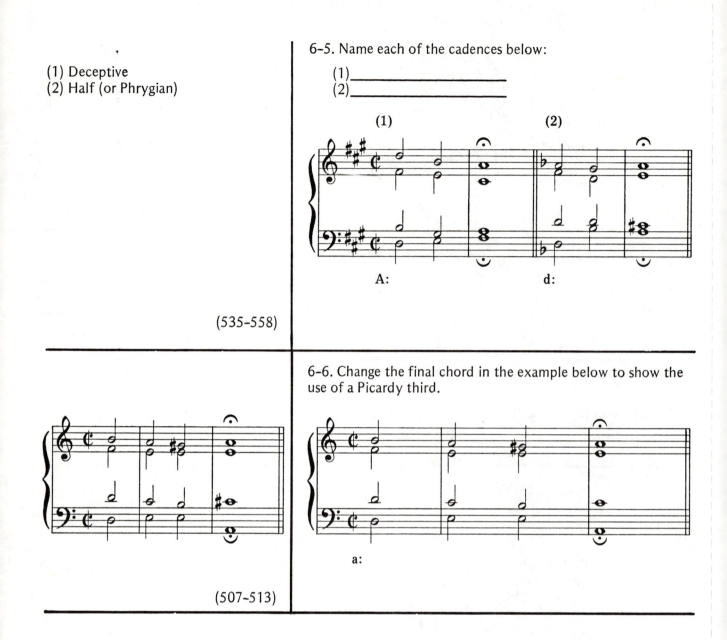

(1)   (2)

A: d:

(535–558)

6-6. Change the final chord in the example below to show the use of a Picardy third.

a:

(507–513)

Supplementary Assignments

ASSIGNMENT 6-1   Name_____

1. Compose single line melodies (four to eight measures long) that illustrate the specified melodic contours. Choose your own keys and meters. Indicate tempo, dynamics, and phrasing.

(1) Ascending

(2) Descending

(3) Arch

(4) Inverted arch

(5) Axial

2. Identify the cadences as final or nonfinal.

Half   _____
Authentic   _____
Deceptive   _____
Plagal   _____

3. Identify the cadences below.

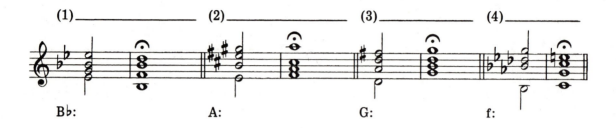

(1)_____ (2)_____ (3)_____ (4)_____

Bb: A: G: f:

Name_____

1. Identify the cadences as either perfect or imperfect.

(1) _____   (2) _____

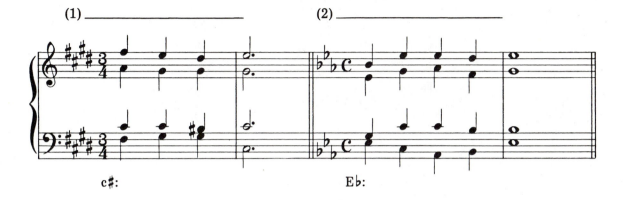

c#:   Eb:

Beethoven, *Symphony No. 8, Op. 93*

(3) _____   (4) _____

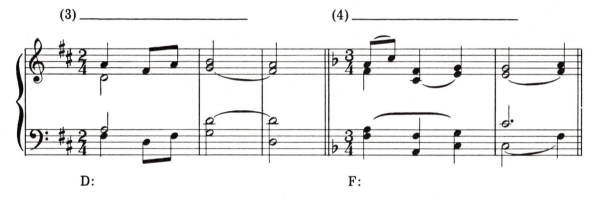

D: F:

2. Which example shows a Phrygian cadence? _____

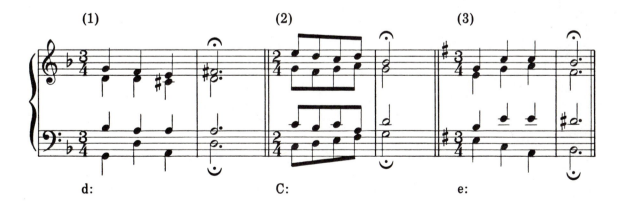

d: C: e:

3. Compose two four-measure phrases based on the harmonic progression below. Write for the piano in homophonic texture. Refer to Appendix B, *Piano Styles*. (For this assignment, styles 6 through 9 and 13 are recommended.)

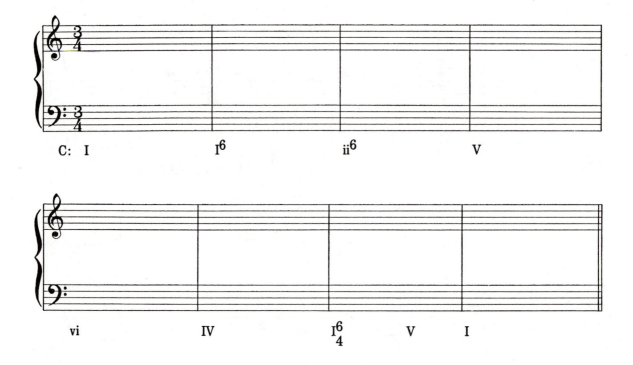

chapter seven

Harmonic Progression

The relation of chords to one another within the structure of tonality was treated in Chapter Two. Our job now is to distinguish between progressive and retrogressive chord movement, and to examine various patterns of harmonic phrase structure. The work in this chapter will shed additional light on the shaping function of harmony, and prepare for the study of harmonization techniques which follows.

568. The manner in which chords relate to one another lies at the heart of the study of tonal harmony. A series of chords is called a HARMONIC PROGRESSION.

During the period of tonal harmony sufficient consistency in harmonic progression was shown that we may refer to a "language of harmony." A language is established by consistent use, and it is the consistencies in the harmonic language which shall be our chief concern.

Even though the music of each composer in the period of tonal harmony speaks with a different "accent," the underlying principles are closely related.

chords

Harmonic progression is concerned with the way _____ relate to one another.

569. The term *harmonic progression* refers in a general way to all harmonic movements. The term PROGRESSION, however, is applied to a particular type of harmonic action: one which gives a sense of "forward motion." Weaker harmonic relations which sometimes give a sense of "backward motion" are called RETROGRESSIONS. The terms PROGRESSION and RETROGRESSION distinguish between relatively "strong" and "weak" harmonic movements.

A "strong," "emphatic" harmonic movement is called a

progression

_____.

570. "Strong" and "weak" are very subjective and inadequate words to describe the effect of various harmonic progressions. Above all, they should not be equated with "good" and "bad," for the expressive purpose of a particular passage may be served better by the use of retrogressions than by progressions. One of the ideals of harmony is variety, and too consistent a use of either progressions or retrogressions is undesirable.

progressions
(and) retrogressions

Harmonic variety is achieved by the use of both _____
_____ and _____.

571. You must now learn to distinguish between progressive
and retrogressive harmonic movements.
    The harmonic relationship of any two chords is classified
according to the interval by which their roots are related.
    Write in the space provided beneath each example the
basic interval (2nd, 3rd, 4th, etc.) *between the roots* of the
two chords.

    (Determine first the root of each chord.)

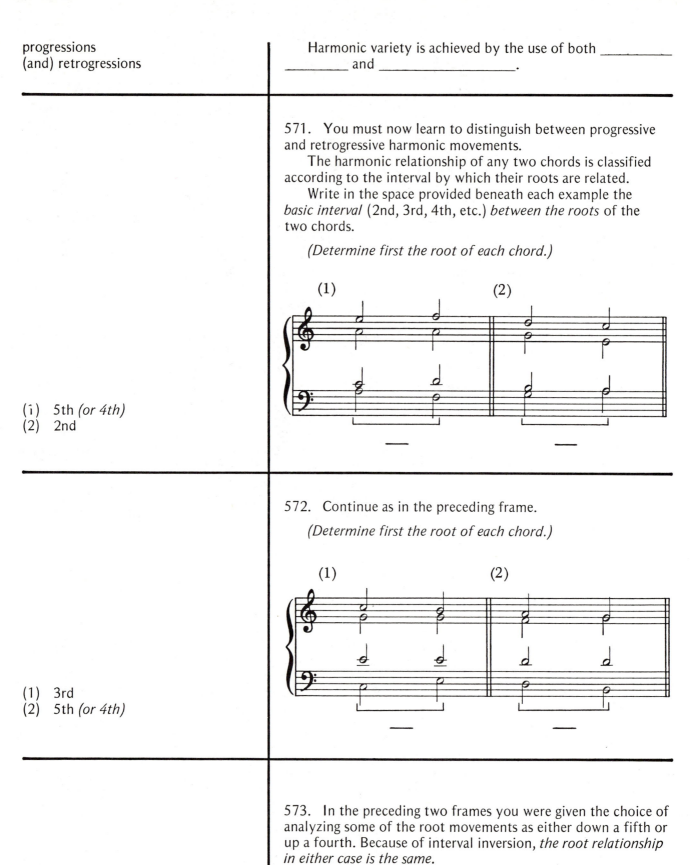

(1)   5th *(or 4th)*
(2)   2nd

572. Continue as in the preceding frame.

    (Determine first the root of each chord.)

(1)   3rd
(2)   5th *(or 4th)*

573. In the preceding two frames you were given the choice of
analyzing some of the root movements as either down a fifth or
up a fourth. Because of interval inversion, *the root relationship
in either case is the same.*
    The following example shows that the interval of a fourth up
is the same as a fifth down, a sixth up is the same as a third down,
and a seventh up is the same as a second down.

In order to simplify references to root movements, we shall speak of only three basic relationships: fifths, thirds, and seconds.

Root movement up a sixth is the same as down a _____

third	

574. Root movement up a seventh is the same as down a _____.

second	

575. Root movement down a fifth is the same as up a _____.

fourth	

576. Root movement down a seventh is the same as _____ a second.

up	

577. Indicate the basic interval between the roots of the chords in each case.

(Remember: The three relationships are fifths, thirds, and seconds.)

(1) 2nd (2) 5th	_____ _____

578. If your answer for (2) in the preceding frame was "4th," remember that a fourth up is the same as a fifth down. In this study, basic root relationships are to be analyzed as fifths, _____, or _____.

thirds, (or) seconds	

579. Indicate the basic interval between the roots of the chords in each case.

(1)   (2)

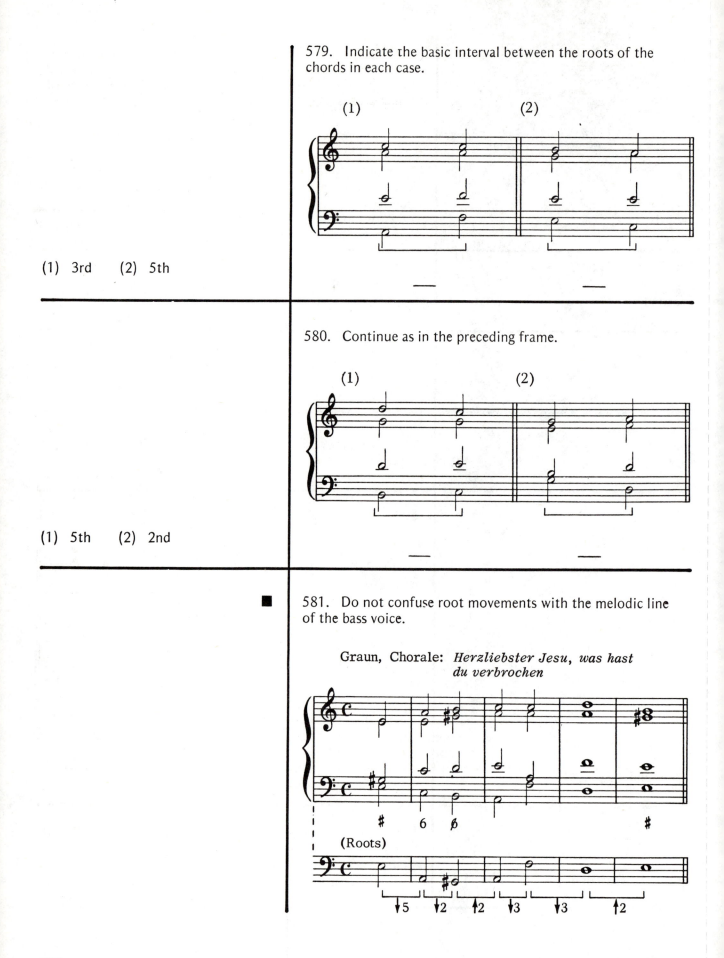

(1) 3rd   (2) 5th

---

580. Continue as in the preceding frame.

(1)   (2)

(1) 5th   (2) 2nd

---

581. Do not confuse root movements with the melodic line of the bass voice.

Graun, Chorale: *Herzliebster Jesu, was hast du verbrochen*

(Roots)

↓5   ↓2   ↑2   ↓3   ↓3   ↑2

Down a second.

The arrows show the direction of the interval. The symbol ↓5, for example, means that the root movement is down a fifth. Notice, too, that the root movement between the fourth and fifth chords is actually *up a sixth*. This is classified as *down a third.*

How would you classify root movement up a seventh?

_____

582. In order to classify root movements accurately you must locate the *root* of each chord. Do not be confused when some chords are in first or second inversion.

Write the roots and analyze with arrows and numbers (as in the preceding frame) each of the root movements in the example below *(Remember: Up a fourth is classified as down a fifth.)*

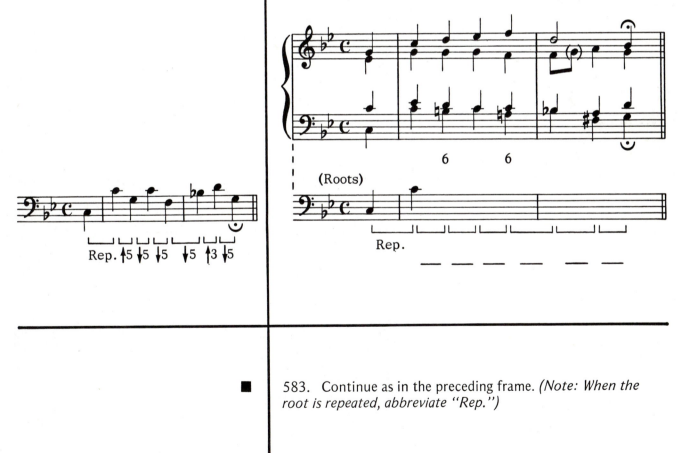

Bach, Chorale: *Von Gott will ich nicht lassen*

(Roots)

Rep.

583. Continue as in the preceding frame. *(Note: When the root is repeated, abbreviate "Rep.")*

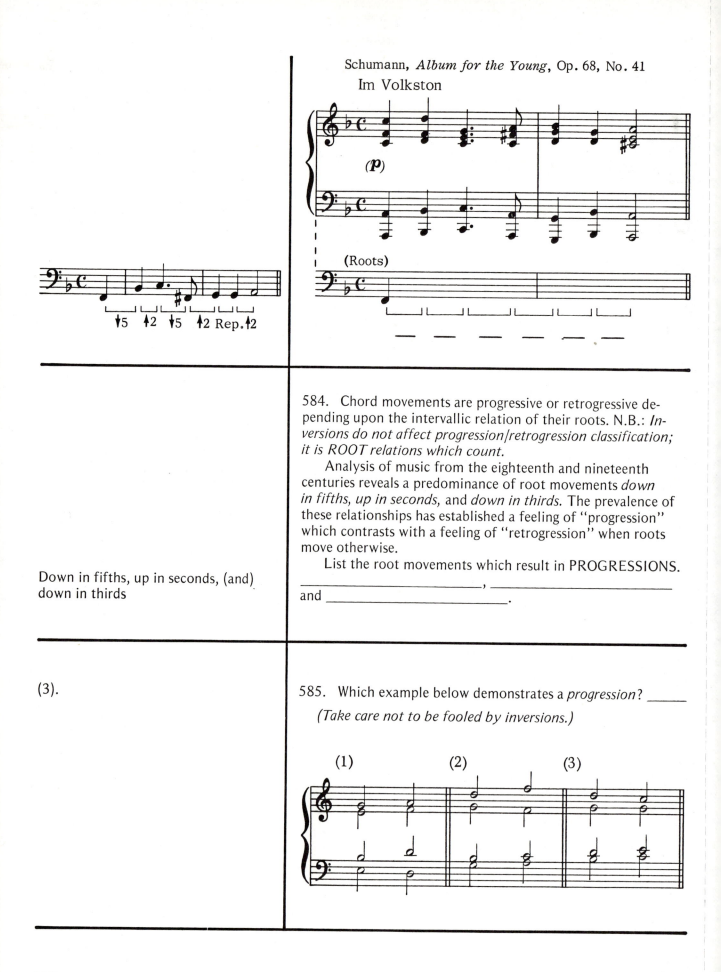

Schumann, *Album for the Young*, Op. 68, No. 41

Im Volkston

(p)

(Roots)

↓5 ↑2 ↓5 ↑2 Rep.↑2

---

584. Chord movements are progressive or retrogressive depending upon the intervallic relation of their roots. N.B.: *Inversions do not affect progression/retrogression classification; it is ROOT relations which count.*

Analysis of music from the eighteenth and nineteenth centuries reveals a predominance of root movements *down in fifths, up in seconds,* and *down in thirds.* The prevalence of these relationships has established a feeling of "progression" which contrasts with a feeling of "retrogression" when roots move otherwise.

List the root movements which result in PROGRESSIONS.

_____, _____

and _____.

Down in fifths, up in seconds, (and) down in thirds

---

(3).

585. Which example below demonstrates a *progression?* _____

(Take care not to be fooled by inversions.)

(1)   (2)   (3)

(2).

586. Which example below demonstrates a *progression* ? _____

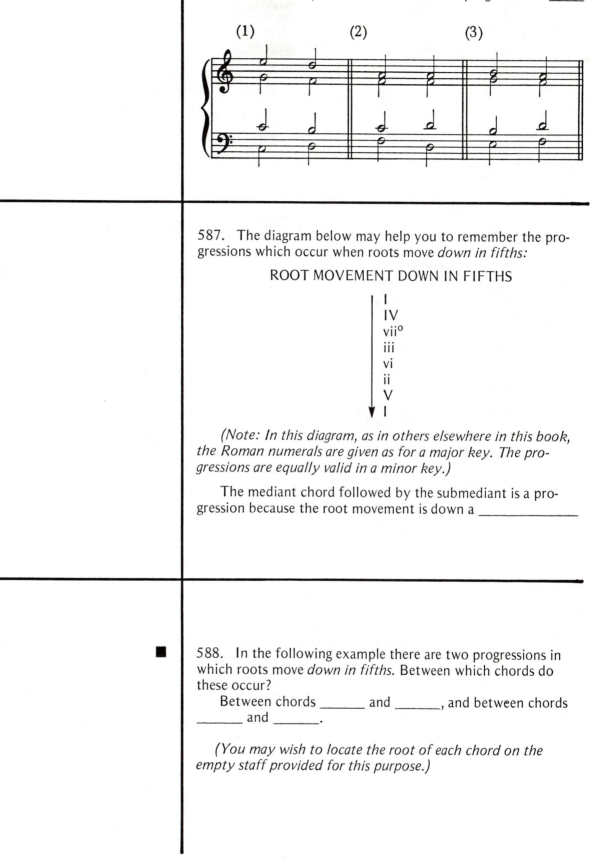

(1)　　　　(2)　　　　(3)

---

587. The diagram below may help you to remember the progressions which occur when roots move *down in fifths:*

ROOT MOVEMENT DOWN IN FIFTHS

I
IV
vii°
iii
vi
ii
V
I

(Note: In this diagram, as in others elsewhere in this book, the Roman numerals are given as for a major key. The progressions are equally valid in a minor key.)

The mediant chord followed by the submediant is a progression because the root movement is down a _____

fifth

---

588. In the following example there are two progressions in which roots move *down in fifths.* Between which chords do these occur?

Between chords _____ and _____, and between chords _____ and _____.

(You may wish to locate the root of each chord on the empty staff provided for this purpose.)

1 (and) 2
4 (and) 5

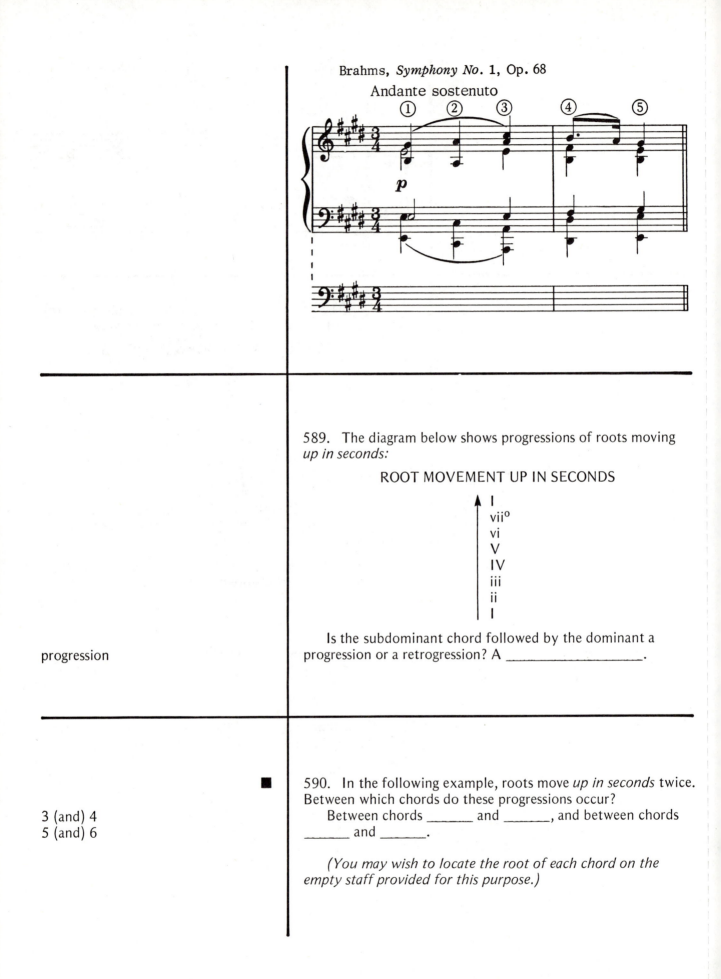

Brahms, *Symphony No. 1, Op. 68*

Andante sostenuto

589. The diagram below shows progressions of roots moving *up in seconds:*

ROOT MOVEMENT UP IN SECONDS

I
viiº
vi
V
IV
iii
ii
I

    Is the subdominant chord followed by the dominant a progression or a retrogression? A _____.

progression

590. In the following example, roots move *up in seconds* twice. Between which chords do these progressions occur?
    Between chords _____ and _____, and between chords _____ and _____.

    (You may wish to locate the root of each chord on the empty staff provided for this purpose.)

3 (and) 4
5 (and) 6

Graun, Chorale: *O Traurigkeit, o Herzeleid*

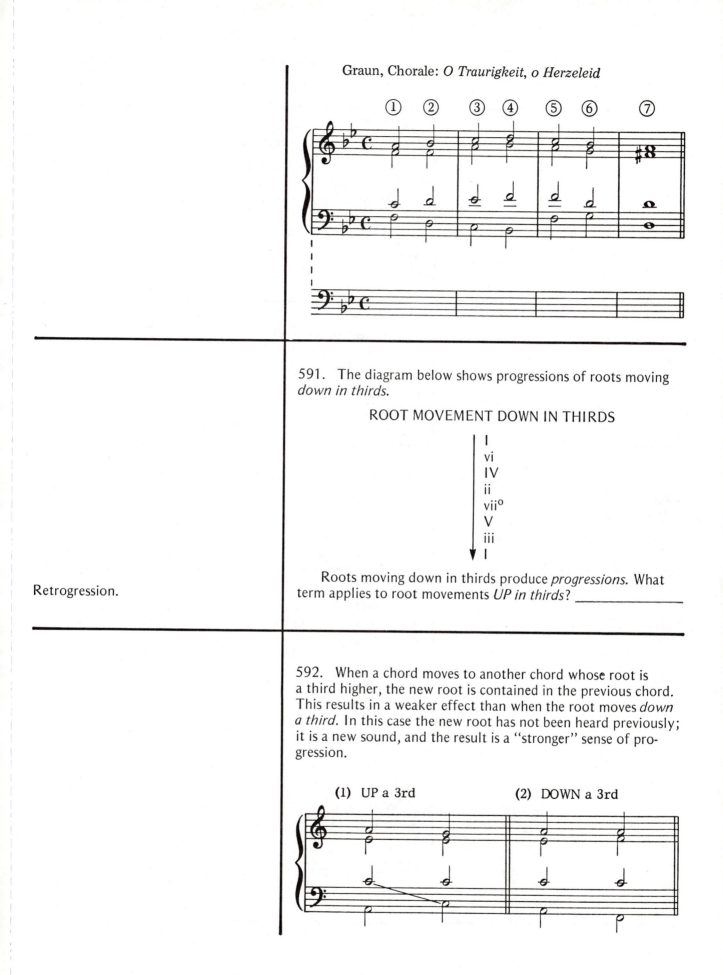

591. The diagram below shows progressions of roots moving *down in thirds*.

ROOT MOVEMENT DOWN IN THIRDS

I
vi
IV
ii
vii°
V
iii
I

Roots moving down in thirds produce *progressions*. What term applies to root movements *UP in thirds*? _____

Retrogression.

592. When a chord moves to another chord whose root is a third higher, the new root is contained in the previous chord. This results in a weaker effect than when the root moves *down a third*. In this case the new root has not been heard previously; it is a new sound, and the result is a "stronger" sense of progression.

(1) UP a 3rd   (2) DOWN a 3rd

subdominant (IV)	What chord follows the submediant (vi) if the root moves down a third? The _____.
	593. Check (√) the correct option: 1. Harmonic movement from one chord to another is classified as either a progression or a retrogression depending upon the root movement. 2. It is desirable that all harmonic movement should be progressions. True statements:
(1) √	(1) _____ (2) _____ Both _____ Neither _____
	594. Check (√) the correct option: 1. Root movement up a sixth is the same as down a third. 2. Root movement up a fourth is the same as down a fifth. True statements:
Both √	(1) _____ (2) _____ Both _____ Neither _____
False. *((2) and (4) are retrogressions.)*	595. All of the root movements listed below are progressions. (True/False) _____ (1) up a 2nd (2) down a 2nd (3) down a 3rd (4) up a 5th
(2).	596. We have learned that *progressive* harmonic movement occurs when roots move down in fifths, up in seconds, or down in thirds. One other important principle remains to be stated: *Harmonic movement from the tonic to any other chord is progressive regardless of the interval involved.* In view of this statement, which case below shows progressive harmonic movement? _____ KEY OF D MAJOR (1) (2)

(1).
((2) is progressive because harmonic movement from the tonic to any other chord is progressive.)

597. Because the tonic triad is built on the key note it is the least active chord in any key. Thus, movement from the tonic to any other triad is movement to a *more active chord*.

   Which example shows *retrogressive* harmonic movement? _____

KEY OF G MINOR

(2).
(Root movement down a 2nd as in (1) is retrogressive.)

598. Which example shows *progressive* harmonic movement? _____

KEY OF A MAJOR

True.

599. No retrogression is possible when moving from the tonic chord. (True/False) _____

True.

600. The sequence of chords represented by Roman numerals below contains progressions only. (True/False) _____

   I   IV   V   vi   IV   ii   V   I

601. Actually, no clear distinction between progression and retrogression can be made. Under most circumstances, harmony functions not as an isolated phenomenon, but in conjunction

with rhythm and melody. The latter two elements may affect harmony so that a succession of chords sounds progressive in one case but retrogressive in another. Nevertheless, you must develop your sensitivity to various degrees of "progressiveness" in harmonic relations to acquire skill in selecting expressive harmonies.

Although the principles of harmonic progression are not absolutely clear, the tendency for roots to progress down in fifths, up in seconds, and down in thirds is prevalent enough in tonal music to serve as a guide in the choice of chords.

Few harmonic phrases consist entirely of either progressions or retrogressions. Fluctuation in the balance between these two types of harmonic movement provides the composer with an expressive tool. A passage in which stability and tonal clarity are desired calls for a large proportion of progressions, while more retrogressions might be used when the opposite effect is desired.

Harmony contributes to musical expression through the fluctuating balance between progressive and retrogressive harmonic movement.

(No response.)

---

602. We shall continue by exploring another approach to harmonic progression.

The structure of tonality rests upon the foundation of the three primary triads: the tonic, subdominant, and dominant. The remaining triads are called secondary triads and are related to the primary triads in the manner shown below:*

Primary triads: ⌈I   ⌈IV ⌈V
Secondary triads: ⌊vi ⌊ii ⌊iii, vii°

Spell the primary triads in the key of E major.

I   - _____
IV - _____
V - _____

*At this point you may wish to review Chapter Two: THE STRUCTURE OF TONALITY.

I - EG♯B
IV - AC♯E
V - BD♯F♯

---

603. Primary and secondary triads provide another approach to harmonic progression.

Learn these two principles:

1. Movement from a primary triad to its secondary triad is *progressive.*
2. A secondary triad may be substituted for its primary triad.

(3).

With respect to (1) above, which case below is a progression? _____

(1) I-iii   (2) vi-I   (3) IV-ii   (4) iii V

---

(2).

604. Which case below is a progression? _____
(1) V-IV   (2) I-vi   (3) vii°-V   (4) vi-V

---

605. Applying the principle that primary triads tend to progress to their secondary triads rather than the reverse, show how each chord below would progress.

(1) vi
(2) ii
(3) iii (or) vii°

(1) I   _____
(2) IV _____
(3) V   _____ or _____

---

606. The harmonic relationships shown in the preceding frame are written out below:

(Play these progressions at the piano.)

Bb: I   vi   IV   ii   V   iii   vii°6

Do you think these progressions are all equally effective?
_____

Your opinion.

---

607. Even when dealing with very simple musical material it is difficult to make absolute judgements; for not only are all elements relative and easily influenced by other factors, but honest and perfectly valid differences of opinion may be held by all of us.

Most of you will probably feel that all of the progressions shown in the preceding frame are effective with the possible exception of V-vii°. This is a relatively weak progression because the harmonic function of these two chords is so similar (vii° is considered by some to be an incomplete V^7) that little harmonic motion results when going from one to the other.*

_____

*Note, too, that v-vii° is root movement up a third—a retrogression.

True.

Except for the progression V-vii°, movement from a primary triad to its secondary triad generally results in a strong harmonic effect. (True/False) _____

---

608. A secondary triad may be substituted for its primary triad at any point in order to provide tonal variety and to prolong the harmonic motion.

Basic progression: I   ⎡V ⎡I
Substitutions: I   ⎣vii° ⎣vi

deceptive

The basic progression (I-V-I) above is changed by substituting vii° for V, and vi for I. Further, the authentic cadence (V-I) has become a _____ cadence (vii°-vi).

---

609. Applying the principle demonstrated in the preceding frame, show the chords which may be substituted where indicated below:

Basic progression: I   ⎡IV ⎡I ⎡V   I

ii-vi-vii° *or* iii

Substitutions: I   ⎣__ ⎣__ ⎣__ I

---

610. Continue as in the preceding frame.

Basic progression: I   V ⎡I ⎡IV V ⎡I

vi-ii-(V)-vi

Substitutions: I   V ⎣__ ⎣__ V ⎣__

---

611. Continue as in the preceding frame.

Basic progression: I ⎡V I ⎡I ⎡IV V ⎡I

vii° *or* iii-(I)-vi-ii-(V)-vi

Substitutions: I ⎣__ I ⎣__ ⎣__ V ⎣__

---

612. The first principle stated in Frame 603 is that *movement from a primary triad to its secondary triad is progressive.* The second principle is that *a secondary triad may be substituted for its primary triad.*

The application of these principles results in a wide variety of chord progressions. This is shown below:

     (1)   (2)

  I   vi   IV   vii°   I

(No response.)

Movement from a primary triad to its secondary triad is shown at (1); at (2), the leading tone triad (vii°) is substituted for the dominant (V).

---

613. Indicate which of the two principles is used at each of the points indicated.

Principle 1. Movement from a primary triad to its secondary triad.

Principle 2. Substitution of a secondary triad for its primary triad.

	(1)		(2)			(3)		(4)	
I	ii	V	iii	IV	I	vi	IV	vii°	I

(1) _____ (3) _____

(2) _____ (4) _____

(1) Principle 2
(2) Principle 1
(3) Principle 1
(4) Principle 2

---

614. Continue as in the preceding frame.

		(1)		(2)		(3)		
I	iii	IV	ii	V	vi	V	iii	I

(1) _____

(2) _____

(3) _____

(1) Principle 1
(2) Principle 2
(3) Principle 1

---

615. The primary triads (I, IV, and V) serve as the structural basis for harmonic progressions, but basic formulas such as I-V-I and I-IV-V-I can be expanded by the use of secondary triads. This is done by moving from a primary triad to its secondary triad before proceeding to the next chord in the basic formula (I-V-I expanded to I-vi-V-I); or by substituting a secondary triad for its primary triad (I-IV-V becomes I-ii-V). The result is greater tonal variety through a wider choice of chords and in some cases, prolongation of the harmonic activity

As we proceed with this study you must bear in mind that harmonic progression is not a science which can be presented in terms of precise laws. We shall make no attempt to relate harmony to natural acoustical phenomena even though much has been made of this approach in the past. This presentation is based upon the observed practices of composers who use the traditional harmonic vocabulary.

In this text principles are not stated as rules, but are intended to serve as guides for the development of your own personal command of harmonic materials.

(No response.)

616. An intimate relation exists between harmonic progression and phrase structure. A phrase has *shape* through melodic contour and *motion* through rhythm. Also it has a beginning, a sense of growth or movement in a particular direction, and finally a point of arrival at the cadence.

Harmonic progressions, like melody, tend to focus upon the cadence. The cadence to which a harmonic phrase moves has a strong influence upon the choice of chords earlier in the phrase.

Cadences are structural points in a composition, and the harmony at these points has special importance in the formal organization. Chords which appear at cadence points usually are chosen so that the tonal organization is stressed.

We have referred frequently to *melodic* phrases. Do you think it would be appropriate to speak of *harmonic* phrases? _____

Yes *(certainly).*

---

617. Some chords in a harmonic phrase are more important to the formal organization of music than others. These include the following:

1. Chords which appear at structural points (cadences).
2. Chords which are stressed rhythmically (on strong beats or strong portions of beats, prolonged, or emphasized by being preceded by a rest).
3. Chords at important points in the phrase (at the peak of the melodic contour, for example).

Melodic contour, phrase structure, and rhythm all have an influence upon the choice of chords.

(No response.)

---

618. Harmony which appears at strategic points and serves to establish the tonal organization is called STRUCTURAL HARMONY.

Examine the excerpt below and on the following page:

Beethoven, *Sonatina in G Major*

G: I——————————   (V)

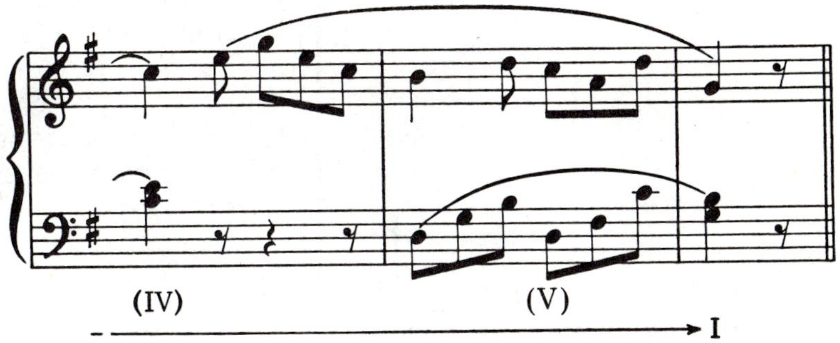

The analysis above shows the basic "structural" harmonic movement from the tonic to the dominant in measure four. This is followed by a phrase which begins and ends with tonic harmony.

Show with Roman numerals the *basic* harmonic organization of this excerpt. _____

I-V-I

---

619. Referring again to the example in the preceding frame, notice that the chords at structural points of lesser importance (Roman numerals in parentheses) also are primary triads (IV and V).

Harmony plays an important role in defining the tonal structure of music. As shown in the previous frame, this occurs at different levels even within the phrase itself. Harmony which is form-defining, and which helps to establish tonal coherence is called _____ harmony.

structural

---

620. Chords which occur more or less incidentally produce embellishing harmony. The first two measures of the excerpt in Frame 618 are shown below to illustrate this type of harmony.

Beethoven, *Sonatina in G Major*

Romanze

The dominant seventh chord on the second beat of the first measure is preceded and followed by tonic harmony. Thus, its function is clearly one of embellishment.

Is it likely that harmony at the end of a phrase would be embellishing? _____

---

621. To achieve the delicate shades of nuance which fine performance demands, it is imperative that you recognize the difference between structural and embellishing harmony. The larger units in the formal organization of a composition are defined, in part, by structural harmony. The importance of this harmony as opposed to embellishing harmony is self-evident. By phrasing, performers must make clear the formal design of the music being played. To do this a sensitivity to the various roles of harmony is vital.

Harmony which is incidental and not form-defining is called _____ harmony.

embellishing

---

622. In this frame you have the delicate task of distinguishing between structural and embellishing harmony. Examine carefully the example below and play it at the piano. Each chord is numbered and analyzed with a Roman numeral. List in the space provided on the next page those chords which seem incidental to the basic harmonic scheme.

(Indicate your answer by recording the appropriate numbers.)

Beethoven, *Sonata*, Op. 49, No. 1

2, 6, 10, 13
(There may be some difference of opinion, but the following frame justifies this list.)

Embellishing harmony: Chords No. _____

---

623. A test which sometimes is useful to distinguish between structural and embellishing harmony is to play the passage omitting all embellishing harmony. Try the version below:

Beethoven, *Sonata*, Op. 49, No. 1 (altered)

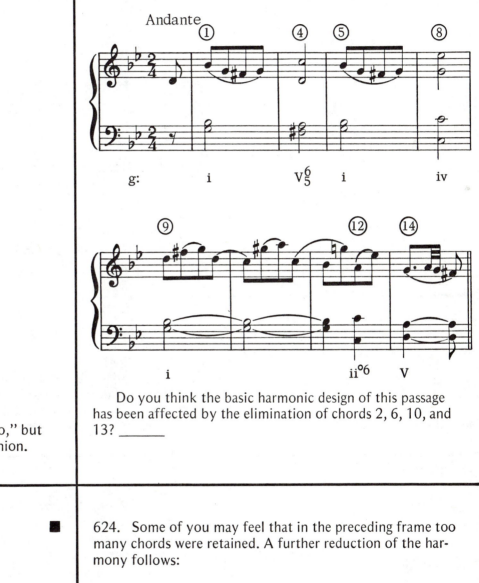

Do you think the basic harmonic design of this passage has been affected by the elimination of chords 2, 6, 10, and 13? _____

Your answer is probably "No," but you are entitled to your opinion.

---

624. Some of you may feel that in the preceding frame too many chords were retained. A further reduction of the harmony follows:

Beethoven, *Sonata*, Op. 49, No. 1 (altered)

Now list (by number) all of the chords which have been deleted from the original version in Frame 622. *Embellishing harmony:* Chords No. _____

2, 3, 4, 5, 6, 7, 10, 11, 12, 13

---

625. In the preceding frame so many chords are deleted from the original version that not all of the melodic notes are accommodated by those which remain. Yet the basic structure of the harmonic phrase is preserved. Further reduction in the number of chords would destroy the sense of harmonic movement.

Structural harmony may be identified by eliminating all _____ harmony.

embellishing

---

626. The structure of music is built up, in part, by harmonic relationships. Harmony operates at many levels, and even the tonal relationships between the parts of multi-movement works are important. At the phrase level, harmony (along with cadences, melodic contour, rhythm, and motivic development) serves to define form and give coherence to music.

The varying roles of harmony can be seen by stripping away the embellishing harmony layer by layer to reveal the different levels of the tonal structure. The harmony which remains is called *structural* harmony. A clear distinction between structural and embellishing harmony cannot always be made. This is a matter of personal opinion, and it also depends

(No response.)

upon the purpose of the analysis. The language of harmony is full of subtleties and there are few passages in music which are not open to a variety of interpretations.

---

627. There is an intimate relationship between harmonic progression and the phrase. An examination of this relationship will shed additional light upon the way chords are related, and will prepare for the technique of harmonization which is the subject of Chapter Eight.

The harmony of the phrase is dominated by the CADENCE; it is the focal point—the "point of arrival"—toward which the melodic contour, rhythm, and harmony are directed.

cadence

The focal point of the phrase is the _____.

---

628. Although phrases seemingly may be harmonized in an infinite number of ways, a few simple practices are the most prevalent. These involve the extent to which the cadence formula dominates the phrase, and how the harmony leads into the cadence itself.

We shall observe three types of phrases:

1. Phrases built on a single chord followed by a cadence.
2. Phrases with harmonic embellishment of a single chord followed by a cadence.
3. Phrases in which a basic progression is spread over the entire phrase.

Harmonic progression is related to the structure of the

phrase

_____.

---

629. The example below shows a phrase which is built on a single chord (the tonic) followed by a cadence.

Verdi, *La Traviata*, Act III, No. 16

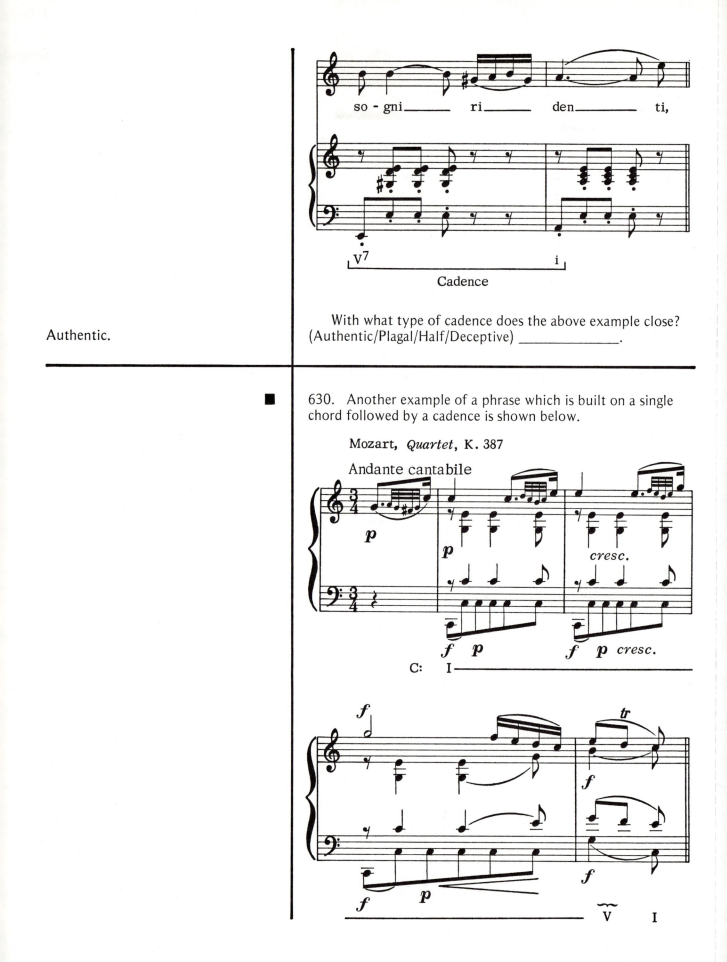

Cadence

With what type of cadence does the above example close?
(Authentic/Plagal/Half/Deceptive) _____.

Authentic.

630. Another example of a phrase which is built on a single chord followed by a cadence is shown below.

Mozart, *Quartet*, K. 387

Andante cantabile

C: I —————————————

———————————— V I

Authentic.

As in the preceding frame, it is the tonic chord which is prolonged. What type of cadence is used to close the phrase? _____

---

631. The example below shows harmonic embellishment of the tonic followed by a cadence.

Haydn, *Capriccio*

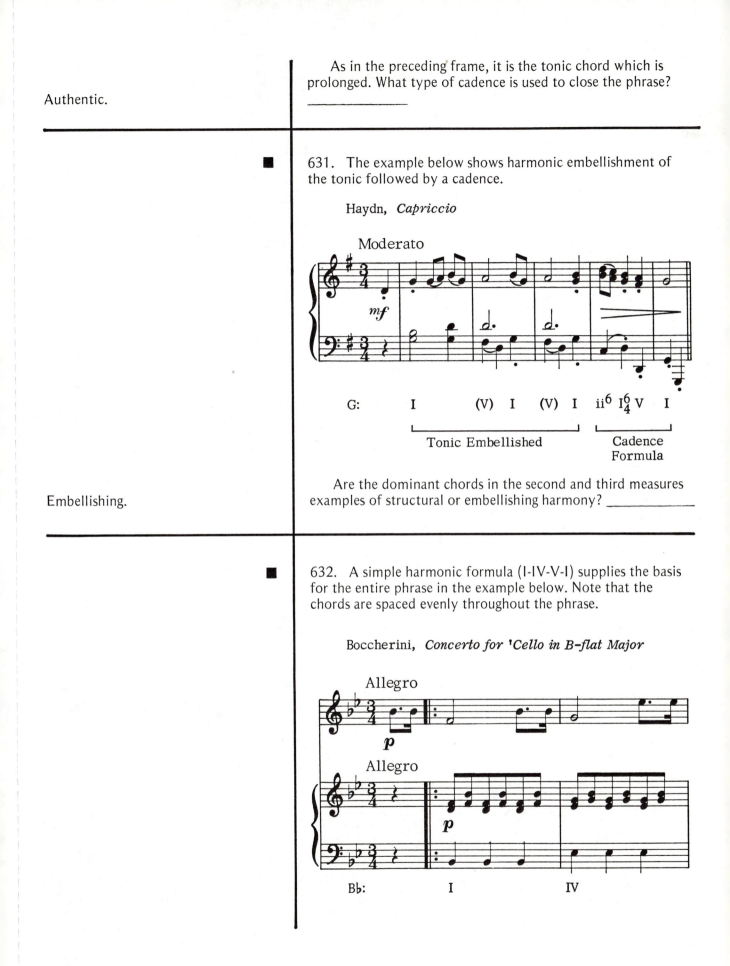

G: I   (V) I   (V) I   ii^6 I$^6_4$ V   I

Tonic Embellished   Cadence Formula

Embellishing.

Are the dominant chords in the second and third measures examples of structural or embellishing harmony? _____

---

632. A simple harmonic formula (I-IV-V-I) supplies the basis for the entire phrase in the example below. Note that the chords are spaced evenly throughout the phrase.

Boccherini, *Concerto for 'Cello in B-flat Major*

Bb: I   IV

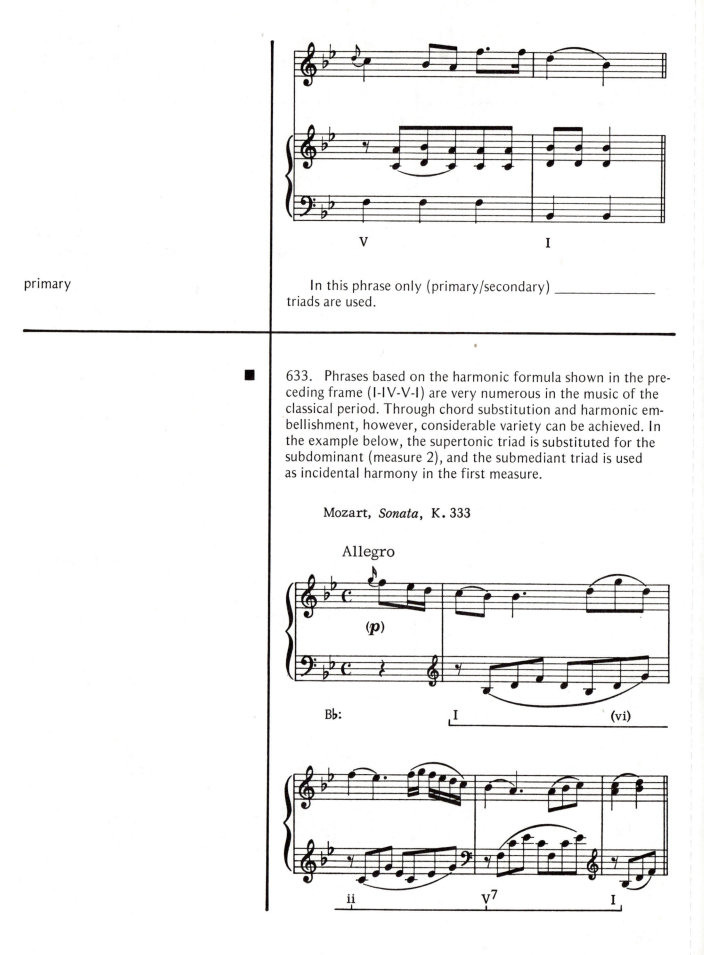

primary

In this phrase only (primary/secondary) _____ triads are used.

■ 633. Phrases based on the harmonic formula shown in the preceding frame (I-IV-V-I) are very numerous in the music of the classical period. Through chord substitution and harmonic embellishment, however, considerable variety can be achieved. In the example below, the supertonic triad is substituted for the subdominant (measure 2), and the submediant triad is used as incidental harmony in the first measure.

Mozart, *Sonata*, K. 333

Allegro

Bb: I   (vi)

ii   V⁷   I

phrase

Variants of the progression I-IV-V-I often serve as the harmonic basis for an entire _____.

■ 634. The harmonic basis of the phrase below is I-IV-V.

Mendelssohn, *Six Pieces for Children*, Op. 72, No. 3

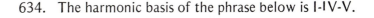

The several chords which are indicated by the bracket above the staff do not serve a structural function; they appear more or less incidentally between those chords which provide the structural harmonic basis for the phrase.

(No response.)

SUMMARY

One of the variable factors in harmonic progression is the relation of a basic harmonic structure to the phrase as a whole. Three types of harmonic structure have been shown: phrases built on a single chord (usually the tonic) followed by a cadence, phrases with harmonic embellishment of a single chord followed by a cadence, and phrases in which a harmonic progression (such as I-IV-V-I) serves as the basis for the entire phrase.

But you must not think that all phrases fall into one of these three types. The harmonic element of music is subtle, and the effect of chord relations is unpredictable. Harmonies are selected for their affective value, and the response they elicit eludes simple rationalization. Also, music resists being ordered into neat patterns of analysis; an approach which serves well for one period or composer may be useless for another. The information contained in this chapter is merely an introduction—the study of harmonic progression continues in the next chapter. Your sensitivity to the language of harmony will increase not only by study and practice, but also through your performing and listening experiences.

Mastery Frames

Up Down		7-1. Check (√) the root movements that result in *progressions*.

	Up	Down
Fifths		√
Seconds	√	
Thirds		√

(587-592)

7-1. Check (√) the root movements that result in *progressions*.

Root Movement	*Up*	*Down*
Fifths	____	____
Seconds	____	____
Thirds	____	____

---

(1) fifth

(2) sixth

(3) seventh

(573-576)

7-2. Complete each statement.

(1) Root movement up a fourth is the same as down a
_____.

(2) Root movement down a third is the same as up a
_____.

(3) Root movement up a second is the same as down a
_____.

True.

(596-599)

7-3. Root movement from the tonic to any other triad is progressive. (True/False)_____

Secondary Triads
Submediant
Supertonic
Mediant, Leading tone

(602-614)

7-4. Give the proper names of the secondary triad(s) related to each primary triad.

Primary Triads	*Secondary Triads*
Tonic	_____
Subdominant	_____
Dominant	_____

Progressive.

(603-605)

7-5. Is movement from a primary triad to its secondary triad progressive or retrogressive?_____

structural   (617–626)

7-6. Harmony that appears at important points in the phrase such as at cadences is called _____ harmony.

Embellishment of a single chord (I) followed by a cadence

7-7. Describe the harmonic structure of the phrase below.
_____
_____

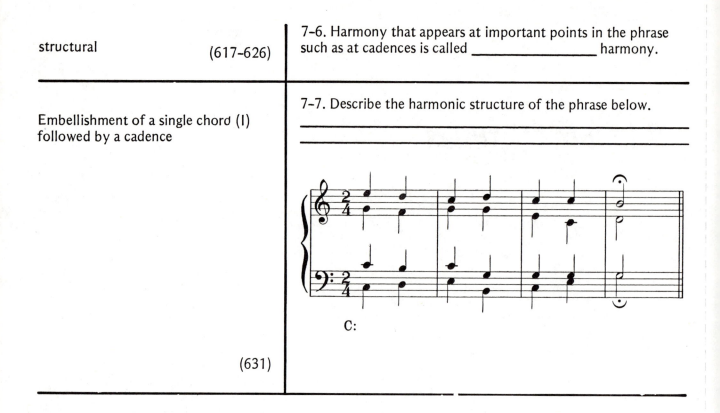

C:

(631)

Supplementary Assignments

ASSIGNMENT 7-1   Name_____

1. Indicate the root movement in each case. Use the signs ↑5, ↓5, ↑2, ↓2, ↑3, and ↓3. *(Be alert for inversions.)*

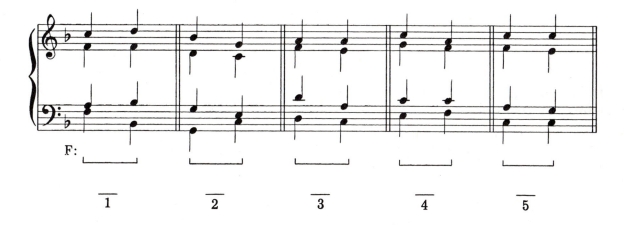

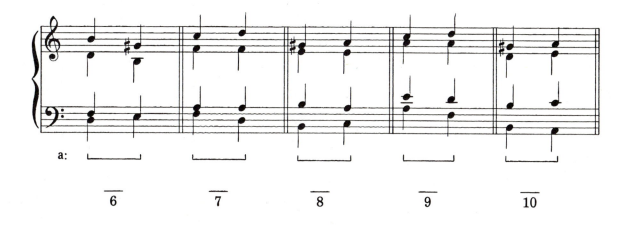

2. Classify each root movement in question 1 as either a *progression* (P) or a *retrogression* (R). Remember: harmonic movement away from the tonic is *progressive* in all cases.

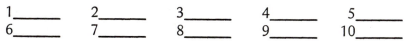

3. For each of the primary triads below write the secondary triad(s) to which they relate. Use correct part writing procedures, and provide the Roman numeral analysis.

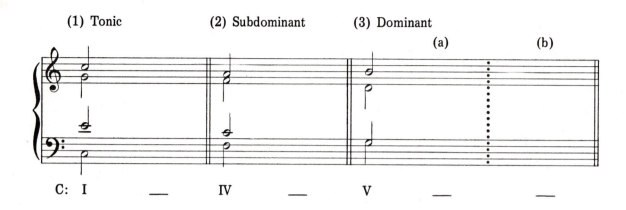

(1) Tonic   (2) Subdominant   (3) Dominant
                                                (a)   (b)

C: I   __   IV   __   V   __   __

4. Indicate each case as either *progressive* (P) or *retrogressive* (R).

(1) Movement from a primary triad to its secondary triad(s)._____
(2) Movement from a secondary triad to its primary triad._____

5. Classify each of the harmonic movements below as a progression or retrogression.

V–vi   _____
I–vii°   _____
IV–iii   _____
iii–V   _____

Name_____

1. Classify each of the harmonic movements below as a progression or retrogression.

vii°–vi _____

iii–IV _____

ii–V _____

IV–vii° _____

I–iii _____

2. Revise the progression below to show substitution of secondary triads for primary triads.

I	V	I	ii	I	IV	V	I
I	___	___	ii	I	___	V	___

3. Compose a phrase for piano based on the given harmonic structure. Choose your own key and meter. Piano styles 2–12 are recommended (see Appendix B).

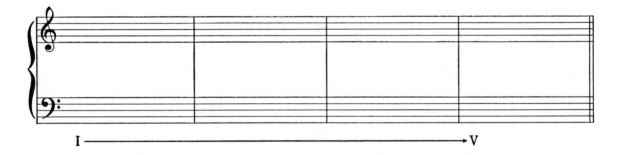

I ⟶ V

4. Compose two phrases for piano based on the harmonic structures given below and on the next page. Keys are given, but you may choose your own meters. Notate completely, including tempo, dynamics, and phrasing indications. Piano styles 13–22 are recommended.

(A)

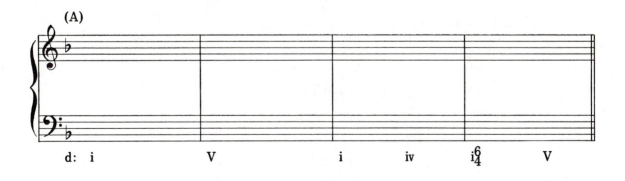

d: i   V   i   iv   i$^6_4$ V

(B)

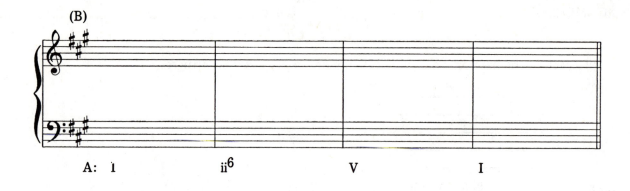

A: I ii⁶ V I

chapter eight

The Technique of Harmonization

The harmonization of a melody involves selecting those chords from the available tonal material that realize the melody's harmonic implications. Even very simple melodies suggest more than one harmonization, so it is not a question of finding the "right" solution, but of selecting one of the alternatives that is stylistically consistent and appropriate to the function of the melody in the composition as a whole. You are not intended to learn to harmonize just like Bach, Mozart, or Schubert even though music by these and other composers is used to illustrate various points throughout this book. You are learning a "technique" of harmonization, not a specific harmonic style. The lessons of this chapter should lead to the development of your own mode of harmonic expression.

635. Our study of the technique of harmonization is based upon the tonal material which has been presented to this point. We are limited, therefore, to the triads of a single tonality; but these may be used in first and second inversions as well as in root position. The technique learned in terms of this limited material will be equally valid when additional resources become available.

The melody below will be used to demonstrate the technique of harmonization.

Sing (or play) this melody to become familiar with its characteristics.

E-flat

This melody is in the key of _____ major.

636. You have just performed the first step in harmonizing a melody: becoming familiar with its characteristics and identifying its tonality. Next you must select an appropriate cadence. The last two notes of this melody suggest two cadences as shown with Roman numerals.

KEY OF E-FLAT MAJOR

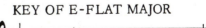

Cadences: { 1. V   I
          2. V   vi

Name these cadences.

Cadence No. 1 _____

Cadence No. 2 _____

■ 637. Melodies often suggest more than one type of cadence. It is important to decide on the cadence which is appropriate for the end of a particular phrase.

Play the melody and try each of the two cadences as notated below:

Eb: V   I   V   vi

Which cadence gives the stronger sense of finality? (1) or (2) _____

(1).

---

638. This demonstration involves only a single phrase, so we shall choose the authentic cadence for its stronger closing effect. The deceptive cadence would imply another phrase to carry forward and complete the musical idea of the first phrase. Contrasting cadences are highly desirable, so they should be chosen with care.

The choice of cadence is dictated entirely by the contour of the melody. (True/False) _____

False.
(The degree of finality desired is important.)

---

639. The cadence has a strong influence upon the harmonies which precede it. The harmonic destination must be known before you can select the chords which will take you there. This is why it is so important to choose the cadence before starting to harmonize the first part of the melody.

The harmony of a phrase is strongly influenced by the

_____ .

cadence

640. Chord changes produce an element of music called HARMONIC RHYTHM. Harmonic rhythm contributes to the motivation of music and plays an important expressive role. Some passages are based on slow changes of harmony, others feature very rapid changes, still others have varying rates of harmonic changes which increase the rhythmic complexity of the composition.

harmonic
rhythm

The temporal element of harmony is called _____ _____.

---

641. Returning to the melody which we are using to demonstrate the technique of harmonization, it is desirable at this point to settle upon an appropriate harmonic rhythm.

The prevailing quarter-note rhythm of the melody suggests the same rhythm for the harmony. This is not the only possibility, for either one or two chords per measure could be employed to good effect. The limited material at our disposal, however, rules out these choices since not all of the melodic notes could be included in such a harmonic scheme.

Most melodies give rise to several possibilities of harmonic

True.

rhythm. (True/False) _____.

---

642. In completing the harmonization of the melody, the prevailing rate of chord change will be the quarter note. Two notes separated by a leap, however, often are harmonized by the same chord. The first two notes (G and B-flat), for example, are both members of the tonic triad. Since it is desirable to begin a phrase with tonic emphasis, it makes good sense to use the tonic triad for these two notes. Our harmonization now stands as below:

Eb: I   I   V   I

Melodic leaps often give a clue to effective chord choice. The two tones of a melodic leap often are harmonized by the

chord

same _____.

---

643. Let us review the steps we have taken to arrive at this point.

We have (1) determined the tonality (E-flat major), (2) chosen an appropriate cadence (authentic), (3) chosen an appropriate harmonic rhythm (principally in quarter-note rhythm), and (4) begun the harmonic phrase with tonic emphasis (suggested by the notes G and B-flat, both of which are members of the tonic triad).

(No response.)

■ **644.** Now play the phrase with the chords which already have been selected.

Three types of harmonic phrase structure were discussed in Chapter Seven: (1) phrases consisting of a single chord followed by a cadence, (2) phrases consisting of the tonic embellished followed by a cadence, and (3) phrases based upon a harmonic formula such as I-IV-V-I.*

Your ear and imagination must be brought into play to decide which of these patterns is best suited to this melody.

Melodies usually are not harmonized by selecting a chord more or less independently for each successive note. The final choice evolves slowly, as a result of careful reference to the cadence and to the _____ as a whole.

phrase *(or melody)*

---

*You may wish to review Chapter Seven, especially Frames 628–634.

■ **645.** Since the fourth scale degree (A-flat) is stressed by appearing on both the first and second beats of the second measure, a subdominant emphasis is appropriate for these notes.

Play the phrase with the additions below:

I-IV-V-I	By now it is clear that the phrase is based on one of the simple harmonic formulas. Write with Roman numerals this formula. _____
	646. Having come this far, and with only three notes yet to be harmonized, your ear should help you complete the harmonization. As an aid in making these final few choices, however, you may wish to list the possibilities for each note. Since the tonal material is limited to triads, a given note can be harmonized by one of three triads. For example, the third note of the melody (C) may be the root of the submediant triad (CE♭G), the third of the subdominant triad (A♭CE♭), or the fifth of the supertonic triad (FA♭C). Applying this method to the other remaining notes, the chords from which you may choose to complete the harmonization are listed below:
root, third, (or) fifth *(Any order.)*	When the tonal material is limited to triads, any note may be harmonized by one of three triads. The note may be either the _____, _____, or _____ of a triad.
	647. The choice between the alternatives listed in the preceding frame is influenced by the balance between progressive and retrogressive harmonic movement which is desired, and also by practical necessities of part writing which may not be revealed until later. But the final choice is based largely upon personal preference. *The basic underlying progression will hold the phrase together regardless of the decisions which are made at this point.* The chords which will be used in this demonstration are shown below:
I-IV-V-I	Although some choices may produce more effective results than others, the harmonic structure which practically guarantees the stability of this phrase consists of the progression (Roman numerals) _____ .

648. It is vital that the bass be an effective melodic line which complements the soprano. The use of some contrary motion between the soprano and bass is desirable as it gives each a measure of independence. The outer voices (soprano and bass) define the "vertical" limits of music, and individuality in these voices contributes greatly to the musical interest.

Compare the soprano and bass of our harmonization as it now stands.

Eb: I - vi iii   IV - I V   I

Evaluate each item:

1. Melodic contour of the bass. (Good/Fair/Poor) _____
2. Effectiveness of the bass in relation to the soprano. (Good/Fair/Poor) _____

Your opinion.

---

649. Regardless how you rated the bass in the preceding frame, it can be improved as a melodic line by eliminating some of the large leaps. The bass usually contains a greater number of leaps than the other voices; but, even so, the angularity in the second measure is not especially good.

Observe the changes below:

Eb: I - vi iii   IV ii I$^6_4$ V   I

Two changes have been made: at (1) the supertonic has been substituted for its primary triad (the subdominant), and at (2) the tonic triad has been placed in second inversion. The cadence formula now includes the use of a _____ six-four chord.

cadential

650. Though slight, these changes bring greater tonal variety to the passage, reduce the angularity of the bass, and avoid the monotonous repetition of A-flat in both the soprano and bass simultaneously (beats one and two of the second measure, Frame 648).

Substitution of secondary for primary triads, and the use of inversions, helps refine the quality of the _____ line.

bass

---

651. You should check the soprano and bass voices against one another for incorrect use of parallel motion. Such errors are easier to detect before the alto and tenor voices are written.

Indicate the type of motion in the spaces provided. Use the following abbreviations: O=oblique; C=contrary; S=similar; P=parallel.

O C S C O C O C

___ ___ ___ ___ ___ ___ ___

---

652. Since no parallel motion occurs between the soprano and bass, the possibility of incorrect parallel motion does not exist. Is all parallel motion between the soprano and bass forbidden? _____

No.
(Parallel thirds and sixths are good.)

---

653. The melodic quality of the bass line and its relation to the soprano is important, as much of the success of the harmonization depends upon a good bass. An effective bass possesses the following features:

1. *Melodic contour.* The bass line should not be too angular even though more leaps are to be expected than in the upper parts.

2. *Contrapuntal interest with the soprano.* The bass and soprano together should make effective two-part writing —some contrary motion is desirable.

3. *Tonal variety.* Inversions help provide a more melodic bass line and contribute to tonal variety.

(No response.)

4. *Parallel motion.* Always check for parallel fifths and octaves between the bass and soprano before writing the remaining voices.

■ 654. Complete the harmonization by writing the alto and tenor voices.

(Use close structure.)

---

655. You should have had no trouble completing the harmonization as the alto and tenor voices fall neatly into place. Sometimes, however, part writing problems arise which can not be solved. When this happens, changes in the bass line, such as the use of different inversions, or even the selection of new chords, will be necessary. Even with only the limited harmonic material with which we are working there are many ways a melody can be harmonized. So do not be reluctant to substitute one chord for another no matter how enamored you are of your first choice.

Part writing difficulties sometimes are solved by the selection of a different chord, or by the use of _____.

inversions

---

656. We have now completed one demonstration of the technique of harmonization. Before trying another, let us review briefly the principal steps taken:

1. Determine the tonality.
2. Choose an appropriate cadence.
3. Choose an appropriate harmonic rhythm.
4. Determine the basic harmonic structure of the phrase. (Look for notes which are emphasized by prolongation, contour, or rhythm.)
5. Select chords for notes which remain from the three possibilities for each.
6. Write the bass.
7. Write the alto and tenor.
8. Make adjustments if necessary.

(No response.)

657. Check (√) the correct option:

1. Harmonic rhythm is always identical with the rhythm of the melody.
2. In four-part writing the bass is a melodic line nearly equal in importance to the soprano.

True statements:
(1) _____   (2) _____   Both _____   Neither _____

(2) √

---

658. We shall continue with another demonstration of the technique of harmonization.

B minor.

What is the tonality of the melody below? _____ ____

Cruger, Chorale: *Herzliebster Jesu, was hast du verbrochen*

---

659. Notice that the melody in the preceding frame does not end on the key note. What cadence is suggested by this phrase?
_____ —

Half cadence.
(See next frame.)

---

660. The melody in Frame 658 ends with the second scale degree. This note is not included in the tonic or submediant chords, so authentic, plagal, and deceptive cadences are not possible. The half cadence is the only one possible in this case.

Show with Roman numerals two chords which produce a half cadence.

i-V, VI-V, or III-V

___ ___

---

661. The final dominant chord can be preceded by i, VI, or III. You may try these three possibilities at the piano to acquaint yourself with the effect of each.

Under proper circumstances any one of these possibilities might be effective. The combination III-V, however, is probably the weakest, because in this case a primary triad (V) is preceded by its secondary triad (III). Our choice shall be i-V.

The tonic (i).

With what chord would you expect the harmonization to begin? _____

■

662. The harmonization now has a beginning and an ending.

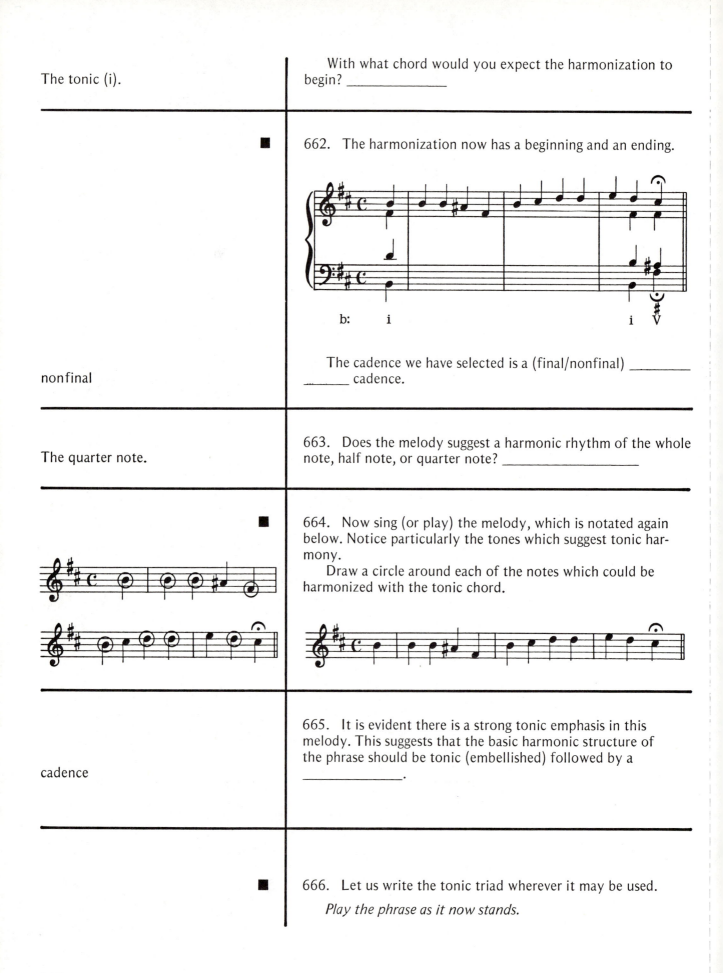

nonfinal

The cadence we have selected is a (final/nonfinal) _____ _____ cadence.

The quarter note.

663. Does the melody suggest a harmonic rhythm of the whole note, half note, or quarter note? _____

■

664. Now sing (or play) the melody, which is notated again below. Notice particularly the tones which suggest tonic harmony.

Draw a circle around each of the notes which could be harmonized with the tonic chord.

---

665. It is evident there is a strong tonic emphasis in this melody. This suggests that the basic harmonic structure of the phrase should be tonic (embellished) followed by a

cadence

_____.

■

666. Let us write the tonic triad wherever it may be used.

Play the phrase as it now stands.

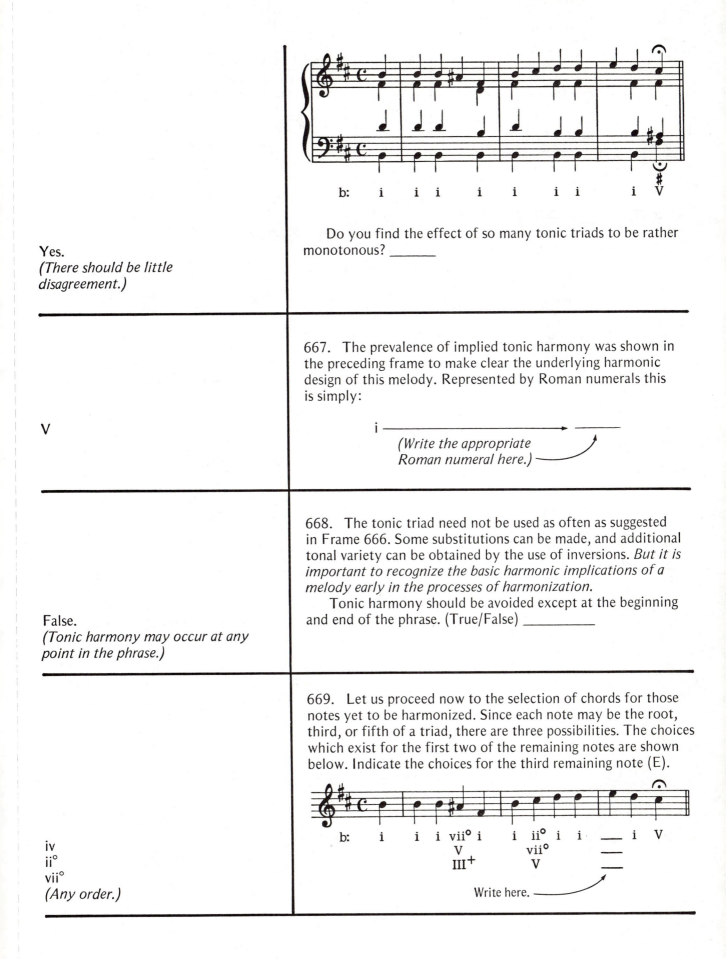

Do you find the effect of so many tonic triads to be rather monotonous? _____

667. The prevalence of implied tonic harmony was shown in the preceding frame to make clear the underlying harmonic design of this melody. Represented by Roman numerals this is simply:

V

i ————————————————→

(Write the appropriate Roman numeral here.) ————

668. The tonic triad need not be used as often as suggested in Frame 666. Some substitutions can be made, and additional tonal variety can be obtained by the use of inversions. *But it is important to recognize the basic harmonic implications of a melody early in the processes of harmonization.*

 Tonic harmony should be avoided except at the beginning and end of the phrase. (True/False) _____

False.
(Tonic harmony may occur at any point in the phrase.)

669. Let us proceed now to the selection of chords for those notes yet to be harmonized. Since each note may be the root, third, or fifth of a triad, there are three possibilities. The choices which exist for the first two of the remaining notes are shown below. Indicate the choices for the third remaining note (E).

iv
ii°
vii°
(Any order.)

b: i   i   i   V   i

i   vii°6   i   i

iv   i   V

670. The choice between these possibilities is influenced by the changes we make in the tonic harmonies. It is at this point that your sense of style and creative imagination must be brought to bear.

To continue the demonstration, the chords shown in the Roman numeral analysis below will be used.

Complete the bass line in accordance with the Roman numerals given.

b: i   i   i   V   i   i vii°6 i   i   iv   i   V

A diminished triad sounds best in first inversion.
(Or equivalent.)

671. There obviously is room for much improvement, both in the choice of chords and in the quality of the bass line. But don't expect a harmonization to take shape instantly; it usually develops slowly with the final product the result of much experimentation and compromise.

Why is it necessary to place the chord at the asterisk in first inversion? _____

_____

---

672. Now follow the steps which are taken to refine the bass line and the choice of chords: We wish to eliminate some of the tonic triads by substituting other chords, and also provide greater tonal variety by the use of inversions. At the beginning of the phrase it would be desirable to have harmonic change to counter the monotony of the repeated notes in the soprano.

Two possibilities are shown below:

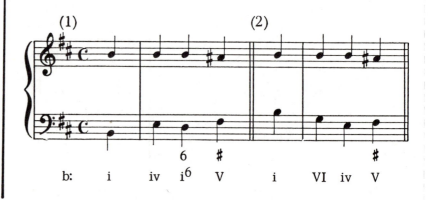

(1)   (2)

b: i   iv   i6   V   i   VI   iv   V

Repeated notes in the melody often call for harmonic changes or the use of _____.

■ 673. We shall choose possibility No. 1 of the preceding frame. So now our harmonization looks like this:

At the asterisk, the repetition of the tonic chord from the fourth beat of the first measure to the first beat of the second measure produces harmonic stagnation. It is usually desirable to have harmonic motion at a point of metric stress (such as the first beat of a measure), so some change is needed. What two chords other than the tonic can be used to harmonize the F-sharp?
(Use Roman numerals) _____ and _____.

V (and) III⁺

■ 674. Since the leap from A-sharp to F-sharp at the asterisk defines the dominant triad, a repetition of this harmony on the fourth beat is appropriate. Also, by using the following tonic chord in first inversion the parallel octaves (B to C-sharp) are eliminated.

Incorrect use of parallel motion often is prevented by the use of _____.

THE TECHNIQUE OF HARMONIZATION

675. Now the first part of the harmonization has been greatly improved. One additional change which will add interest to the latter part is shown at the asterisk below:

b: i   iv i6 V -   i6 vii°6 i VI   iv i V

The submediant triad (VI) may often be substituted for the tonic because it is the tonic's _____ triad.

secondary

---

676. Now that all of the chords have been chosen, it is necessary to examine the bass line and its relation to the soprano. Evaluate the bass as written in the preceding frame.

1. Is the bass a good melodic line? _____
2. Is there any incorrect parallel motion between the bass and soprano? _____
3. Does the bass complement the soprano (is there effective use of contrary motion)? _____

1. Your opinion.

2. No.

3. Yes.

---

677. Write the alto and tenor voices.

The fifths are not both perfect. (A-sharp to E is a diminished fifth.) *(Or equivalent.)*

678.   Notice in the solution given in the preceding frame that consecutive fifths occur in the second measure (beats two and three) between the alto and tenor voices. Why is this not an error? _____

---

perfect

679.   Consecutive fifths are incorrect only if both intervals are _____.

(No response.)

680.   An effective harmonization rarely appears instantly, but develops slowly and by successive stages. Compare, for example, our final version in the preceding frame with that of Frame 670. It is obvious that considerable improvement has taken place. Additional experience in harmonization will make it possible for you to proceed more quickly to the final version; *but until your technique becomes more highly developed, it would be unwise to omit any of the steps which are demonstrated in this chapter.*

1st   3
2nd   1
3rd   5
4th   7
5th   4
6th   2
7th   6

(Unless all of your answers were correct review Frame 656.)

681.   Some of the steps which are associated with the process of harmonization are listed at the left below. Arrange these steps in proper sequence by writing the number of each step in the appropriate space at the right.

1. Choose an appropriate cadence.
2. Write the bass.
3. Determine the tonality.
4. Select chords for notes not associated with the basic harmonic structure.
5. Choose an appropriate harmonic rhythm.
6. Check for incorrect parallel motion between bass and soprano.
7. Determine the basic harmonic structure of the phrase.

1st   _____
2nd   _____
3rd   _____
4th   _____
5th   _____
6th   _____
7th   _____

---

authentic

682.   The choice of chords is influenced by the cadence, so do not begin to harmonize until the cadence has been selected. If the melody consists of several phrases, there should be variety in the types of cadences used. The final cadence, of course, should be the most conclusive. For this reason the final cadence usually is a perfect _____ cadence.

THE TECHNIQUE OF HARMONIZATION

If your choice was:
(a) go to Frame 684.
(b) go to Frame 685.
(c) go to Frame 686.

683. For the remainder of this chapter you must draw on the knowledge you have acquired regarding effective chord choice and part writing procedures. Which chord ((a), (b), or (c)) most effectively continues the progression? _____

Bb: I   V   I   IV   vi   V   ii

(No response.)

684. The harmonic movement IV-vi is a retrogression (the bass moves up a third). While retrogressions are not entirely ruled out, there is a better choice. *Return to Frame 683 and try again.*

(No response.)

685. The progression IV-V is very strong, but the parallel fifths and octaves (between the bass and soprano, and between the bass and tenor) make this a poor choice. *Return to Frame 683 and try again.*

(No response.)

686. This is the best choice. The harmonic movement IV-ii is a progression (the root moves down a third), and the part writing is correct. *Proceed with the next frame.*

If your choice was:
(a) go to Frame 688.
(b) go to Frame 689.
(c) go to Frame 690.

687. Which chord ((a), (b), or (c)) most effectively continues the progression? _____

c#:   iv   i⁶₄   V   iv   VI   VI

(No response.)	**688.** Several things are wrong with this choice. Not only is the harmonic movement V-iv weak, but there are parallel fifths between the bass and soprano. Notice, also, the incorrect doubling in the subdominant chord. *Return to Frame 687 and try again.*
deceptive *(Skip to Frame 691.)*	**689.** This is the best choice. Notice that the third is doubled in the submediant triad. This is to avoid the augmented second which would have occurred if the tenor had taken an A (as in chord (c)). What type of cadence is illustrated in this example? A _____ cadence.
(No response.)	**690.** The progression V-VI is good, but the augmented second between B-sharp and A in the tenor makes this a bad choice. *Return to Frame 687 to find a better solution.*
If your choice was: (a) go to Frame 692. (b) go to Frame 693. (c) go to Frame 694.	**691.** Which fragment ((a), (b), or (c)) most effectively continues the progression? _____
(No response.)	**692.** The use of the leading tone triad (vii°) in root position makes this a poor choice. *Return to Frame 691 and try again.*
(No response.)	**693.** The progression I-iii-IV-V-vi is a good one. Incorrect parallel motion between the second and third chords, however, makes this a bad choice. *Return to Frame 691 and try again.*
Imperfect authentic.	**694.** This is the best choice. Identify the type of cadence used. *(Be specific.)* _____

The final chord does not have the keynote in the soprano.
(Or equivalent.)

695. Why is the cadence in Frame 691 (choice (c)) not a perfect authentic cadence? _____
_____

If your choice was:
(a) go to Frame 698.
(b) go to Frame 697.

696. Which fragment ((a) or (b)) most effectively continues the progression? _____

D: I   V⁶ IV⁶ I   V   I⁶ IV⁶   V

(No response.)

697. The harmonic progression of (b) is a good one. There are, however, several flaws. The most serious of these is parallel octaves which occur between the second and third chords in the soprano and tenor voices (E to D). The bass line is excessively angular; also, it is undesirable to leap too often in the bass from triads in first inversion. *Continue with the next frame to learn why (a) was the better choice.*

True.

698. You may have been reluctant to make this choice because of the retrogression V-IV. Retrogressions, however, often provide good harmonic interest, and you should not be afraid to use them if good voice leading results.

You may refer to Frame 697 to learn why (b) is weak.

If not used to excess, retrogressions are equal in effectiveness to progressions. (True/False) _____

Weaken.

699. There should be an appropriate balance between progressions and retrogressions. This balance fluctuates drastically depending upon the wishes of the composer at a given moment. Merely as an arbitrary norm for an appropriate balance, let us suggest two-thirds progression and one-third retrogression as reasonable.
Does an excess of retrogressive harmonic relationships weaken or strengthen the sense of forward motion? _____

If your choice was:
(a) go to Frame 701.
(b) go to Frame 702.

700. Which fragment ((a) or (b)) most effectively continues the progression? _____

f: i i⁶ iv⁶   i ii°⁶ V   VI   i V⁶ V   i

(No response.)

701. There is actually nothing wrong with either (a) or (b). This example is given to show that there are more ways than one to harmonize even a simple melodic line. The choice between these two possibilities is one of personal preference, as well as the type of cadence desired. *Continue with Frame 702 for comment on choice (b).*

(No response.)

702. Although there is nothing wrong with this choice, many of you may prefer (a). The reason is that in (b) the dominant chord (V) is used on both the second and third beats immediately prior to the cadence chord. This reiteration of dominant harmony results in a stagnation of the harmonic rhythm. The greater sense of motion which results from the progression ii-V in (a) is desirable.

Read the comments in Frame 701 before continuing with Frame 703.

---

(2) √

703. Check (√) the correct option:

1. Structural harmony occurs only at cadence points.
2. Relatively rapid chord changes produce animated harmonic rhythm.

True statements:
(1) _____   (2) _____   Both _____   Neither _____

SUMMARY

The finished harmonization evolves from an assessment of the basic harmonic implications of the melody. Structural harmony—chords which constitute the tonal framework of the phrase—should be chosen first. Remember that tonal stability and modal clarity result chiefly from the use of primary triads in important structural positions. If used to excess, secondary triads weaken the tonality.

The steps to harmonizing a melody that are presented in this chapter are summarized below:

1. Familiarize yourself with the melody by singing or playing it.
2. Determine the key to be used. Some melodies may be harmonized in more than one key
3. Select an appropriate cadence. If the phrase is one of a group of phrases, cadences should complement one another.
4. Choose an appropriate harmonic rhythm. The melody may suggest a particular rate of chord change, such as one or two per measure, or perhaps call for a chord for each note.
5. Determine the basic harmonic structure of the phrase. The three structures that have been presented are:
    a. A single chord followed by a cadence.
    b. Harmonic embellishment of a single chord followed by a cadence.
    c. A cadence formula (or a basic harmonic progression such as I-IV-V-I) spread over the entire phrase.
6. Select the remaining chords. Any note may be the root, third, or fifth of a triad. Progressions should predominate over retrogressions.
7. Write the bass voice. Produce an effective melodic line by using first and second inversions when appropriate. The bass should complement the melody. A variety of relative motion is desirable Contrary motion contributes to the individuality of voices.
8. Check for incorrect parallel motion between the bass and soprano voices.
9. Write the alto and tenor voices. Each should produce an agreeable melodic line.
10. Check for part writing errors, including incorrect doubling, spacing, and parallel perfect intervals.

Mastery Frames

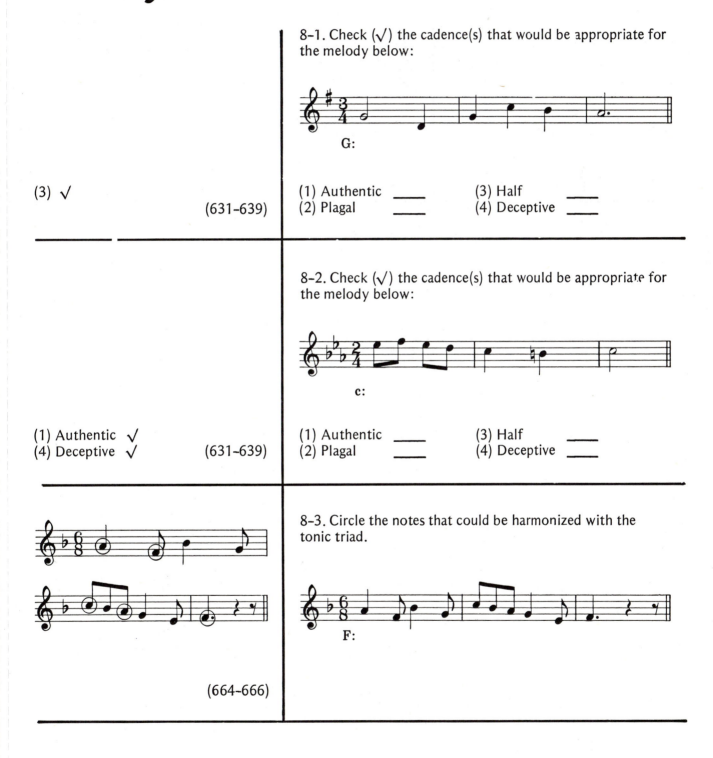

8-1. Check (√) the cadence(s) that would be appropriate for the melody below:

G:

(3) √   (631–639)

(1) Authentic ____   (3) Half ____
(2) Plagal ____   (4) Deceptive ____

8-2. Check (√) the cadence(s) that would be appropriate for the melody below:

c:

(1) Authentic √
(4) Deceptive √   (631–639)

(1) Authentic ____   (3) Half ____
(2) Plagal ____   (4) Deceptive ____

8-3. Circle the notes that could be harmonized with the tonic triad.

F:

(664–666)

(2).

(644)

8-4. Which harmonic phrase structure is suggested by the melody in the preceding frame?_____

(1) A single chord followed by a cadence.
(2) The tonic embellished followed by a cadence.
(3) A harmonic formula spread over the entire phrase.

(1)	(2)
IV	ii
ii	vii°
vii°	V

(646)

8-5. Indicate with Roman numerals the three triads that might be used at (1) and (2).

Eb: ___   ___

___   ___

___   ___

Supplementary Assignments

ASSIGNMENT 8–1   Name_____

1. Write chord symbols and identify the cadences that are appropriate for the melodic lines.

(A)

C:

       __ __

       __ __

CADENCE TYPE

_____

_____

(B)

A♭:

       __ __

_____

(C)

g:

       __ __

_____

2. Check (√) the note value of the prevalent harmonic rhythm suggested by each of the melodies below.

3. The three chords provided in the example below indicate the basic harmonic structure of the phrase. Complete the harmonization by selecting chords for the remaining notes of the melody that produce mostly progressive harmonic movement. Use inversions and employ correct part writing procedures.

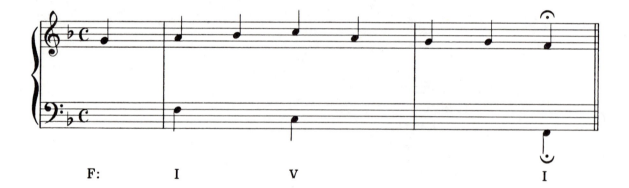

4. Complete the harmonization and supply the Roman numeral analysis.

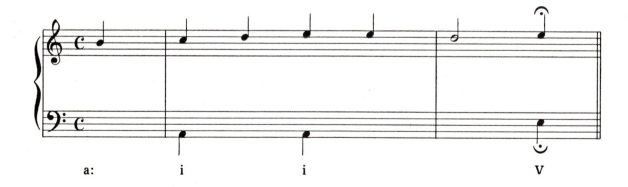

Name_____

1. Show with Roman numerals the three triads that may be used to harmonize each note of the major scale.

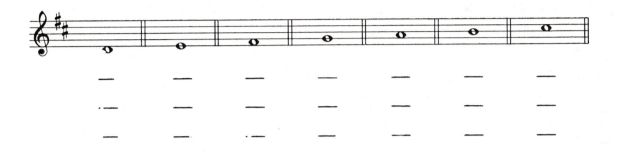

2. Show with Roman numerals the three triads that may be used to harmonize each note of the harmonic minor scale.

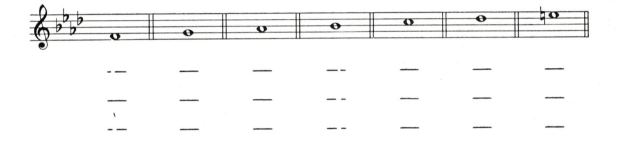

3. Complete the harmonization and supply the chord symbols.

B♭: I   vii°6   V

4. Harmonize the melodies below using the method that is summarized in Frame 656. Analyze with Roman numerals.

(A)

G:

(B)

a:

chapter nine

Nonharmonic Tones

The tones of a musical composition belong to one of two groups: *harmonic tones*—those which constitute chords; and *nonharmonic tones*—those which are extraneous to the harmony. If all tones were harmonic, music would be excessively consonant. Although not all nonharmonic tones are dissonant, most are, and motivation results from the dissonant tensions they produce. Nonharmonic tones also contribute to smoother melodic lines, and greater rhythmic animation.

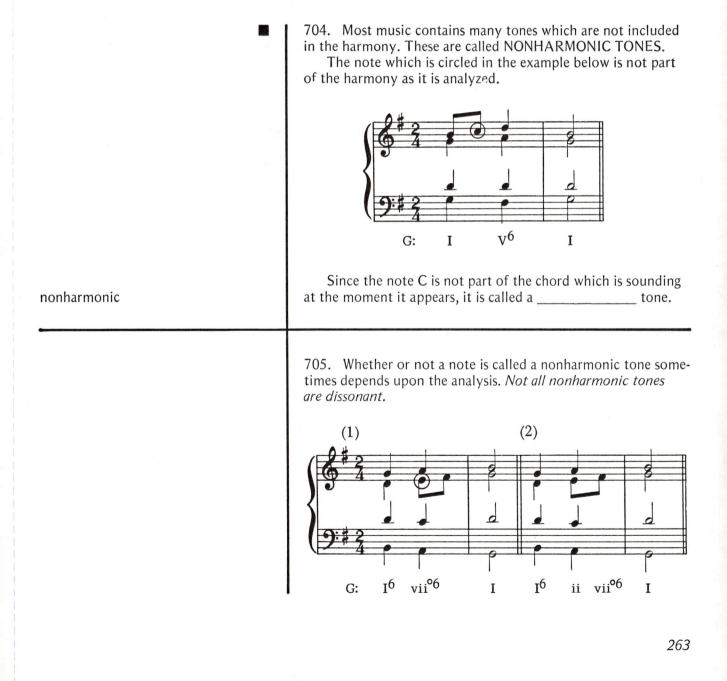

704. Most music contains many tones which are not included in the harmony. These are called NONHARMONIC TONES.

The note which is circled in the example below is not part of the harmony as it is analyzed.

G: I   V⁶   I

Since the note C is not part of the chord which is sounding at the moment it appears, it is called a _____ tone.

nonharmonic

705. Whether or not a note is called a nonharmonic tone sometimes depends upon the analysis. *Not all nonharmonic tones are dissonant.*

(1)   (2)

G: I⁶   vii°⁶   I   I⁶   ii   vii°⁶   I

In (1) the note E is called a nonharmonic tone because it is not part of the harmony as it is analyzed. In (2), however, two chords (ii and vii°⁶) are analyzed on the second beat; this causes both the E and F-sharp to be included in the harmony.

Any tone which is not part of the harmony as it is analyzed is called a nonharmonic tone. (True/False) _____

True.

■ 706. Nonharmonic tones originate in the melodic and rhythmic aspects of music. Melodies often contain a greater number of notes than can be accommodated by the harmony. Occasionally very rapid harmonic rhythm is used to harmonize each note of a melody, but such practice becomes tiresome if carried on too long.

Schumann, *Symphonic Studies*, Op. 13

Presto possible

All of the notes in the above example are included in the harmony; thus, in spite of very rapid melodic movement, there are no nonharmonic tones.

Rapid harmonic rhythm tends to reduce the number of nonharmonic tones. (True/False) _____

True.

■ 707. The harmonic rhythm of the following example is much slower than that shown in the preceding frame. The circled notes are not included in the harmony.

Allegro

Allegro

F: I

vi

ii

Music which has slow harmonic rhythm generally contains
(few/many) _____ nonharmonic tones.

many

708. Nonharmonic tones contribute to the smoothness of
melodic lines by reducing the number of leaps. They also increase the rhythmic activity. By staggering rhythmic activity
in each of the voices, greater individuality results.

Each voice has little individuality in the example below as
the rhythm is the same for each.

Bach, Chorale: *Ach Gott, wie manches Herzeleid*
(altered)

No.	

Are there any nonharmonic tones in the above example?

_____

---

709. Compare the example below with that in the preceding frame.

Bach, Chorale: *Ach Gott, wie manches Herzeleid*

Certainly you will agree that the example above (with non-harmonic tones) is much more interesting than the version in the preceding frame. Each voice receives greater individuality through the use of _____ tones.

nonharmonic

---

710. In addition to greater individuality through rhythmic activity, each voice (Frame 709) is a better melodic line. Nonharmonic tones reduce the number of leaps and give the music a more "flowing" quality.

Is it desirable for melodic lines to be entirely free of leaps?

_____

No.
(Melodies without leaps are monotonous and quite rare.)

---

711. The use of nonharmonic tones often causes irregularities of doubling or in the distribution of the voices. Refer again to Frame 708. In the third chord the alto is below the tenor. There would be no reason to cross the voices in this fashion if no nonharmonic tones were employed. Frame 709, however, shows why this is desirable. The momentum of the ascending scale line in the tenor carries it up to the note E, and the alto drops down to A to improve the sonority of the chord. Normal distribution of the voices is resumed in the fourth chord.

In order to produce expressive melodic lines in each of the voices, irregularities of doubling or an occasional crossing of the voices is tolerated.

(No response.)

1, 5, (and) 7	712. In the example of Frame 709 there are three chords which contain irregular doubling. Indicate these chords (by number). _____, _____, and _____.
nonharmonic	713. In chord 1 (Frame 709) there are three roots and one third, but no fifth; chord 5 is in root position, so it would be normal to double the bass rather than the soprano as has been done here; chord 7 has two roots and two thirds, but no fifth. All of these irregularities result from the desire to write more expressive melodic lines through the use of _____ tones.
(No response.)	714. While the use of nonharmonic tones permits greater freedom of part writing, not all of the "rules" are thrown to the winds. Nonharmonic tones normally do not justify the use of parallel fifths or octaves, nor is it desirable to double active tones (the leading tone, in particular). In fact, you will find that nonharmonic tones added to part writing which otherwise is correct often produce incorrect parallel motion, so you must check more carefully than ever for such errors.
(2) √	715. Check (√) the correct option: 1. Nonharmonic tones must be analyzed as part of the harmony. 2. Nonharmonic tones give rhythmic interest to the voices. True statements: (1) _____ (2) _____ Both _____ Neither _____
Both √	716. Check (√) the correct option: 1. Nonharmonic tones often cause irregularities of doubling. 2. A tone which is not part of the harmony as analyzed is a nonharmonic tone. True statements: (1) _____ (2) _____ Both _____ Neither _____
	717. There are several kinds of nonharmonic tones and the remainder of this chapter is devoted to naming them and learning to write them correctly. Unfortunately the terminology of nonharmonic tones is not standardized. Writers in the field of music theory often use different terms for the same device, or use the same term in conflicting ways. Even the term

"nonharmonic tone" is not universal. Other terms are *accessory tone, bytone, nonchord tone,* and *foreign tone.*

Actually, the name given to a particular nonharmonic tone is of little importance as long as its musical significance and correct interpretation are appreciated. Labels given to musical events are not an end in themselves; they make verbalization possible. Although standardization of terminology would be desirable, and communication greatly facilitated, the fact remains that we must accommodate ourselves to different sets of terms when comparing the writings of various authors. You will find this is not difficult once an understanding of a particular device has been acquired.

Nonharmonic tones are usually classified according to the way they are approached and left. Further classification is made with reference to rhythmic placement.

(No response.)

---

  718. A nonharmonic tone which is approached and left by step in the same direction is called a PASSING TONE (symbol: PT).

Schumann, *Album for the Young,* Op. 68, No. 11

step

Since the circled note (A) is not part of the harmony, it must be analyzed as a nonharmonic tone. It is called a passing tone because it is approached and left by _____ in the same direction.

---

  719. Passing tones may occur in either ascending or descending direction, and two or more may occur simultaneously.

In the following example, there are nine passing tones; draw a circle around each. *(Refer to the Roman numeral analysis to identify the notes which are not part of the harmony.)*

C: vi   I⁶ IV I⁶ I   V

Bach, Chorale: *Allein, zu dir, Herr Jesu Christ*

C: vi   I⁶   IV   I⁶   I   V

direction

720. Notice in the preceding frame that when two or more passing tones occur simultaneously they produce consonant intervals with each other.

Passing tones may occur singly or in groups of two or more. All passing tones are approached and left by step in the same _____

721. Figured bass symbols are used to indicate melodic movement over a single bass note.

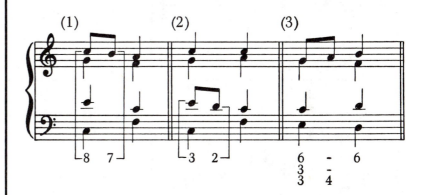

(1)   (2)   (3)

8 7   3 2   6   -   6
                    3   -
                    3   4

In (1) the numbers 8 7 refer to the notes C and B which occur over the bass note C; in (2) the numbers 3 2 list the intervals between the bass and tenor (the actual intervals of a tenth and ninth are reduced to avoid the use of unnecessarily large numbers); the figuration in (3) is more complete to show the doubled third above the bass and the melodic movement in the soprano.

Numbers in the figured bass which occur *horizontally* beneath a single bass note indicate melodic movement in one of the upper voices.

(No response.)

722. Refer again to (3) in the preceding frame. Note that the dashes which follow the numbers 6 and 3 show that the notes indicated by these figures are held while melodic movement occurs in another voice.

Write the alto and tenor voices.

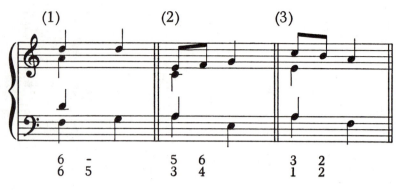

$$\begin{matrix} 6 & - \\ 6 & 5 \end{matrix} \qquad \begin{matrix} 5 & 6 \\ 3 & 4 \end{matrix} \qquad \begin{matrix} 3 & 2 \\ 1 & 2 \end{matrix}$$

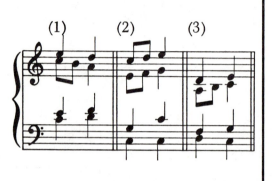

723. Write the alto and tenor voices.

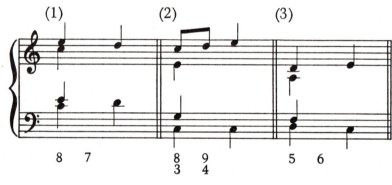

$$8 \quad 7 \qquad \begin{matrix} 8 \\ 3 \end{matrix} \quad \begin{matrix} 9 \\ 4 \end{matrix} \qquad 5 \quad 6$$

724. Write the alto and tenor voices. *(Note that the chord at the asterisk is a diminished triad—double accordingly.)*

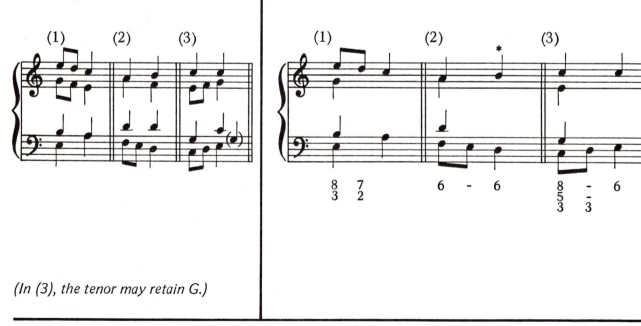

$$\begin{matrix} 8 & 7 \\ 3 & 2 \end{matrix} \qquad 6 \quad - \quad 6 \qquad \begin{matrix} 8 & - \\ 5 & \\ 3 & 3 \end{matrix} \quad 6$$

(In (3), the tenor may retain G.)

725. Examples (2) and (3) in the preceding frame show that when melodic movement occurs in the bass, dashes are used to indicate notes which are sustained while the bass moves. Complete the alto and tenor voices. (Remember: numbers in the figured bass represent intervals above the notes *under which the numbers occur.*)

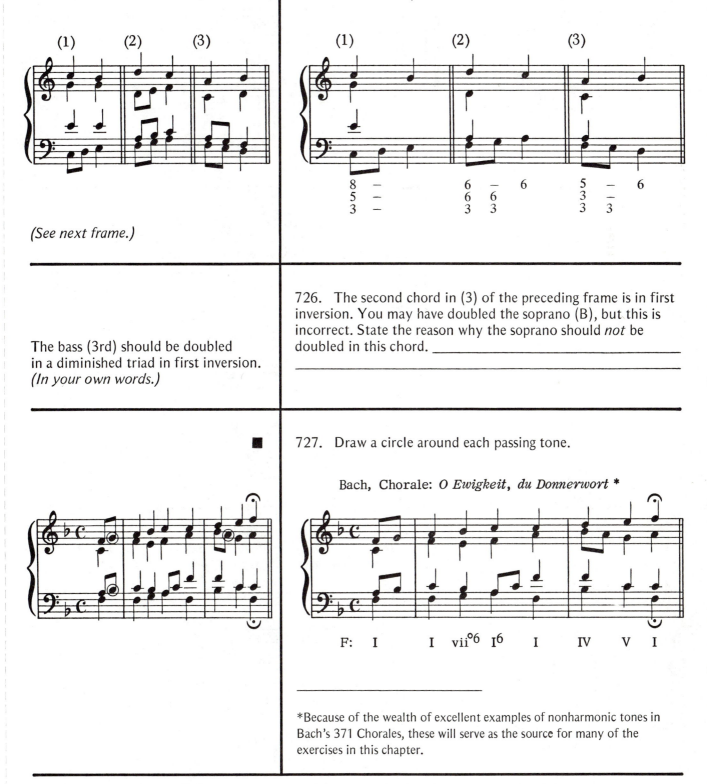

(See next frame.)

The bass (3rd) should be doubled in a diminished triad in first inversion. *(In your own words.)*

726. The second chord in (3) of the preceding frame is in first inversion. You may have doubled the soprano (B), but this is incorrect. State the reason why the soprano should *not* be doubled in this chord. _____

_____

727. Draw a circle around each passing tone.

Bach, Chorale: *O Ewigkeit, du Donnerwort* *

F: I   I   vii°6 I6   I   IV   V   I

———————————

*Because of the wealth of excellent examples of nonharmonic tones in Bach's 371 Chorales, these will serve as the source for many of the exercises in this chapter.

728. Complete the alto and tenor voices and draw a circle around each passing tone.

Bach, Chorale: *Was mein Gott will, das g'scheh'*

$$
\begin{array}{llllllllll}
8 & 7 & 5 & 6 & 5 & - & 6 & - & & 6 & 5 & 4 \\
 & & 3 & 4 & 3 & 3 & 6 & 6 & & 4 & & \\
 & & 3 & - & & & & & & &
\end{array}
$$

729. All of the passing tones to this point have appeared on the weak portion of the beat. These are called UNACCENTED passing tones. Passing tones may also coincide with the strong portion of the beat, in which case they are called ACCENTED passing tones. Which example shows an accented passing tone?

(2). _____

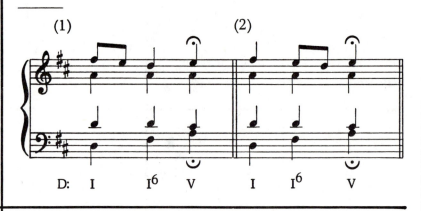

(1)   (2)

D: I   I^6 V   I   I^6 V

730. Draw a circle around the *accented* passing tones. *(Refer to the Roman numeral analysis to find the notes which are not part of the harmony.)*

Bach, Chorale: *Helft mir Gott's Güte preisen*

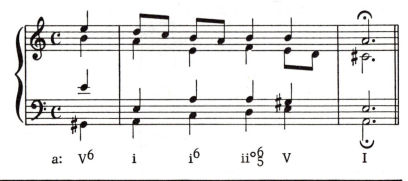

a: V^6 i   i^6 ii$^{\circ6}_5$ V   I

731. Both of the accented passing tones in the preceding frame occur in descending motion. Although used most frequently in this fashion, accented passing tones may also occur in ascending motion.

Bach, Chorale: *Du grosser Schmerzensmann*

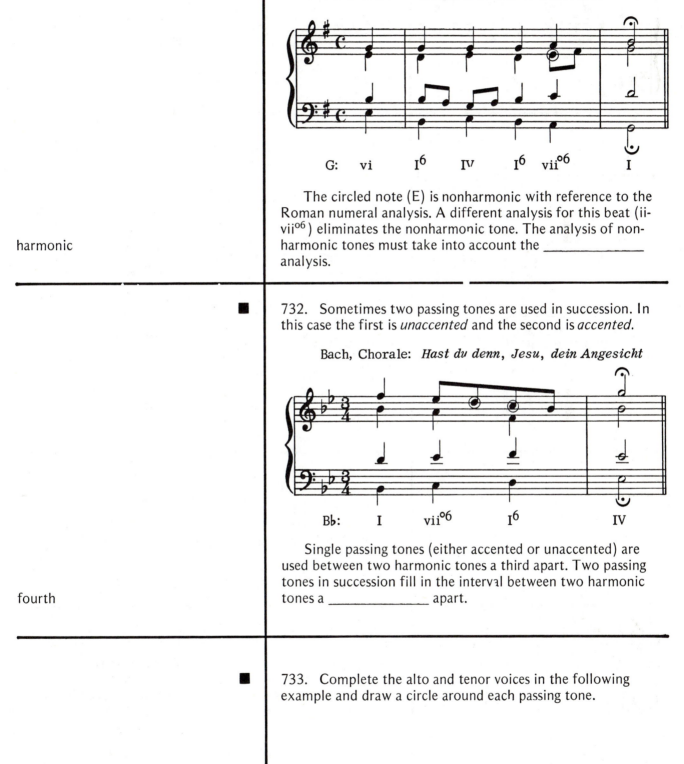

G: vi   I⁶   IV   I⁶   vii°⁶   I

The circled note (E) is nonharmonic with reference to the Roman numeral analysis. A different analysis for this beat (ii-vii°⁶) eliminates the nonharmonic tone. The analysis of nonharmonic tones must take into account the _____ analysis.

harmonic

---

732. Sometimes two passing tones are used in succession. In this case the first is *unaccented* and the second is *accented*.

Bach, Chorale: *Hast du denn, Jesu, dein Angesicht*

Bb: I   vii°⁶   I⁶   IV

Single passing tones (either accented or unaccented) are used between two harmonic tones a third apart. Two passing tones in succession fill in the interval between two harmonic tones a _____ apart.

fourth

---

733. Complete the alto and tenor voices in the following example and draw a circle around each passing tone.

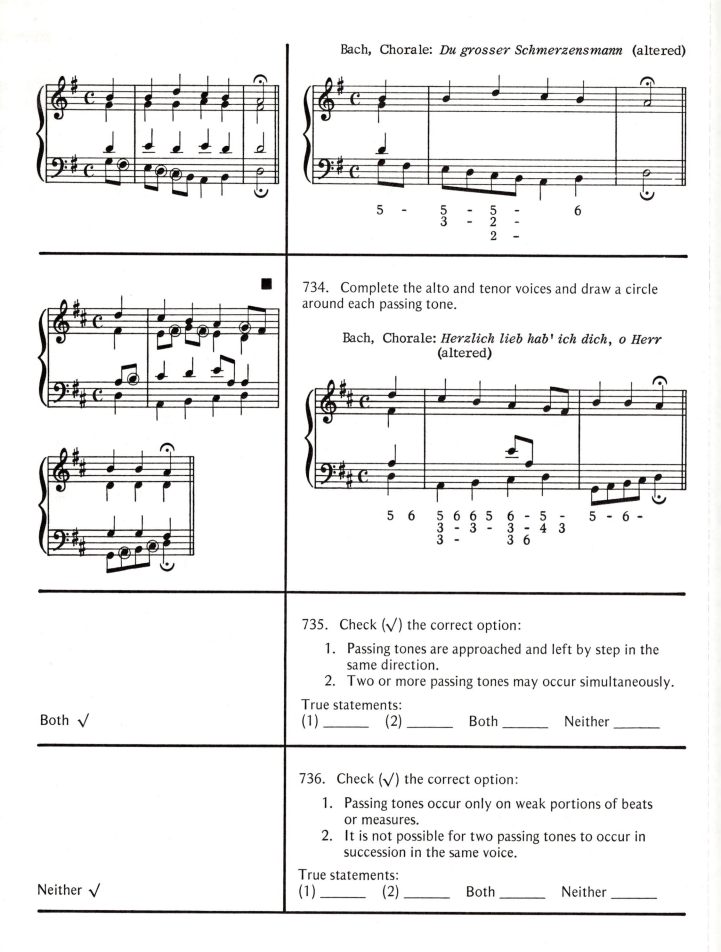

Bach, Chorale: *Du grosser Schmerzensmann* (altered)

5 -   5 - 5 -   6
      3 - 2 -
          2 -

734. Complete the alto and tenor voices and draw a circle around each passing tone.

Bach, Chorale: *Herzlich lieb hab' ich dich, o Herr* (altered)

5 6   5 6 6 5   6 - 5 -   5 - 6 -
      3 - 3 - 3 - 4 3
      3 -   3 6

Both √

735. Check (√) the correct option:

1. Passing tones are approached and left by step in the same direction.
2. Two or more passing tones may occur simultaneously.

True statements:
(1) _____   (2) _____   Both _____   Neither _____

Neither √

736. Check (√) the correct option:

1. Passing tones occur only on weak portions of beats or measures.
2. It is not possible for two passing tones to occur in succession in the same voice.

True statements:
(1) _____   (2) _____   Both _____   Neither _____

737. A nonharmonic tone which is approached and left by step with a change of direction is called a NEIGHBORING TONE (symbol: NT).*

Beethoven, *Sonata*, Op. 49, No. 2

Tempo di Minuetto

Whereas the passing tone leads by step from one harmonic note to another a third away, the neighboring tone appears between two harmonic notes of the _____ pitch.

same

_____

*Other terms for this device are *returning note, changing tone,* and *auxiliary tone.*

738. Most neighboring tones occur on weak portions of beats or measures (as in the preceding frame). Accented neighboring tones, although less common, can sometimes be used effectively.

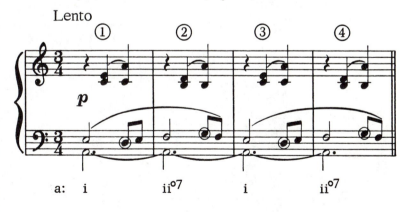

Chopin, *Valse Brillante*, Op. 34, No. 2

Lento

Neighboring tones may be either a step *above* or *below* the harmonic tone. Lower neighboring tones are shown in the first and third measures of the above example. Which measures contain upper neighboring tones? _____ and _____.

Two (and) four

739. Frames 737 and 738 show that neighboring tones may be accented or unaccented, and occur (by step) either above or below the harmonic tone to which they relate.

Are most neighboring tones accented or unaccented? _____

Unaccented.

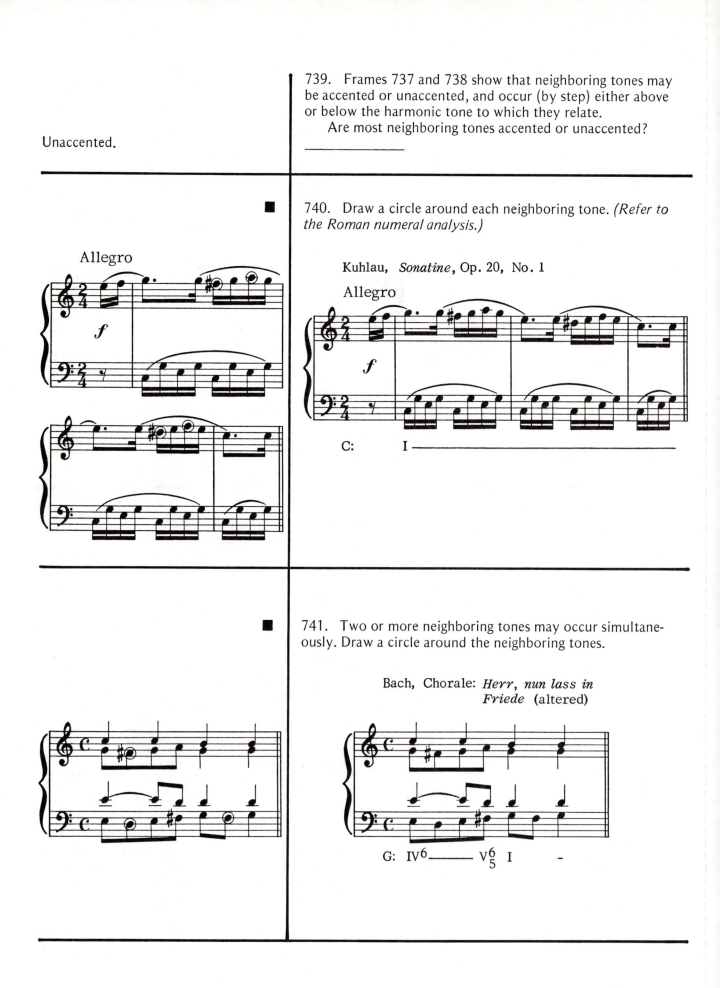

740. Draw a circle around each neighboring tone. *(Refer to the Roman numeral analysis.)*

Kuhlau, *Sonatine*, Op. 20, No. 1

Allegro

C: I ——————————————

741. Two or more neighboring tones may occur simultaneously. Draw a circle around the neighboring tones.

Bach, Chorale: *Herr, nun lass in Friede* (altered)

G: IV6 ——— V6/5 I   -

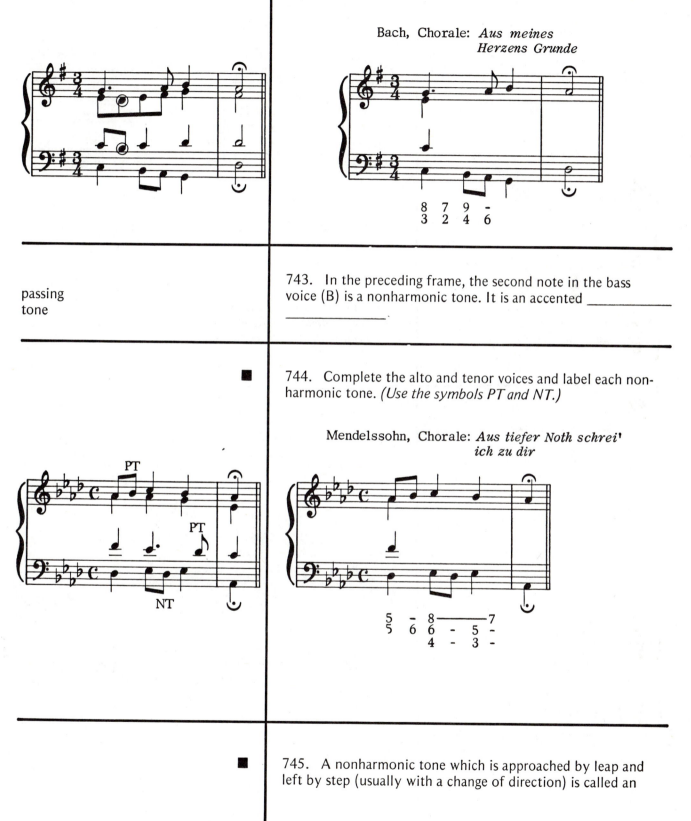

742. Complete the alto and tenor voices and draw a circle around each neighboring tone.

Bach, Chorale: *Aus meines Herzens Grunde*

743. In the preceding frame, the second note in the bass voice (B) is a nonharmonic tone. It is an accented _____ _____.

passing
tone

744. Complete the alto and tenor voices and label each non-harmonic tone. *(Use the symbols PT and NT.)*

Mendelssohn, Chorale: *Aus tiefer Noth schrei' ich zu dir*

745. A nonharmonic tone which is approached by leap and left by step (usually with a change of direction) is called an

APPOGGIATURA (symbol: App).*

Beethoven, *Sonata*, Op. 10, No. 1

The feature which distinguishes the appoggiatura from both the passing tone and the neighboring tone is that it is approached by _____.

leap

_____

*The term appoggiatura comes from the Italian *appoggiare,* to lean. It describes the effect of this nonharmonic tone, which is that of "leaning" upon the tone to which it resolves.

---

746.   The appoggiatura occurs most often in a position of rhythmic stress (as in the preceding frame). The example below, however, shows *unaccented* appoggiaturas.

Tchaikovsky, *Symphony No.* 5, Op. 64

Andante cantabile, con alcuna licenza

The appoggiatura is a nonharmonic tone which is approached by leap and left by _____.

step

747. Double appoggiaturas are shown in the example below.

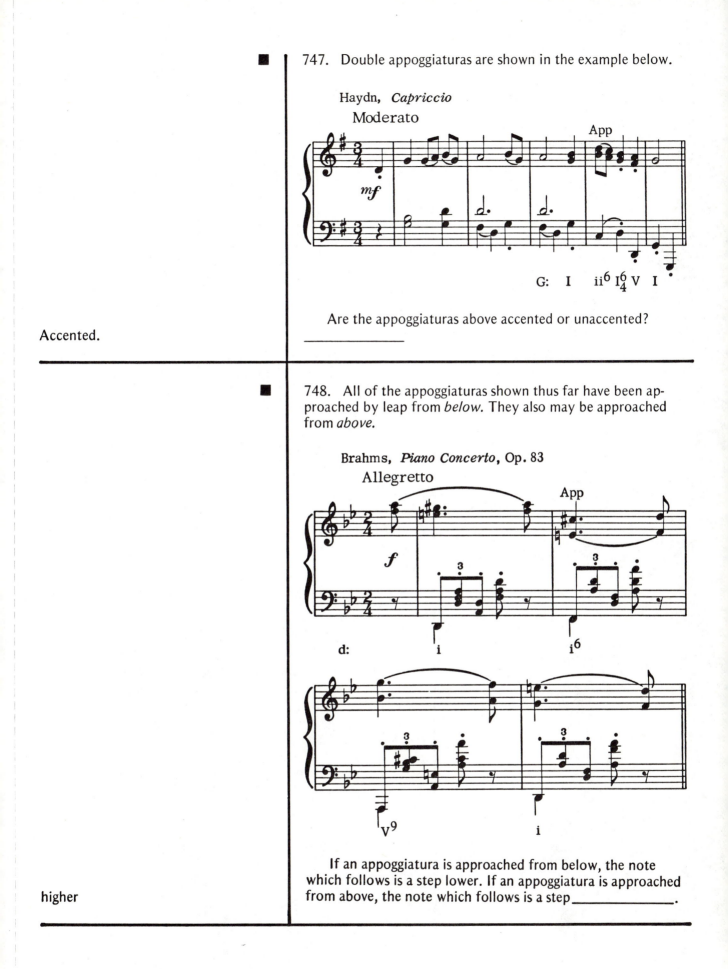

Haydn, *Capriccio*
Moderato

G: I   ii⁶ I⁶₄ V   I

Are the appoggiaturas above accented or unaccented?

Accented.
_____

748. All of the appoggiaturas shown thus far have been approached by leap from *below*. They also may be approached from *above*.

Brahms, *Piano Concerto*, Op. 83
Allegretto

d: i   i⁶

V⁹   i

If an appoggiatura is approached from below, the note which follows is a step lower. If an appoggiatura is approached from above, the note which follows is a step_____.

higher

■ 749. The appoggiatura sometimes appears without preparation.

Bach, *French Suite No. 3*

step

With or without preparation, the appoggiatura is followed by tone a which is a half- or whole _____ away.

■ 750. Without preparation, the appoggiatura's effect of "leaning" upon the harmonic tone which follows is heightened. The appoggiatura at the asterisk below is an echo of that heard in the preceding measure. This produces a dramatic effect of emotional tension.

Tchaikovsky, *Romeo and Juliet*, *Overture–Fantasy*

poco a poco string. accel.

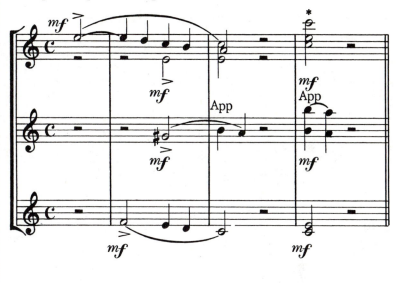

The appoggiaturas above are accented. Are the appoggiaturas in Frame 749 accented or unaccented? _____

Unaccented.

---

751.   Although the appoggiatura sometimes appears without preparation, it usually is approached by leap. In all cases it is left by step—usually in the direction opposite to its approach (if any). Some of the possible forms of the approggiatura are shown below:

WITH PREPARATION

(Accented)   (Unaccented)

WITHOUT PREPARATION

(Accented)   (Unaccented)

downward

An appoggiatura which is approached from below will usually be left by step in a(n) (upward/downward) _____ _____ direction.

752. Complete the alto and tenor voices and label each non-harmonic tone. *(Use the symbols PT, NT, and App.)*

Bach, Chorale: *Jesu, nun sei gepreist*

3   -   6————9 - 6   8 - 5 -
6— 6 - 4 -   4   7 6 4 3
3 -

---

753. A nonharmonic tone which is approached by step and left by leap (usually with a change of direction) is called an ESCAPE TONE (symbol: ET).*

Mozart, *Quartet*, K. 575

Allegretto

ET   ET

A: I   -   V⁷   I

The escape tone's melodic movement is the opposite of the appoggiatura's. Whereas the appoggiatura is approached by leap and left by step, the escape tone is approached by step and left by _____.

leap

---

*The escape tone is also known by its French name *échappée*.

754. The most common form of the escape tone is shown in the preceding frame (an ascending step followed by a descending leap). The reverse form, however, is also used.

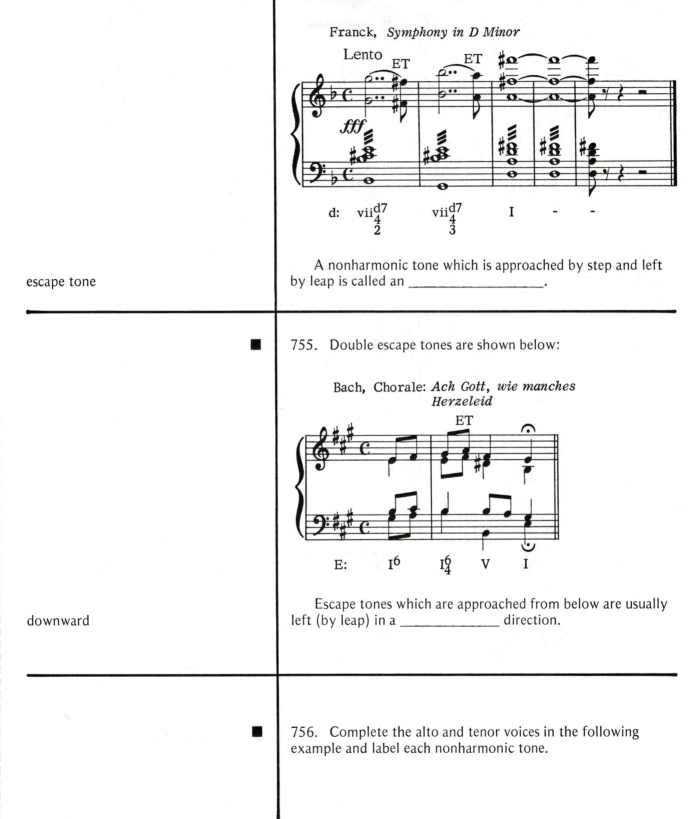

Franck, *Symphony in D Minor*

A nonharmonic tone which is approached by step and left by leap is called an _____.

escape tone

755. Double escape tones are shown below:

Bach, Chorale: *Ach Gott, wie manches Herzeleid*

Escape tones which are approached from below are usually left (by leap) in a _____ direction.

downward

756. Complete the alto and tenor voices in the following example and label each nonharmonic tone.

6 - 5 - 8 7
    3 4

---

757. Complete the alto and tenor voices and label each non-harmonic tone.

Bach, Chorale: *Nicht so traurig, nicht so sehr* (altered)

8 7   8 9 5 - 6 5 -   ♮
♮6 -   6 - 4 3 3 4

---

758. Complete the alto and tenor voices and label each non-harmonic tone.

Bach, Chorale: *Gott des Himmels und der Erden* (altered)

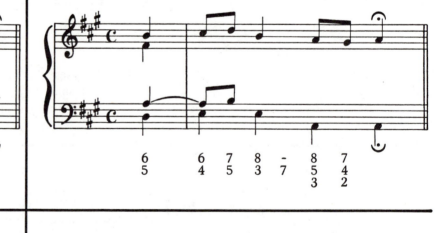

6   6 7 8 - 8 7
5   4 5 3 7 5 4
              3 2

(No response.)

759. The example in the preceding frame shows that several nonharmonic tones may occur simultaneously. Not only are there double escape tones, but also triple neighboring tones.

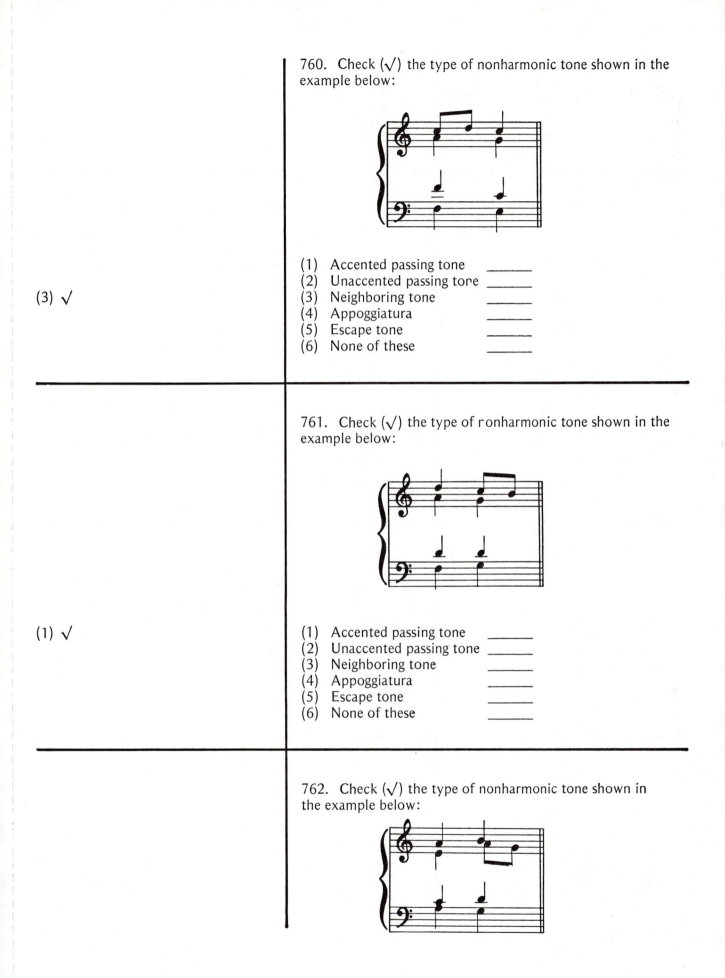

760. Check (√) the type of nonharmonic tone shown in the example below:

(1)   Accented passing tone   _____
(2)   Unaccented passing tone   _____
(3)   Neighboring tone   _____
(4)   Appoggiatura   _____
(5)   Escape tone   _____
(6)   None of these   _____

(3) √

761. Check (√) the type of nonharmonic tone shown in the example below:

(1)   Accented passing tone   _____
(2)   Unaccented passing tone   _____
(3)   Neighboring tone   _____
(4)   Appoggiatura   _____
(5)   Escape tone   _____
(6)   None of these   _____

(1) √

762. Check (√) the type of nonharmonic tone shown in the example below:

(1) Accented passing tone _____
(2) Unaccented passing tone _____
(3) Neighboring tone _____
(4) Appoggiatura _____
(5) Escape tone _____
(6) None of these _____

(4) √

---

763. Check (√) the type of nonharmonic tone shown in the example below:

(1) Accented passing tone _____
(2) Unaccented passing tone _____
(3) Neighboring tone _____
(4) Appoggiatura _____
(5) Escape tone _____
(6) None of these _____

(6) √

---

764. The nonharmonic tone in the preceding frame does not fall into any of the patterns presented thus far. It is approached by step and left by repetition. This type of nonharmonic tone is called an ANTICIPATION (symbol: A).

The name of this nonharmonic tone is an apt description of its musical function. It is a *premature* sounding of a harmonic tone to follow.

The anticipation is always left by repetition of the same note.

(No response.)

■

765. The approach to the anticipation is usually by step. Double anticipations approached from *above* by step are shown:

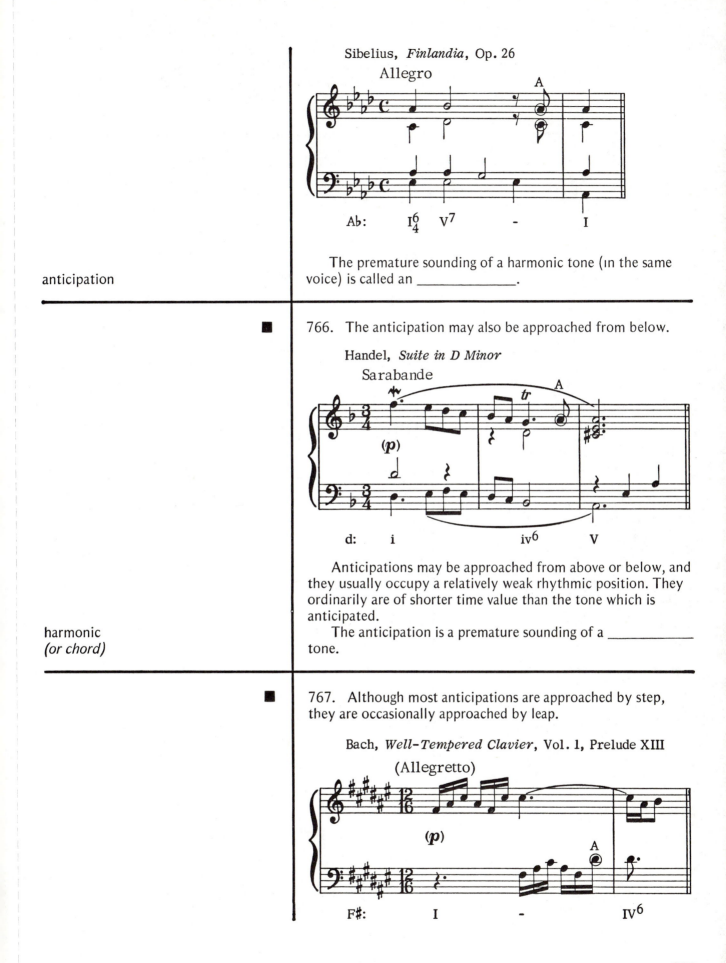

Sibelius, *Finlandia*, Op. 26

Allegro

Ab: I$^6_4$ V^7 — I

The premature sounding of a harmonic tone (in the same voice) is called an _____.

anticipation

---

766. The anticipation may also be approached from below.

Handel, *Suite in D Minor*

Sarabande

d: i iv^6 V

Anticipations may be approached from above or below, and they usually occupy a relatively weak rhythmic position. They ordinarily are of shorter time value than the tone which is anticipated.

The anticipation is a premature sounding of a _____ tone.

harmonic
(or chord)

---

767. Although most anticipations are approached by step, they are occasionally approached by leap.

Bach, *Well-Tempered Clavier*, Vol. 1, Prelude XIII

(Allegretto)

F#: I — IV^6

same

Regardless of the approach, the tone following the antici-pation is always the _____ pitch.

---

768. Most anticipations occur as part of a cadence pattern over the dominant chord. It is usually the tonic note which is anticipated.

Handel, *Sonata No. 1 for Oboe and Harpsichord*

Anticipations may occur at any point in a phrase, but the majority are found at the _____.

cadence

---

769. Check (√) the type of nonharmonic tone shown in the example below:

(4) √

(1) Passing tone _____
(2) Neighboring tone _____
(3) Appoggiatura _____
(4) Escape tone _____
(5) Anticipation _____
(6) None of these _____

770. Check (√) the type of nonharmonic tone shown in the example below:

(1) Passing tone _____
(2) Neighboring tone _____
(3) Appoggiatura _____
(4) Escape tone _____
(5) Anticipation _____
(6) None of these _____

(5) √

771. Check (√) the type of nonharmonic tone shown in the example below:

(1) Passing tone _____
(2) Neighboring tone _____
(3) Appoggiatura _____
(4) Escape tone _____
(5) Anticipation _____
(6) None of these _____

(3) √

772. A nonharmonic tone which is approached by the same tone and left by step (upward or downward) is called a SUSPENSION (symbol: S). Both of the nonharmonic tones shown below meet these conditions.

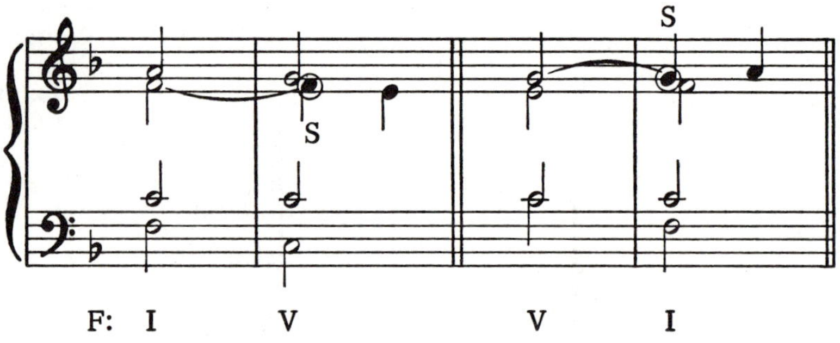

F: I   V   V   I

same

The approach to a suspension is from a tone of the _____ _____ pitch.

773. The suspension is best understood as a figure composed of three parts: preparation, suspension, and resolution. Whether the motion is upward or downward, the suspension proceeds to the resolution by _____.

step

P   S   R

6   7   6

774. Label the three parts of each suspension figure. (P= preparation, S=suspension, and R=resolution.)

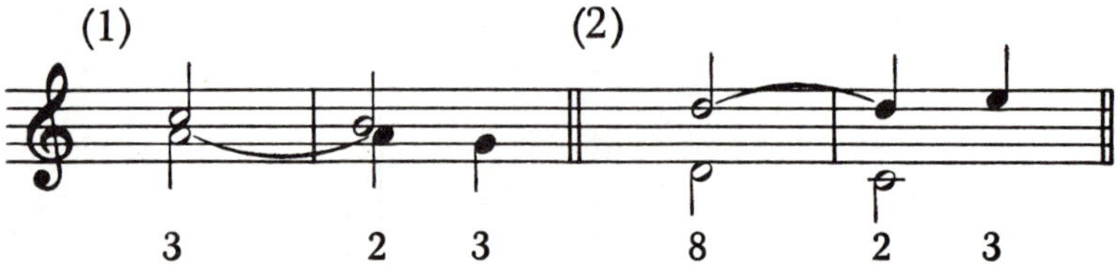

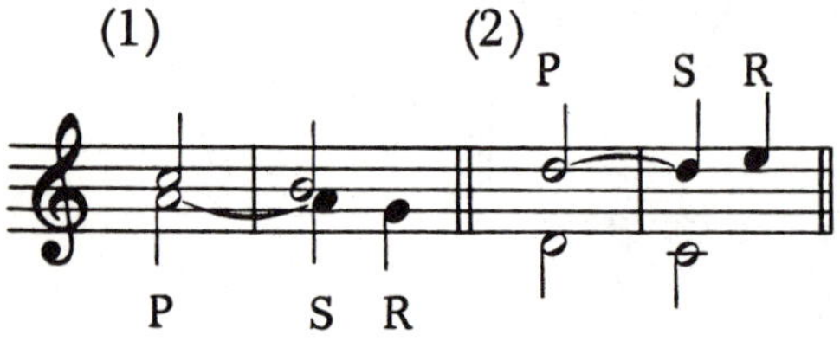

(1)   (2) P   S   R

P   S   R

(1)   (2)

3   2   3   8   2   3

775. Check (√) the correct option:

1. The suspension is prepared by a tone of the same pitch.
2. The suspension may resolve to any tone (higher or lower).

(1) √
((2) is incorrect because the
resolution must be by STEP.)

True statements:
(1) _____   (2) _____   Both _____   Neither _____

---

776. In most cases the preparation is sustained into the suspension by a tie or the note values used.

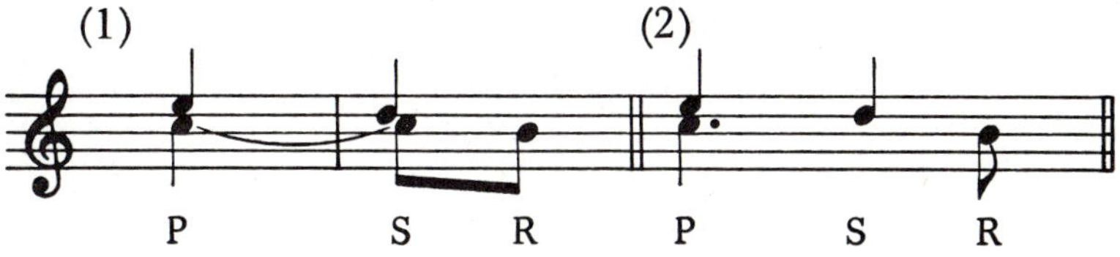

Continuous sounding (without repetition) of the preparation and suspension is considered by some to be an integral feature of the suspension. Current preference, however, is to classify nonharmonic tones according to the direction of movement preceding and following them. This approach simplifies terminology.

The preparation may be sustained into the suspension, or the suspension may be re-sounded. (True/False) _____

True.

---

777. Suspensions not tied to their preparation are shown below:

Brahms, *Ein deutsches Requiem*, Op. 45, I
Ziemlich langsam und mit Ausdruck

(No response.)	Suspensions such as these are sometimes called *appoggiaturas.* You must be prepared to accept alternate terms for several nonharmonic tones, as terminology is not standardized in this area of music theory.

■ 778. Most suspensions resolve DOWNWARD by step. Suspensions which resolve upward are relatively rare and sometimes are called RETARDATIONS.

Bach, *Well-Tempered Clavier*, Vol. 2, Prelude XII
(Moderato)

retardations

Since all of these suspensions are restruck, some theorists refer to them as appoggiaturas. The suspensions at the asterisks resolve upward. These are also known as _____.

---

779. Because suspensions are handled the same whether they resolve upward or downward, are sustained or re-sounded, it seems unnecessary to apply different terms in each case.

To summarize:

The suspension is a nonharmonic tone which is approached by the same pitch and left by step (usually downward). The preparation may be sustained (usually by tie) into the suspension, or the suspension may be re-sounded. The term *retardation* refers to a suspension which resolves upward.

(No response.)

---

780. We must now turn to a study of the rhythmic organization of the suspension figure.

Learn these principles:

1. The suspension occurs on an *accented* portion of the measure (or beat).
2. The resolution usually occurs on the weak beat (or portion of the beat) immediately following the suspension.
3. The preparation is usually equal to or double the time value of the suspension.

The metric organization of the suspension figure is in accordance with either the unit or the division of the unit, and there is notable consistency within a composition once a rate has been established.

(1) UNIT RHYTHM   **(2) DIVISION RHYTHM**

8 7 6   6 - 4 3 3 6 7 6

In (1) the rhythmic value of the preparation is double that of the suspension. Is this true in each case in (2)? _____

No.

---

781. The preparation often is twice as long as the suspension; but, as shown by the second suspension in example (2) of the preceding frame, it may also be _____ in value.

equal

---

782. Whereas the preparation is usually equal to or double the time value of the suspension, this is not a binding rule. The example below shows a suspension whose preparation is six times as long.

Bach, *Well-Tempered Clavier*, Vol. 2, Fugue I
(Vivace)

Does the rhythmic movement of the suspension above coincide with the unit or with the division? _____

The unit.

783. Below is an example of a suspension whose preparation is one-half as long.

Bach, *Well-Tempered Clavier*, Vol. 2, Fugue XI (Allegretto)

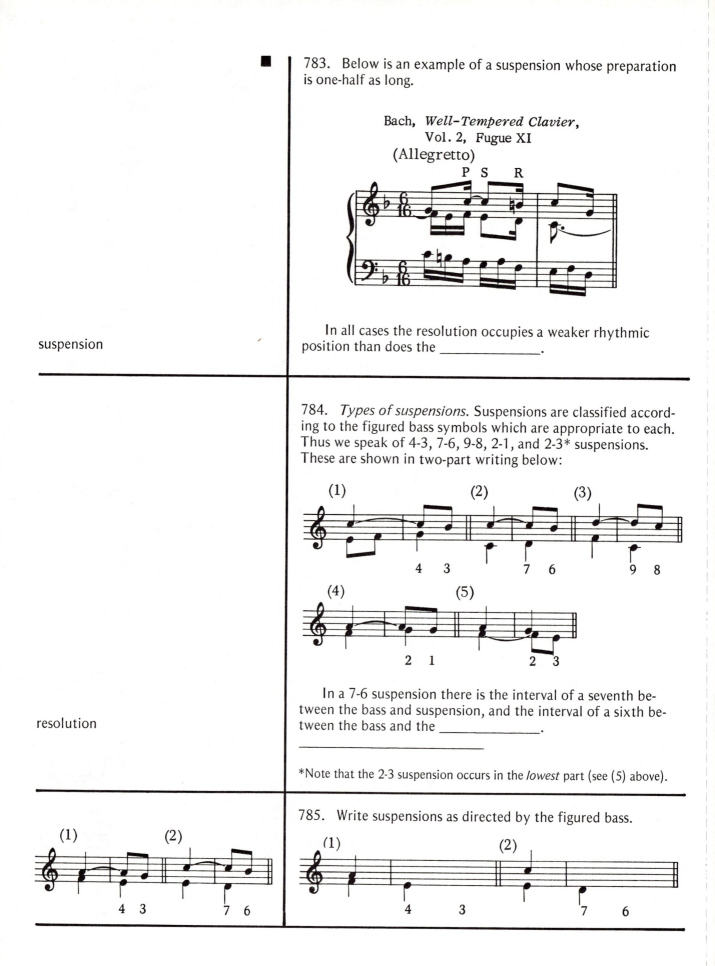

In all cases the resolution occupies a weaker rhythmic position than does the _____.

suspension

784. *Types of suspensions.* Suspensions are classified according to the figured bass symbols which are appropriate to each. Thus we speak of 4-3, 7-6, 9-8, 2-1, and 2-3* suspensions. These are shown in two-part writing below:

(1)   (2)   (3)

       4 3   7 6   9 8

(4)   (5)

       2 1   2 3

In a 7-6 suspension there is the interval of a seventh between the bass and suspension, and the interval of a sixth between the bass and the _____.

resolution

_____

*Note that the 2-3 suspension occurs in the *lowest* part (see (5) above).

(1)   (2)

       4 3   7 6

785. Write suspensions as directed by the figured bass.

(1)   (2)

       4   3   7   6

294

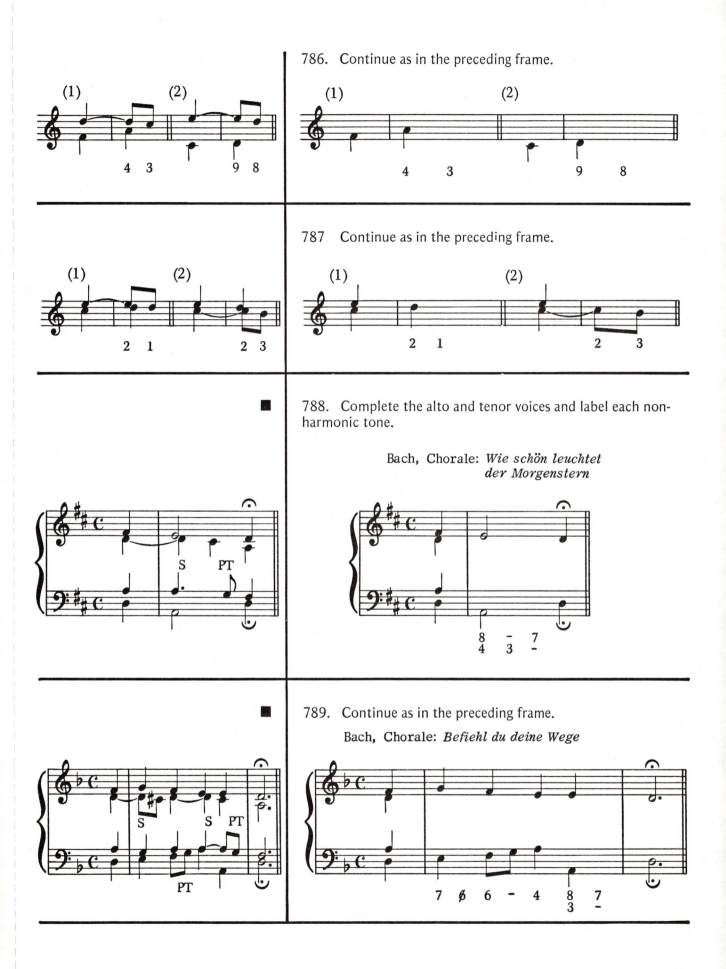

786. Continue as in the preceding frame.

787 Continue as in the preceding frame.

788. Complete the alto and tenor voices and label each nonharmonic tone.

Bach, Chorale: *Wie schön leuchtet der Morgenstern*

789. Continue as in the preceding frame.

Bach, Chorale: *Befiehl du deine Wege*

4-3.

790. The first suspension in the preceding frame is a 7-6 suspension. Of what type is the second? _____

791. Complete the alto and tenor voices and label each non-harmonic tone.

Bach, Chorale: *Es wird schier der letzte Tag herkommen*

792. Sometimes the resolution of one suspension becomes the preparation of another. This results in a "chain of suspensions."

Haydn, *Symphony No. 101* (*The Clock*)

Chains of suspensions are usually part of a harmonic and/or melodic sequence.* The brackets in the above example identify the sequence pattern.

_____

*Sequence is the repetition of a musical pattern at a different pitch level.

(No response.)

793. Complete the alto and tenor voices and label all non-harmonic tones.

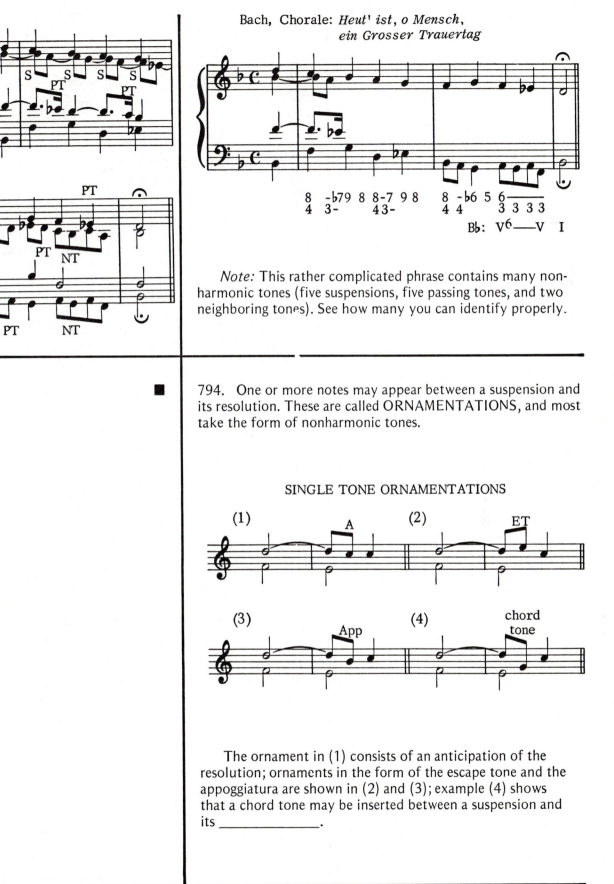

Bach, Chorale: *Heut' ist, o Mensch,*
ein Grosser Trauertag

8 -♭79 8 8-7 9 8   8 -♭6 5 6——
4 3-   43-   4 4   3 3 3 3

B♭: V⁶——V I

Note: This rather complicated phrase contains many non-harmonic tones (five suspensions, five passing tones, and two neighboring tones). See how many you can identify properly.

794. One or more notes may appear between a suspension and its resolution. These are called ORNAMENTATIONS, and most take the form of nonharmonic tones.

SINGLE TONE ORNAMENTATIONS

The ornament in (1) consists of an anticipation of the resolution; ornaments in the form of the escape tone and the appoggiatura are shown in (2) and (3); example (4) shows that a chord tone may be inserted between a suspension and its _____.

resolution

795. Ornamentations may consist of two or more tones.

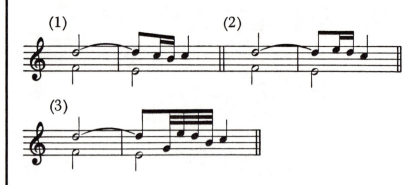

In (1) the B is a lower neighboring tone to the anticipation (C); the E in example (2) is an upper neighboring tone; although rare, florid ornamentations such as in (3) are sometimes encountered (see the following frame).

Ornamentations introduce melodic activity between a suspension and its resolution, and may in some cases delay the resolution; but no matter how it is ornamented, the resolution (in relation to the suspension) is by step. Do the majority of suspensions resolve upward or downward? _____

Downward.

---

796. Ornamentations occur frequently when suspensions are woven into a complex contrapuntal fabric. Such a case is shown below where the florid ornamentation is part of the imitative procedure as is shown by the brackets.

Bach, *Well-Tempered Clavier*, Vol. 1, Fugue XXIV

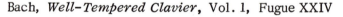
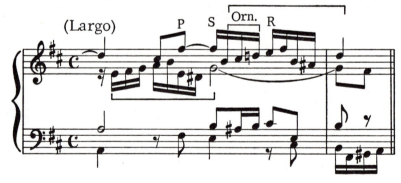

Ornamentation is used to increase melodic activity and give variety to suspension figures. Suspensions are ornamented by inserting a note (or notes) between the preparation and the suspension. (True/False) _____

False.
(Ornamentation occurs between the suspension and its resolution.)

797. Complete the alto and tenor voices and label each non-harmonic tone. In the case of suspensions indicate the preparation (P), suspension (S), and ornamentation (O).

Bach, Chorale: *Das alte Jahr vergangen ist*

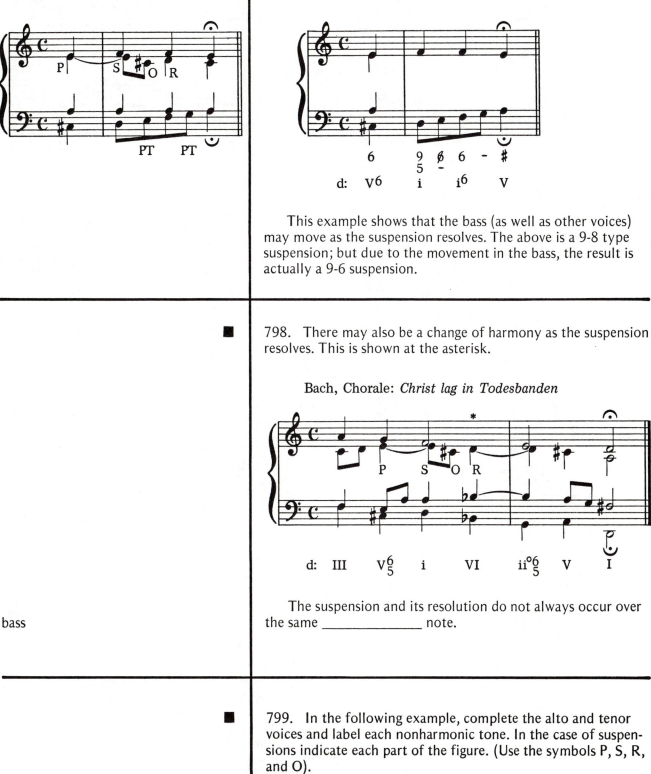

This example shows that the bass (as well as other voices) may move as the suspension resolves. The above is a 9-8 type suspension; but due to the movement in the bass, the result is actually a 9-6 suspension.

798. There may also be a change of harmony as the suspension resolves. This is shown at the asterisk.

Bach, Chorale: *Christ lag in Todesbanden*

bass

The suspension and its resolution do not always occur over the same _____ note.

799. In the following example, complete the alto and tenor voices and label each nonharmonic tone. In the case of suspensions indicate each part of the figure. (Use the symbols P, S, R, and O).

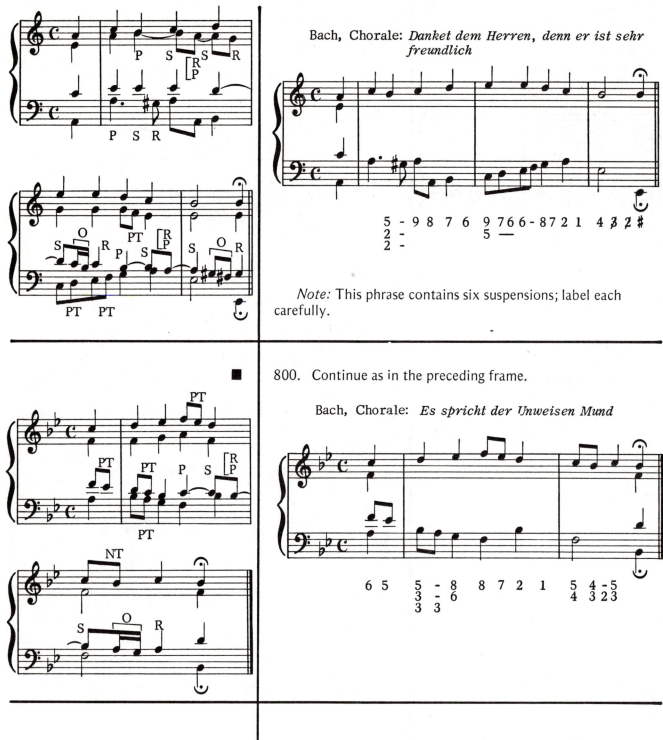

Bach, Chorale: *Danket dem Herren, denn er ist sehr freundlich*

Note: This phrase contains six suspensions; label each carefully.

800. Continue as in the preceding frame.

Bach, Chorale: *Es spricht der Unweisen Mund*

801. Suspensions cause dissonance to occur on the accented portions of the beat or measure; thus they contribute to a higher level of tension than unaccented nonharmonic tones. But since suspensions resolve by step, the result is a smooth, satisfying release from tension. The suspension is the most complex nonharmonic tone, so review carefully the principles which govern its use as stated below:

1. The suspension occurs on a *strong* beat or portion of a beat.
2. The resolution usually occurs on the *weak* beat (or portion of a beat) immediately following the suspension.
3. The preparation is the same pitch as the suspension and is usually equal to or double the time value of the suspension.
4. The suspension resolves by step either upward or downward, but the majority resolve downward. (Suspensions which resolve upward are sometimes called *retardations*.)
5. The preparation is usually sustained into the suspension (often by the use of a tie), but the suspension may also be re-sounded. (Some writers refer to such suspensions as *appoggiaturas*.)
6. Suspensions are classified according to the intervals which occur above the bass. The following types result: 4-3, 7-6, 9-8, 2-1, and 2-3.
7. Ornamentation consisting of one, two, or more tones may appear between the suspension and its resolution.

(No response.)

■ 802.   The example below shows nonharmonic tones which are called CHANGING TONES (symbol: CT):

Changing tones fall into a pattern of four notes, *the first and last of which are harmonic.* The second tone of the figure is approached by step and is left by a leap of a third in the opposite direction. The third tone (also nonharmonic) resolves by step to the final tone of the figure.

(No response.)

leap

803. In the changing tone figure the *first* nonharmonic tone is approached by step and the *second* by _____.

---

step

804. The resolution of the *second* nonharmonic tone in the changing tone figure is by _____.

---

(3).

805. Which example below shows changing tones? _____

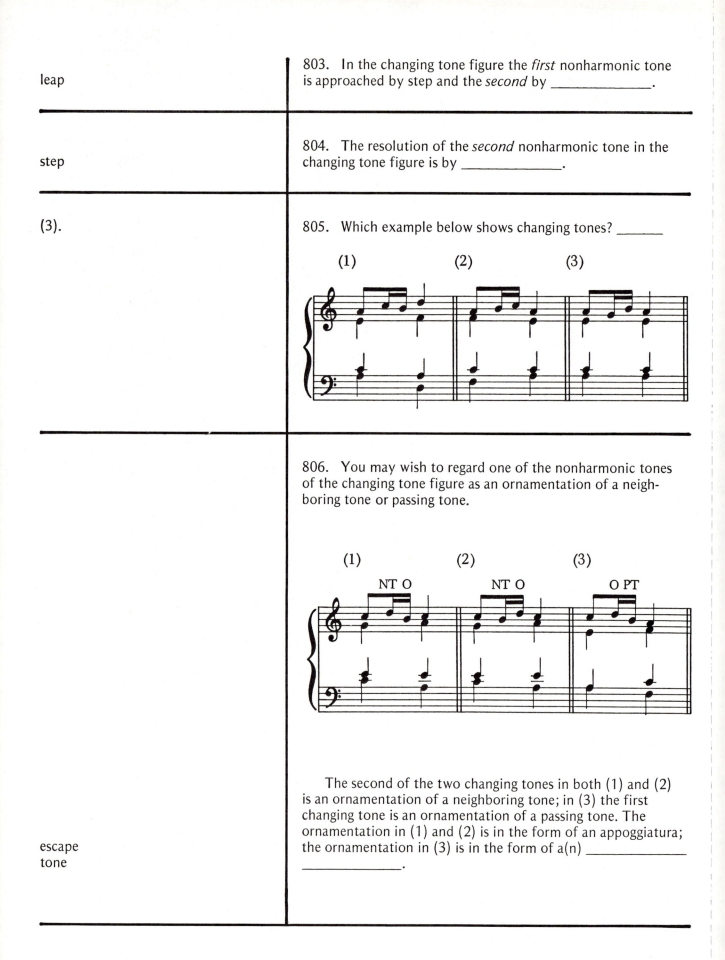

806. You may wish to regard one of the nonharmonic tones of the changing tone figure as an ornamentation of a neighboring tone or passing tone.

The second of the two changing tones in both (1) and (2) is an ornamentation of a neighboring tone; in (3) the first changing tone is an ornamentation of a passing tone. The ornamentation in (1) and (2) is in the form of an appoggiatura; the ornamentation in (3) is in the form of a(n) _____ _____.

escape
tone

■ **807.** Circle and label all of the nonharmonic tones in the example below:

Berlioz, *Symphonie Fantastique*

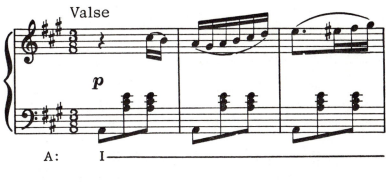

A: I ——————————————————————

—————————————————— IV

■ **808.** When a tone is retained in one part while harmonies which are foreign to it are produced by other parts the effect is called a PEDAL (symbol: Ped).*

Bach, *French Suite No. 1,* Allemande

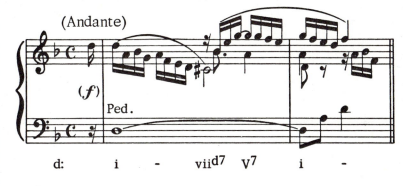

d: i   -   vii°7 V7   i   -

The tone D in the lowest part is sustained while the upper parts produce independent harmonies. What relation does the pedal (D) have to the tonality of this example? It is the

_____.

tonic

*This device is also called *pedal point,* or *organ point.*

809. The pedal device derives its name from the organist's technique of holding down a pedal while playing other harmonies above it. Pedals occur most frequently in the bass part. However, they may also occur in the upper or middle parts. The terms *inverted pedal* and *inner pedal* are sometimes used in such cases.

Bach, Chorale Prelude: *Vor deinen Thron tret' ich*

The pedal in the example above occurs in the highest voice. (True/False) _____

True

810. The pedal may be any scale degree, but it is usually either the tonic or dominant. Occasionally both the tonic and dominant are used simultaneously. The result is a double pedal.

Schumann, *Album for the Young*, Op. 68, No. 18

Nicht sehr schnell

C: I   ii   V⁷   I

The pedal device gives a static quality in contrast to the harmonies with which it is associated. It tends to (strengthen/ weaken) _____ the tonality.

strengthen

---

811.   The pedal usually begins and ends as a harmonic tone. In this way its presence in the musical texture is "legitimized." Before proceeding to another tone, a pedal must be included once again as part of the harmony.

A nonharmonic tone which is approached and left by the same tone is called a pedal. (True/False) _____

True.

---

812.   The pedal is sometimes more than just a sustained tone. The example below shows a double pedal (A-A) which is part of a melodic figure. Note that the higher pedal is embellished by lower neighbors (G-sharps) to give added rhythmic interest.

Bach, *Well-Tempered Clavier*, Vol. 1 Prelude XX

(Vivace)

a: i   vii^d7

vii^d7   i

first

Rhythmic and melodic figuration is used to counteract the tonally static quality of the pedal.

Which scale degree is stressed by the double pedal in the above example? The _____.

■ 813.   Since the pedal contributes greatly to tonal stability, accompanying harmony may be in sharp contrast to it. When double or triple pedals, or pedals with melodic significance are used, the effect is often of polyharmony or polytonality. Passages such as the one below are common in twentieth-century music.

Stravinsky, *Le Sacre du Printemps*

Più mosso (♩=60)

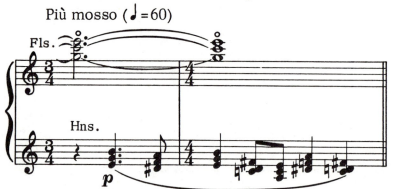

Copyright 1921 by Edition Russe de Musique.
Copyright assigned to Boosey and Hawkes, Inc. 1947.
Reprinted by permission.

The triad sounded by the flutes is an example of a (single/double/triple) _____ pedal.

triple

■ 814.   All of the nonharmonic tones presented thus far have been no more than a second away from either the preceding or succeeding tone. One nonharmonic tone, however, is both approached and left by leap. This type of nonharmonic tone is called a FREE TONE (symbol: FT).

Chopin, *Valse Brillante, Op. 34, No. 2*

Lento

leap	The free tone is the only nonharmonic tone which is approached and left by _____.
(3).	815. The free tone is the rarest of all nonharmonic tones so it will not be stressed here. In most cases it can be analyzed as part of a more complex sonority. The free tone in the preceding frame, for example, could be considered the eleventh of an expanded dominant sonority. Which example below shows a free tone? _____ 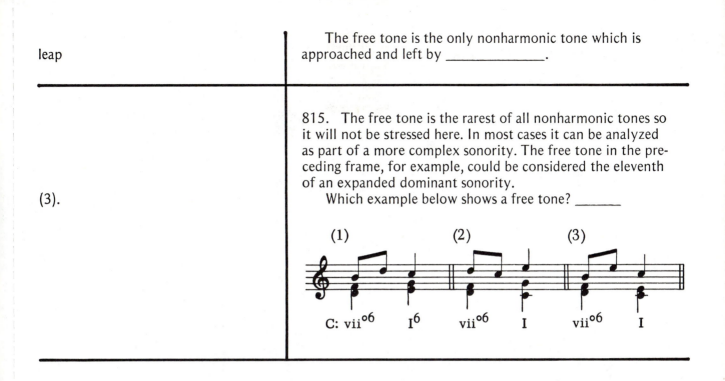

SUMMARY

Nonharmonic tones are extraneous to the harmony. Most nonharmonic tones appear in such a way that chords retain their integrity. In other words, the nonharmonic tone cannot be mistaken for a chord tone. Some tones, however, can be analyzed as being either harmonic or nonharmonic. For this reason, the chord first should be identified clearly. Thus, any tone that does not fall into the chord *as analyzed* must be a nonharmonic tone.

The rhythmic activity which nonharmonic tones give to each part contributes to the independence of the melodic lines. Greater smoothness is another result of good nonharmonic tone usage. Of still greater importance, however, is the introduction of dissonance to the musical texture. Although not all nonharmonic tones are dissonant, most are. Dissonant tones which immediately resolve into more consonant ones cause an ebb and flow of tensions, which help produce the effect of forward motion.

Nonharmonic tones provide the composer with the means of introducing dissonance into music to whatever degree desired. Nonharmonic dissonance, however, is fleeting; it is tightly controlled in accordance with established practice, and is readily tolerated by the listener.

The various types of nonharmonic tones are summarized in the chart that follows.

NONHARMONIC TONES

Name	Symbol	Example	Approach	Left	Direction of Resolution
Passing tone (unaccented or accented)	PT		By step	By step	Same as approach
Neighboring tone (unaccented or accented)	NT		By step	By step	Opposite to approach
Appoggiatura (unaccented or accented)	App		By leap (The App. may be the initial tone)	By step	Usually opposite to approach
Escape tone	ET		By step	By leap	Usually opposite to approach
Anticipation	A		Usually by step	By the same tone	Same tone

Name	Symbol	Example	Approach	Left	Direction of Resolution
Suspension	S		By the same tone (tied or reiterated)	By step	Up or down
Changing tones	CT		By step or leap	By step or leap	Usually the same tone as the approach
Pedal	Ped		By the same tone	By the same tone	Same tone
Free tone	FT		By leap	By leap	Usually opposite to approach

Mastery Frames

(1) Anticipation   (764–768)

(2) Passing tone   (718–736)

(3) Escape tone   (753–758)

(4) Appoggiatura   (745–752)

(5) Neighboring tone   (737–744)

(6) Suspension   (772–801)

9-1. Name the nonharmonic tone described in each case.

(1) Approached by step and left by repetition.
_____

(2) Approached and left by step in the same direction.
_____

(3) Approached by step and left by leap.
_____

(4) Approached by leap and left by step.
_____

(5) Approached and left by step with a change of direction.
_____

(6) Approached by the same tone and left by step.
_____

(1) Preparation
(2) Suspension
(3) Resolution

(773–776)

9-2. Identify the three parts of the suspension figure shown below.

(1)_____
(2)_____
(3)_____

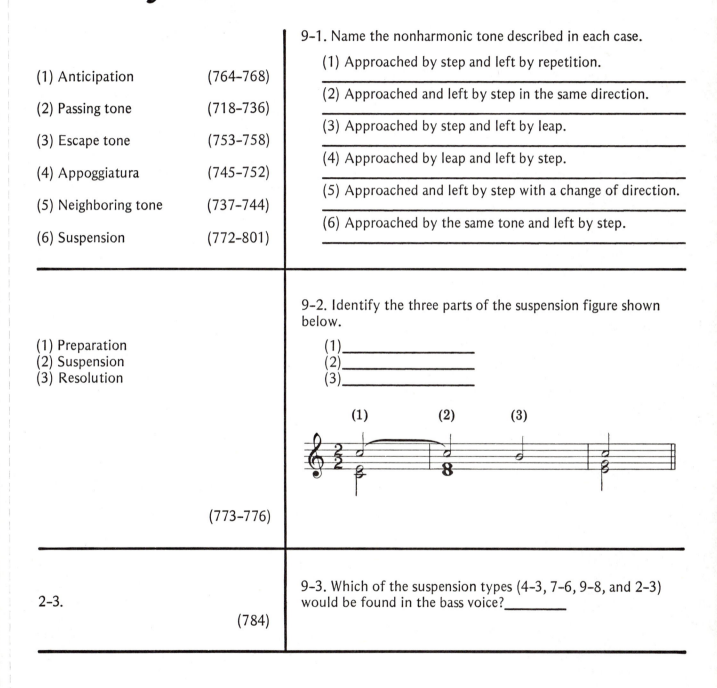

2-3.

(784)

9-3. Which of the suspension types (4–3, 7–6, 9–8, and 2–3) would be found in the bass voice?_____

		9-4. Name the nonharmonic tones at the asterisks.
(1) Changing tones	(802–807)	(1)_____
(2) Free tone	(814–815)	(2)_____
(3) Retardation	(778)	(3)_____

d: i ——————————— C: I   V⁶   G: V   I⁶   I

		9-5. A tone that is retained in one part (usually the bass) while harmonies which are foreign to it are produced by other parts is called a _____.
pedal	(803–813)	

Supplementary Assignments

ASSIGNMENT 9–1   Name_____

1. Circle all nonharmonic tones and label with abbreviations (PT, NT, etc.).

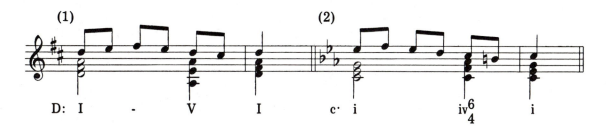

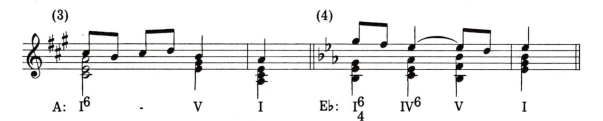

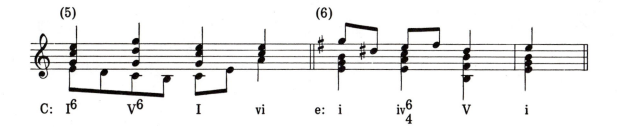

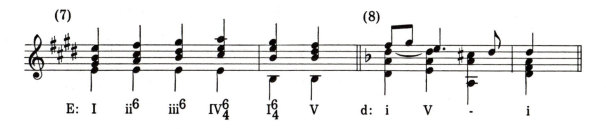

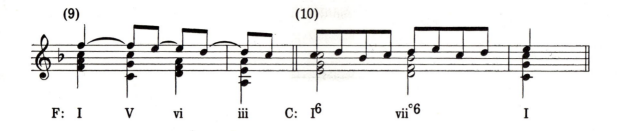

F: I   V   vi   iii   C: I⁶   vii°⁶   I

2. Write nonharmonic tones as directed. *(Notes may be added to the soprano or bass parts. Also, use accidentals when needed to produce the chord quality indicated by the Roman numerals.)*

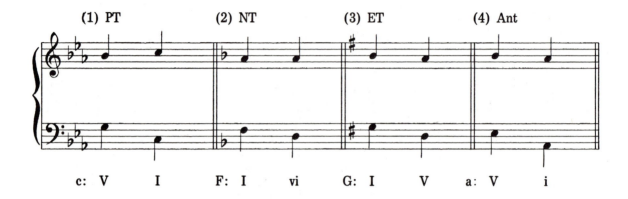

(1) PT   (2) NT   (3) ET   (4) Ant

c: V   I   F: I   vi   G: I   V   a: V   i

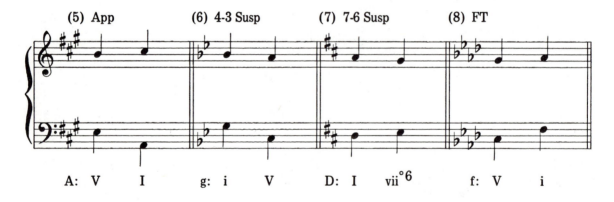

(5) App   (6) 4-3 Susp   (7) 7-6 Susp   (8) FT

A: V   I   g: i   V   D: I   vii°⁶   f: V   i

 Name________________________________

1. Rewrite the soprano part to show three different ornamentations of the suspension.

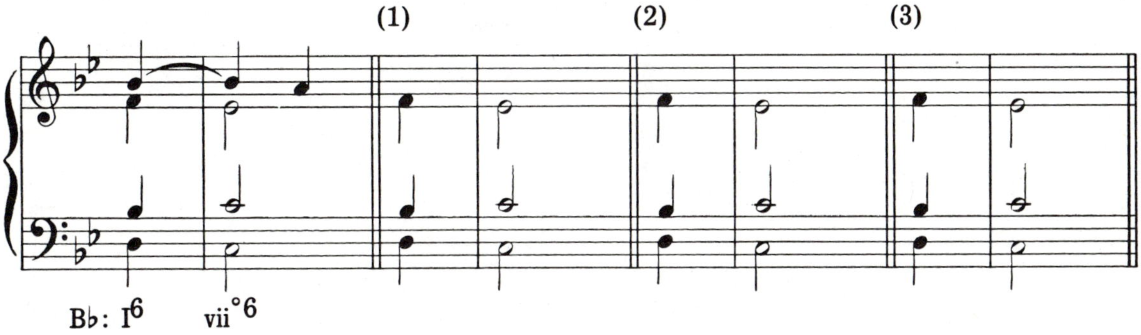
(1)
(2)
(3)
B♭: I6 vii°6

2. Write the alto and tenor voices according to the figured bass symbols. Label all nonharmonic tones and provide the Roman numeral analysis.

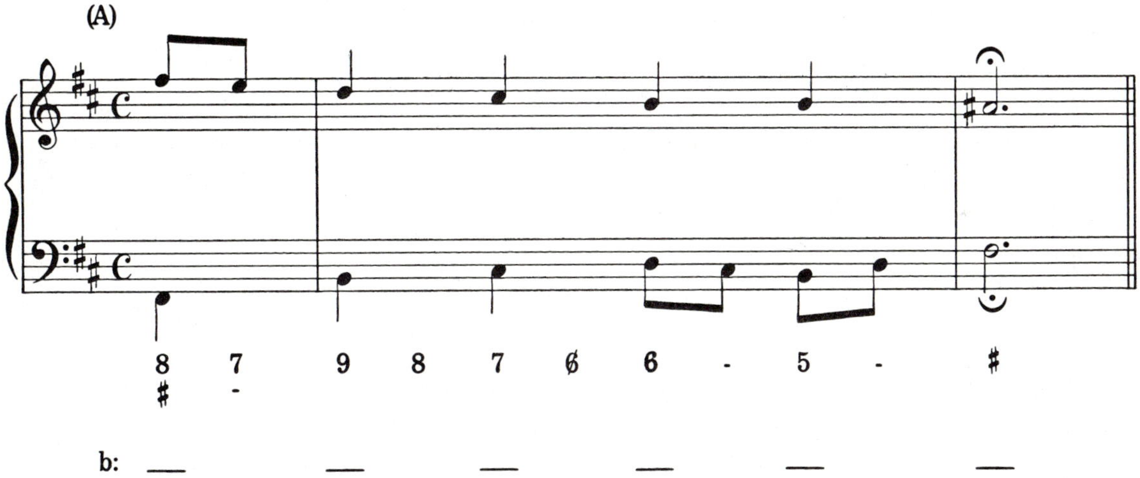
(A)
8 7 9 8 7 6 6 - 5 - ♯
♯ -
b: __ __ __ __ __ __

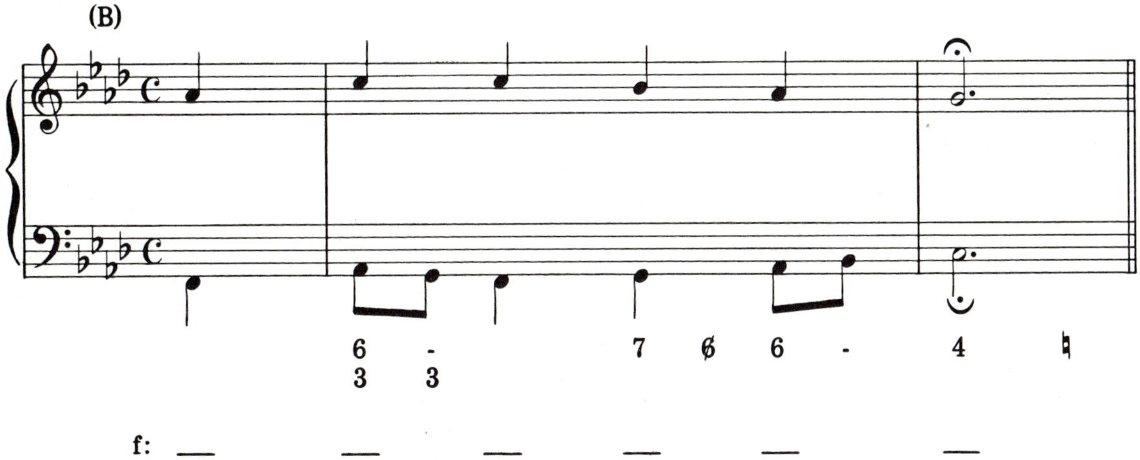
(B)
6 - 7 6 6 - 4 ♮
3 3
f: __ __ __ __ __ __

3. Supply four-voice harmonizations for the melodies below which include the nonharmonic tones indicated. Also provide the Roman numeral analysis.

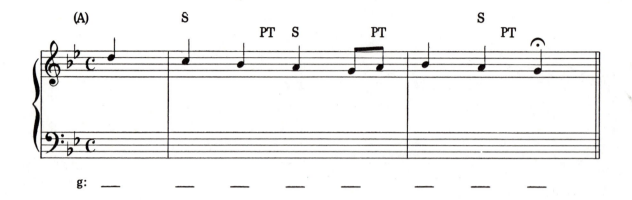

appendix a

Chord Symbols

Since early in the nineteenth century, symbols have been used to show the harmonic function of chords. These symbols consist of Roman and Arabic numerals as well as letters, accidentals, and figures such as the circle and plus sign. Chord symbols provide a vocabulary for verbal and written reference, and serve as a quick means of identifying not only a chord's relation to the tonal center, but also its quality and structure.

Musical analysis may take many forms, ranging from mere descriptive observation to complex interpretations made with reference to some explanatory system. Symbolism varies with the degree of exactness required by the analysis. The symbols used in this book are a compromise between simplicity and exactness; they may easily be adapted to serve the purpose of a particular type of analysis. Inversions, for example, generally are shown as part of the chord symbol; but, if the purpose of analysis is served merely by showing how chords function in a progression, symbols may be simplified by representing chords in root position only. Chord symbols are not precise enough to permit music to be reconstructed from them alone. They do, however, indicate the specific quality of diatonic triads and seventh chords (either directly or by inference), and usually show inversions. Thus the basic harmonic structure may readily be traced. In the case of certain altered chords, undue complexity is avoided at the expense of precision. To be completely consistent, logical, and devoid of ambiguity, chord symbols would be so complex that many no longer would serve as convenient references to harmonic entities.

As in many areas of music theory, there is a lack of standardization regarding chord symbols. Whenever possible, the most widely accepted practices have been observed. The following information summarizes the symbols used in this book.

DIATONIC TRIADS

Roman numerals are used to identify triads and are directly related to scale degrees. Further, the quality of triads is shown by the form of the symbols (capital letters = major, small letters = minor, small letters with circle = diminished, and capital letters with plus sign = augmented).

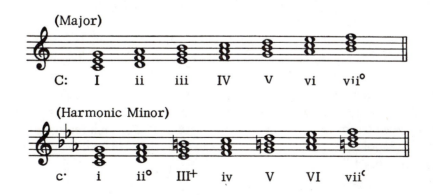

First and second inversions of triads are shown by adding the figured bass symbols 6 or $^6_4$ to the Roman numerals.

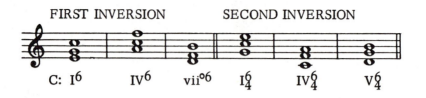

FIRST INVERSION   SECOND INVERSION

C: I⁶   IV⁶   vii°⁶   I$^6_4$ IV$^6_4$ V$^6_4$

Notice that the figures are placed at the upper right-hand corner of the Roman numerals. When more than one number is involved, the largest appears at the top and the remainder are placed in descending order.

SYMBOLS FOR CHORDS NOT PRESENTED IN THIS BOOK

Some of the examples in this book include chords which are not treated fully until Part II. In no case does comprehension of the material depend upon an understanding of these chords.

DIATONIC SEVENTH CHORDS

The figure 7 added to the Roman numeral indicates a seventh chord in root position. In a major key the form of the Roman numeral is the same as for the corresponding triad.

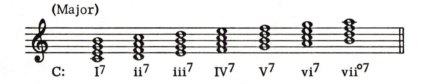

(Major)

C: I⁷   ii⁷   iii⁷   IV⁷   V⁷   vi⁷   vii°⁷

The symbols used in harmonic minor are shown below:

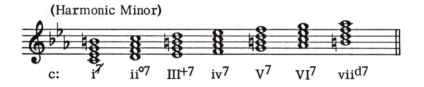

(Harmonic Minor)

c: i⁷   ii°⁷   III⁺⁷   iv⁷   V⁷   VI⁷   vii^d7

Notice that for the diminished seventh chord (vii^d7) the circle which denotes the diminished triad is replaced by a small d. All diminished seventh chords are shown in this way regardless of their use. This is to simplify nomenclature when the diminished seventh chord is used as an altered chord. Although not a traditional figured bass symbol, the small d is appropriate as it reflects the name commonly given to this chord: "diminished seventh chord."

Inversions of seventh chords are shown by figured bass symbols.

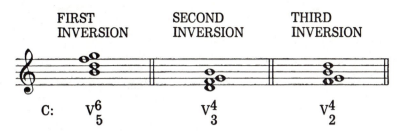

$$V_5^6 \qquad V_3^4 \qquad V_2^4$$

FIRST INVERSION — SECOND INVERSION — THIRD INVERSION

C:

THE DOMINANT NINTH CHORD

The symbol V^9 is used to represent a dominant chord consisting of four superimposed thirds.

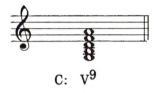

C: V^9

THE MEDIANT MAJOR TRIAD IN MINOR KEYS

The mediant triad generated by the descending form of the melodic minor scale is a major triad. The chord symbol is an upper-case Roman numeral. For example:

c: III

appendix b

Piano Styles

Creative writing is possibly the best way to demonstrate command of the concepts and materials presented in this text. In original compositions students may apply the knowledge gained in terms of their own creativity. It is desirable that a variety of media (piano, voice, small ensembles, etc.) be used, but because of its availability, the piano is the most practical. The brief exposition of piano styles presented here provides a guide for those who have had little experience with keyboard techniques.* Effective writing is possible—even by non-pianists—if typical styles are utilized. The material which follows—used in conjunction with the suggested supplementary assignments—facilitates the creative work which helps develop a heightened sensitivity to the rhetoric of harmonic music.

There are three textures into which all music falls: *monophonic* (a single melodic line) *homophonic* (a melody with accompaniment); and *polyphonic* (several voices approximately equal in melodic interest). Of these, homophonic texture is the most practical for music in which the harmonic element is stressed. Thus we shall concentrate on various homophonic piano styles.

I. FIGURATED BLOCK CHORDS. In the example below, the melody is provided a simple accompaniment in block chords.

Mozart: *Sonata*, K 545 (altered)

---

*The information included in Appendix B is provided to serve both Parts I and II of this course. Some of the examples contain harmonic materials presented in Part II.

Block chords are easy to play because the left hand does not move over the keyboard. Care should be taken that principles of doubling and voice leading are applied. Active tones (the leading tone and chord sevenths) should not be doubled, and should be resolved properly. Notice in measure two, for example, that the leading tone (B) is omitted from the left hand, and also that the chord seventh (F) is resolved down by step to E.

Figuration patterns give rhythmic interest to block chords.

Mozart: *Sonata,* K 545

The way that the three notes of the block chords are transcribed into the figuration pattern is clear.

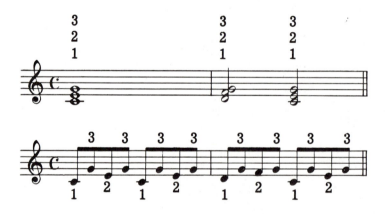

This technique of providing rhythmic animation for block chords is called "Alberti bass," after the Venetian composer Domenico Alberti (1710-1740?), who used such patterns extensively, perhaps even to excess.

Styles 3-12 show some of the many figurations which may be devised. The meter, as well as the degree of animation desired, affects the choice of pattern.

II. JUMP BASS (AFTER-BEAT PATTERNS).

In these styles the left hand jumps from bass notes to block chords. The best sonority results when the block chords are set in the vicinity of middle C.

Schubert: *Waltz in A minor*

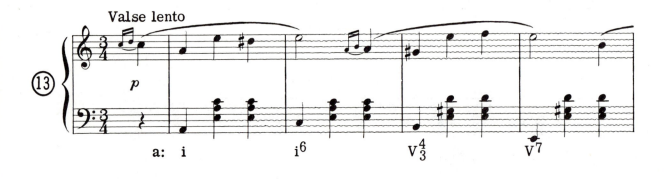

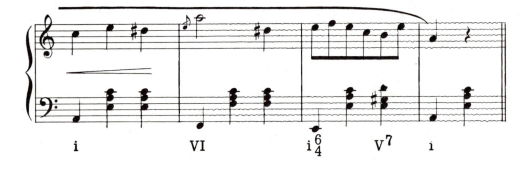

As in figurated block chords, care must be taken that principles of part writing are observed. In the above example there are four voices in the left hand. Notice how each of these traces a smooth line, and also the way active tones resolve properly.

Of course the relation of the accompanying voices to the melody must also be considered. *Undesirable doubling and incorrect parallel motion must be avoided.*

Jump bass patterns are exploited mostly in waltzes and mazurkas, but are also useful in duple or quadruple meter for march-like effects. Some typical patterns are shown in styles 14-18.

III. ARPEGGIATION. The succsssive sounding of chord tones over a more or less extended range is called arpeggiation. Compared with previously presented styles, arpeggiation generally produces more sonorous effects. This is due to the vibration of more strings. Rhythmic animation and richer texture also result from arpeggiation.

There is scarcely any limit to the arpeggiation patterns which can be devised. The examples which follow demonstrate a few typical patterns; these may suggest others which satisfy specific expressive needs as they arise.

In style 19, arpeggiation is used exclusively throughout the entire composition. The effect is of figurated harmonies.

Schumann: *Album für die Jugend* ("Kleine Studie")

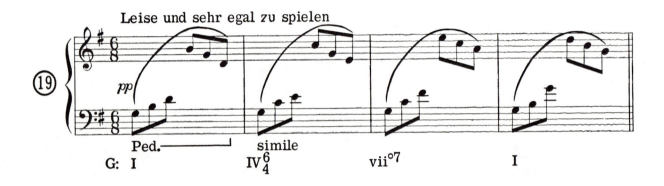

The example below shows fairly simple left hand arpeggiation, which supports a melody in the right hand.

Chopin: *Nocturne,* Posthumous

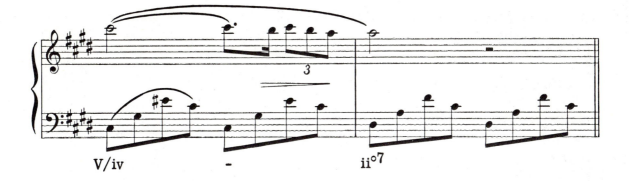

V/iv   -   ii°7

The arpeggiation in the next example is more extended in range.

Leybach: *Nocturne,* Op. 52

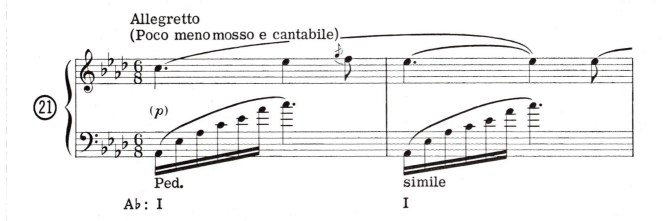

Allegretto
(Poco meno mosso e cantabile)

(p)

Ped.   simile

A♭: I   I

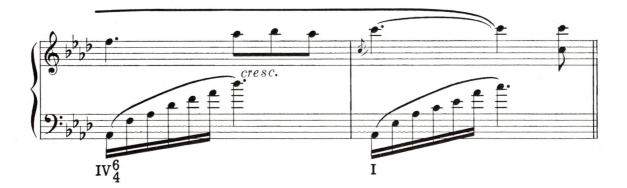

cresc.

IV$^6_4$ I

Style 22 has an arpeggiation pattern in the left hand while the right hand not only plays the melody, but also fills in the harmony for additional sonority.

Brahms· *Intermezzo*, Op. 119, No. 2

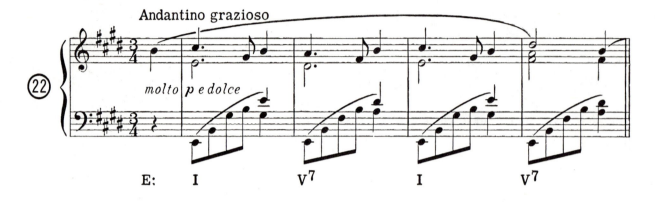

Arpeggiation takes a different form in the next example. The treble and bass move mostly in parallel tenths, while the middle voice completes the harmony, and fills in the eighth note rhythm.

Mendelssohn, *Lieder ohne Worte*, Op. 85, No. 2

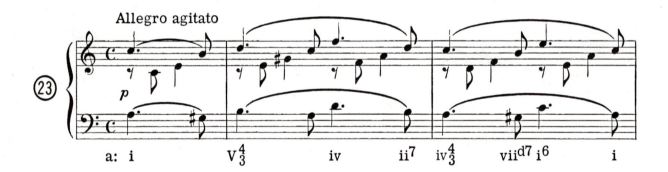

In style 24 the arpeggiation is in the tenor register divided between the right and left hands.

Schumann: *Kinderscenen* ("Von Fremden Ländern und Menschen")

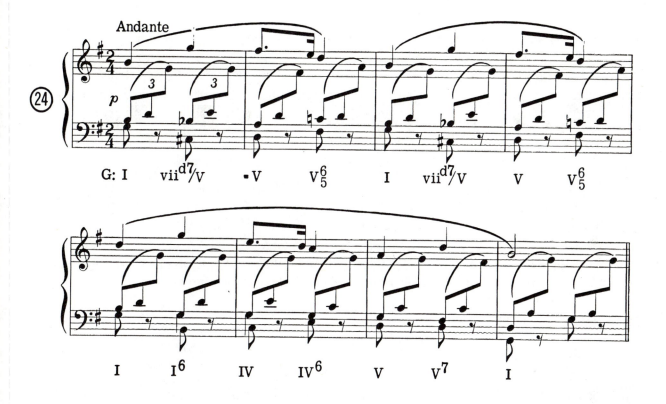

In the next example the arpeggiation is in descending motion, divided between the two hands.

Burgmüller: *Lullaby*

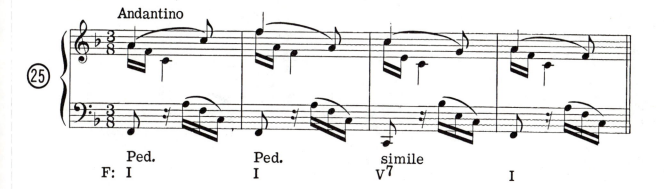

IV. HYMN STYLE. For serious, dignified, or stately effects, melodies may be accompanied in a fashion similar to vocal settings of hymns. In this style chords change for almost every melody note. The resulting rapid harmonic rhythm makes figuration impractical. The number of voices may be consistent, or fluctuate to produce the desired sonorities.

Close style: The example below shows octave doubling of the bass, with the remaining voices in the right hand.

Schumann: *Album für die Jugend* ("Nordisches Lied"), Op. 26

Open style: In this case the voices are divided equally between the two hands, and open structure predominates Only once is the four-part texture enriched by the addition of a fifth tone.

Chopin: *Mazurka*, Op. 68, No. 3

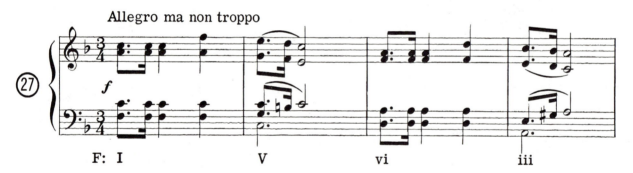

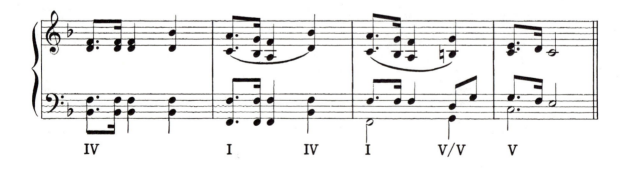

V. RIGHT-HAND PATTERNS.
Of the several typical ways to treat the right hand, the single line melody is the simplest. This style has been amply demonstrated in previous examples (see styles 2, 13, 20, and 21). A few others are shown in the remaining examples.

Added alto in thirds and sixths:

Mozart: *Sonata,* K 333

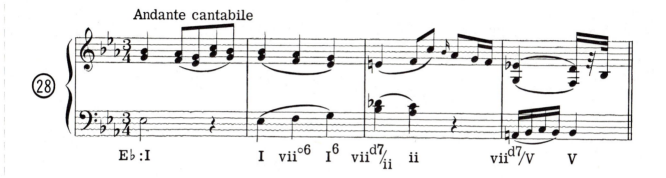

Filled in chords:

Schubert: *Waltz in B-flat Major*

Melody in octaves: Increased sonority and prominence for the melodic line can be supplied by octave doubling.

Beethoven: *Sonata,* Op. 10, No. 1

Melody with after beats: This technique is used when fuller sonorities are desired. Such patterns also produce a more intricate rhythmic texture.

Mendelssohn: *Lieder ohne Worte,* Op. 102, No. 1

Polyphonic texture has not been touched on here, but even casual use of imitation between melodic and accompaniment elements is effective. In addition, placement of the melody in the tenor or bass registers with the accompaniment above, provides variety. Above all, avoid using only a limited range. The compass of the piano is more than seven octaves, and effective writing requires that the hands range rather widely over the keyboard. In this way the color contrasts of the various registers are exploited.

appendix c

Glossary of Terms

Accessory tone *See* Nonharmonic tone.
Accidental A sign that affects the pitch of a note.
Acoustics The science that deals with sound.
Active tone A tone that has a strong tendency to resolve in a specific direction, *e.g.*, the leading tone.
Alto A low female voice The next-to-the-highest voice of the four-part chorus.
Amen cadence *See* Plagal cadence.
Anticipation A nonharmonic tone that is approached by step and left by repetition.
Appoggiatura A nonharmonic tone that is approached by leap and left by step, usually with a change of direction.
Arpeggiation Sounding the tones of a chord in succession, rather than simultaneously.
Arpeggio six-four chord A second inversion chord formed by arpeggiated movement in the lowest voice.
Augmented fourth An interval that is a half step larger than a perfect fourth.
Augmented second An interval that is a half step larger than a major second.
Augmented triad A chord consisting of two major thirds.
Authentic cadence A closing harmonic progression consisting of the dominant chord (sometimes the leading tone) followed by the tonic chord.
Auxilliary six-four chord *See* Pedal six-four chord.
Auxilliary tone *See* Neighboring tone.

Baroque era The musical period from 1600 to 1750 characterized by elaborate ornamentation, strict forms, and the establishment of functional harmonic tonality.
Bass A low male voice. The lowest voice of the four-part chorus.
Bass staff The staff modified by the bass clef sign, which designates F below middle C as occurring on the fourth line.
Borrowed chord A diatonic chord in one mode (major or minor), which appears as an altered chord in the opposite parallel mode. Most borrowed chords appear in major, borrowed from the parallel minor key.

Bytone *See* Nonharmonic tone.

Cadence A melodic-harmonic formula that brings a phrase to a more or less definite close.
Cadential six-four chord A second inversion chord that is part of a cadence formula—most frequently, the tonic chord in second inversion followed by the dominant.
Chain of suspensions Several suspensions in succession in which the resolution of one suspension becomes the preparation for the following.
Changing tone *See* Neighboring tone.
Changing tones The middle two notes of a four-note figure, of which the first and fourth are chord tones, and the second and third are nonharmonic tones.
Chord A combination of several tones sounded simultaneously.
Chord function Chords function differently depending upon the relation of their root to the tonal center. The tonic chord, for example, is relatively static, whereas the dominant chord is active.
Chord of repose The tonic triad.
Chord quality Chords differ in quality according to their intervallic structure. Diatonic triads, for example, may be major, minor, diminished, or augmented.
Chord spacing The placement of the various chord members in part writing. *See* Close structure; Open structure.
Chord tone One of the tones that constitute a chord.
Classical era The musical period from about 1750 to 1800, characterized by simplicity and order.
Close structure The spacing of voices so that no vacant chord members occur between the three upper voices.
Common tone A tone that occurs in two or more chords.
Consecutive perfect intervals Perfect unisons, fourths, fifths, or octaves that occur in succession between the same two voices.
Contrary motion Two voices that move in opposite directions.

Crossed voices   The abnormal vertical distribution of voices in a chord, *e.g.*, the alto placed above the soprano.

Damper pedal   The right-hand pedal of the piano, which, when depressed, allows the strings to continue vibrating.

Deceptive cadence   A nonfinal cadence consisting of the dominant chord followed by the submediant chord.

Diatonic   Literally "by step"—having to do with scale tones; tonal material derived from a scale.

Diatonic triad   A triad consisting of tones included in a scale.

Diminished triad   A chord consisting of two diminished thirds.

Dissonance   Auditory tension produced by two or more tones when sounding intervals of the major or minor second, major or minor seventh, or tritone.

Dominant   The fifth degree of the scale, or the chord built thereupon.

Double flat   A sign that causes a basic note to be lowered in pitch a whole step.

Double pedal   Two tones (usually tonic and dominant) used simultaneously as a pedal.

Double sharp   A sign that causes a basic note to be raised in pitch a whole step.

Doubled tones   The same chord member sung by two or more voices.

Doubling   The assignment of the same chord member to two or more voices. This is necessary when a triad is set for four or more voices.

Downward stem   A stem that extends downward from a notehead. When the grand staff is used for the four-voice chorus, alto and bass stems go downward.

Dyad   A two-note chord.

Dynamics   The aspect of music concerning varying degrees of loudness and softness.

Echappée   *See* Escape tone.

Elements of music   The basic properties of music, which include rhythm, melody, timbre, texture, and harmony.

Embellishing harmony   The chords that are not vital to the stability of the phrase, in contrast to structural harmony.

Embellishing six-four chord   *See* Pedal six-four chord.

Escape tone   A nonharmonic tone that is approached by step and left by leap, usually with a change of direction.

Essential chord   A chord that serves a structural function; often one of the three primary triads (tonic, subdominant, or dominant).

Figured bass   A shorthand notation widely used during the baroque era. *See* Figured bass symbols.

Figured bass symbols   Various signs, including numerals and accidentals, placed beneath the bass to indicate chords and melodic motion in the upper voices. Figured bass symbols basically show the intervals that occur above the lowest voice.

Final cadences   The cadences that produce a sufficient sense of closure to conclude principal sections of the music. The two final cadences are the authentic and plagal.

First inversion   A chord that employs the third in the lowest voice.

Flat   A sign that causes a basic note to be lowered in pitch a half step.

Foreign tone   *See* Nonharmonic tone.

Four-part texture   Music set in four parts. *See* Four-voice chorus.

Four-voice chorus   A chorus consisting of soprano, alto, tenor, and bass.

Free tone   A nonharmonic tone that is approached and left by leap.

Grand staff   Two staves joined together, usually with the treble clef sign on the upper and the bass clef sign on the lower.

Gregorian chant   The monodic liturgical music of the Roman Catholic Church.

Half cadence   A nonfinal cadence, usually terminating with the dominant chord.

Half step   The smallest interval of the tempered scale, equivalent to a minor second.

Harmonic action   The effect of chords moving from one to another.

Harmonic analysis   The process of examining critically the harmonic element of music. The identification of tonalities and the labeling of chords are basic types of harmonic analysis.

Harmonic cadence   Closure produced by harmonic action. The strong dominant-tonic progression, for example, contributes to the positive effect of the authentic cadence irrespective of the rhythmic and melodic elements.

Harmonic function   The movement of chords to one another defines tonal space and delineates form. Harmonic function basically is either "structural" or "embellishing."

Harmonic interval The interval produced by two tones sounding simultaneously.

Harmonic minor scale A scale that consists of the following half- and whole-step pattern: W H W W H W+H H.

Harmonic phrase A succession of chords that constitutes a phrase.

Harmonic progression The movement from one chord to another.

Harmonic rhythm The rhythm defined by chord changes.

Harmonic tonality The definition of a tonal center by means of chords relating in various ways to the tonic.

Harmonic tone A tone that is included as part of a chord.

Harmonization The technique of selecting chords to accompany a melody.

Harmony The element of music concerning chords and their relation to one another.

Horizontal aspect of harmony Successions of chords.

Imperfect cadence An authentic or plagal cadence that lacks a complete sense of finality. *See* perfect cadence.

Inner pedal An alternate term for a pedal that occurs in an inner voice. *See* Pedal.

Interval The difference in pitch between two tones.

Inversion 1) Altering an interval so that the higher note becomes the lower. This is usually done by moving the upper note an octave lower, or vice versa. 2) Placing a chord member other than the root in the bass.

Inverted pedal An alternate term for a pedal that occurs in an upper voice. *See* Pedal.

Irregular doubling The exigencies of part writing sometimes make it necessary to employ an alternate doubling to avoid a more serious weakness.

Iteration Emphasis by repetition, immediate or delayed.

Key The tonality of a composition or segment thereof.

Key center The tonal center; the first degree of the scale upon which the music is based.

Key signature A group of sharps or flats that produce the desired half- and whole-step pattern of a given scale.

Keynote *See* tonal center.

Leading tone The seventh scale degree, a half step below the tonic.

Major scale A scale that consists of the following half- and whole-step pattern: W W H W W W H.

Major triad A chord consisting of a major third and a superimposed minor third.

Mediant The third scale degree, or the chord built thereupon.

Melodic contour The shape defined by the rising and falling pitches of a melody.

Melodic line *See* Melodic contour.

Melodic phrase A phrase etched by the melodic contour.

Melody A musical line produced by a series of single tones.

Minor triad A chord consisting of a minor third and a superimposed major third.

Natural minor scale A minor scale that uses the same tones as its relative major scale. It consists of the following half- and whole-step pattern W H W W H W W.

Neighboring tone A nonharmonic tone that is approached and left by step with a change of direction. Neighboring tones usually occur on an unaccented portion of the beat and may be either a step above or below the harmonic tone.

Nonchord tone *See* Nonharmonic tone.

Nonfinal cadences Cadences that are incapable of bringing a composition to a close. The two nonfinal cadences are the half and the deceptive.

Nonharmonic tone A tone that is extraneous to the harmony.

Notehead The part of a note that indicates the pitch.

Oblique motion Movement of two voices, one of which remains stationary while the other moves either upward or downward.

Octave An interval in which the frequency of the higher note is double that of the lower.

Open structure The spacing of voices so that there is a vacant chord member between the tenor and alto, and between the alto and soprano.

Opening progression Harmonic movement away from the tonic at the beginning of the phrase.

Organ point *See* Pedal.

Ornamentation One or more notes appearing between a suspension and its resolution.

Parallel fifths Movement in fifths between the same two voices. If both fifths are perfect, the individuality of the voices is diminished. Such movement is generally avoided.

Parallel motion Two or more voices moving by the same intervals in the same direction.

Part writing The technique of writing chords and leading voices from one to another.

Passing six-four chord A second-inversion chord that usually occurs between a triad in first inversion and the same triad in root position. Typical is the following: tonic in first inversion—dominant in second inversion—tonic in root position.

Passing tone A nonharmonic tone that is approached and left by step in the same direction. It may occur either ascending or descending, and may be either accented or unaccented.

Pedal A nonharmonic tone consisting of a sustained tone (usually in the bass), against which other voices produce harmonies that are foreign to it.

Pedal point *See* Pedal.

Pedal six-four chord A second-inversion chord that occurs over the same (or repeated) bass note, *e.g.*, the subdominant six-four preceded and followed by the tonic in root position.

Perfect cadence An authentic or plagal cadence that meets the following conditions:
1. Both the final and penultimate chords must be in root position.
2. The final (tonic) chord must have the keynote in the highest voice.

Phrase A basic unit in the formal organization of music, usually four measures in length, used especially during the classical period.

Phrase structure The underlying harmonies stripped of embellishing chords. Most phrases fall into one of three types:
1. A single chord followed by a cadence
2. Harmonic embellishment of a single chord followed by a cadence
3. A cadence formula (or basic harmonic progression) spread over the entire phrase.

Phrygian cadence In traditional harmony, a type of half cadence. The subdominant in first inversion moving to the dominant (in a minor key) is a typical example.

Picardy third The raised third in the tonic chord of a minor key. This effect is usually reserved for the final chord, to provide a more emphatic conclusion.

Pitch The "highness" or "lowness" of sound.

Plagal cadence A closing harmonic progression consisting of the subdominant chord followed by the tonic chord.

Polyharmony Two or more chords that occur simultaneously.

Polytonality The simultaneous occurrence of two or more tonalities.

Preparation The initial note of the suspension figure. *See* Suspension.

Primary triads The tonic, subdominant, and dominant triads.

Progression 1) The movement from one chord to another. 2) More specifically, harmonic movement that creates a sense of forward motion. Root movements down in fifths, up in seconds, and down in thirds generally produce strong effects. *See also* Retrogression.

Range The normal compass of a given voice or instrument.

Resolution 1) The movement from one chord to another; the term often denotes movement from an active chord to a less active one. 2) The final note of the suspension figure. *See also* Suspension.

Retardation A suspension that resolves upward. *See also* Suspension.

Retrogression A relatively weak harmonic movement. *See also* Progression.

Returning note *See* Neighboring tone.

Rhythm The temporal aspect of music. Involved is the division of time into beats, accent patterns of meter, and rhythmic figures.

Roman numerals Symbols used to identify chords built on the various degrees of the scale.

Romantic era The musical period from about 1800 to 1900 characterized by emphasis on emotional qualities, freedom of form, increased use of chromaticism, and expanded tonality.

Root The note on which a chord is built.

Root movement The intervallic relationship of the root of a chord to the root of an adjoining chord.

Root position The arrangement of a chord so that the root is in the lowest voice.

Scale A stepwise arrangement (ascending or descending) of the tones contained in an octave.

Scale degrees The tones contained in a scale.

Second inversion The arrangement of a triad so that the fifth is in the lowest voice.

Secondary triads Triads that are built on the second, third, sixth, and seventh scale degrees.

Sequence The repetition of a musical pattern (harmonic or melodic) at a different pitch level.

Sharp A sign that causes a basic note to be raised a half step.

Similar motion Two voices that move in the same direction, but not by the same interval.

Six-four chord *See* Second inversion.

Slash (/) A sign that is used in connection with figured bass symbols. When drawn through a number, the note presented by the number is raised a half step.

Sonority The aural effect of a tone or group of tones.

Soprano A high female voice. The highest voice of the four-voice chorus.

Spacing *See* Chord spacing.

Staff The five parallel horizontal lines and intervening spaces upon which musical symbols are placed.

Stationary six-four chord *See* Pedal six-four chord.

Stem The vertical line attached to a notehead.

Stepwise motion Melodic movement to adjacent scale degrees.

Strong beat A beat that has relatively strong metric stress, *e.g.*, the first beat of the measure.

Structural harmony Harmony that appears at strategic formal points and serves to establish the tonal organization.

Structural points Locations that have special formal significance, *e.g.*, the beginning and end of the phrase.

Structure of tonality The tonal pattern created by the three principal triads: the tonic, the dominant (a perfect fifth above), and the subdominant (a perfect fifth below).

Subdominant The fourth scale degree, or the chord built thereupon

Submediant The sixth degree of the scale, or the chord built thereupon.

Subtonic The tone a whole step below the tonic, or the chord built thereupon.

Supertonic The second scale degree, or the chord built thereupon.

Suspension A nonharmonic tone that is approached by the same note (usually tied) and left by step (usually downward).

Tenor A high male voice. The next-to-the-lowest voice of the four-voice chorus.

Texture The structure of sound created by tones sounding together.

Timbre The quality of a sound determined by the number and relative intensity of its overtones.

Tonal center The first degree of a scale; the tonic.

Tonal harmony Harmony based on diatonic scales that demonstrates loyalty toward the tonic.

Tonal music Music that adheres to a central tone, the tonic.

Tonal system *See* Tonality.

Tonality The organization of the tones and chords of a key with reference to the tonic.

Tonic The first degree of the scale, or the chord built thereupon.

Treble staff The staff modified by the treble clef sign, which designates G above middle C as occurring on the second line.

Triad A chord of three tones. Most triads are built in thirds.

Triad tone A tone that is part of a triad.

Triple pedal Three tones used simultaneously as a pedal. *See also* Pedal

Unessential chord A chord that is not vital to the stability of the phrase. *See also* Embellishing harmony.

Upper voices All voices other than the lowest.

Upward stem A stem that is attached to the right-hand side of the notehead and extends upward. When the grand staff is used for the four-voice chorus, soprano and tenor stems go upward.

Vertical aspect of harmony Chords, as opposed to chord progressions.

Voice leading The technique of moving the various voices from one chord to another.

Weak beat A beat that has relatively light metric stress.

Whole step The major second; two halfsteps.

index

Musical Examples

(Numbers refer to frames, except where page numbers are indicated (p. or pp.))

index

Subjects